Luminos is the Open Access monograph publishing program from UC Press. Luminos provides a framework for preserving and reinvigorating monograph publishing for the future and increases the reach and visibility of important scholarly work. Titles published in the UC Press Luminos model are published with the same high standards for selection, peer review, production, and marketing as those in our traditional program. *www.luminosoa.org*

A

Philip E. Lilienthal

B O O K

The Philip E. Lilienthal imprint
honors special books
in commemoration of a man whose work
at University of California Press from 1954 to 1979
was marked by dedication to young authors
and to high standards in the field of Asian Studies.
Friends, family, authors, and foundations have together
endowed the Lilienthal Fund, which enables UC Press
to publish under this imprint selected books
in a way that reflects the taste and judgment
of a great and beloved editor.

The publisher and the University of California Press Foundation gratefully acknowledge the generous support of the Philip E. Lilienthal Imprint in Asian Studies, established by a major gift from Sally Lilienthal.

Parameters of Disavowal

Parameters of Disavowal

Colonial Representation in South Korean Cinema

———

Jinsoo An

UNIVERSITY OF CALIFORNIA PRESS

University of California Press, one of the most distinguished university presses in the United States, enriches lives around the world by advancing scholarship in the humanities, social sciences, and natural sciences. Its activities are supported by the UC Press Foundation and by philanthropic contributions from individuals and institutions. For more information, visit www.ucpress.edu.

University of California Press
Oakland, California

Suggested citation: An, J. *Parameters of Disavowal: Colonial Representation in South Korean Cinema*. Oakland: University of California Press, 2018. DOI: https://doi.org/10.1525/luminos.51

Library of Congress Cataloging-in-Publication Data

Names: An, Jinsoo, 1968– author.
Title: Parameters of disavowal : colonial representation in South Korean
    cinema / Jinsoo An.
Description: Oakland, California : University of California Press, [2018] |
    Series: Global Korea ; 1 | Includes bibliographical references and index.
Identifiers: LCCN 2018002008 (print) | LCCN 2018004386 (ebook) |
    ISBN 9780520968103 (Pub) | ISBN 9780520295308 (pbk. : alk. paper)
Subjects: LCSH: Motion pictures—Korea (South)—History—20th century. |
    Imperialism in motion pictures—20th century. | Nationalism in motion
    pictures—20th century.
Classification: LCC PN1993.5.K6 (ebook) | LCC PN1993.5.K6 A74 2018
    (print) | DDC 791.430951/95—dc23
LC record available at https://lccn.loc.gov/2018002008

25   24   23   22   21   20   19   18
10   9   8   7   6   5   4   3   2   1

CONTENTS

ILLUSTRATIONS

ACKNOWLEDGMENTS

I have been very fortunate and blessed to receive tremendous help and support from many people and institutions throughout my writing of this book. I express my deepest gratitude to my mentors Nick Browne, John Duncan, Marilyn Fabe, Elaine Kim, Soyoung Kim, and John Lie for their inspiration, intellectual encouragement, and professional advice over the years. I am also profoundly indebted to the inspiring teachings of the late professors Teshome Gabriel and Nancy Abelmann.

I extend equal gratitude to my colleagues at the Department of East Asian Languages and Cultures of the University of California, Berkeley, who have welcomed me and offered me thorough support and guidance. I am deeply indebted to the generosity of Robert Ashmore, Weihong Bao, Mark Blum, Mark Csikszentmihalyi, Jacob Dalton, Yoko Hasegawa, H. Mack Horton, Andrew F. Jones, Youngmin Kwon, Ling Hon Lam, Dan O'Neill, Robert Sharf, Alan Tansman, Paula Varsano, and Sophie Volpp.

I was also fortunate to have joined a welcoming community of colleagues at UC Berkeley. Russell Ahn, Jaeyong Chang, Jack Davey, Stephanie Kim, Hong Yung Lee, Steven Lee, Taeku Lee, Hannah Michell, Laura C. Nelson, Kyung-nyun Kim Richards, and Clare You taught me the value of teaching, service, and collaboration. I also value deeply the friendship and camaraderie I have developed with Seung-eun Chang, Minsook Kim, Kijoo Ko, Meehyei Lee, Soojin Lee, and Junghee Park over the years.

Many people in various fields have inspired me with their distinguished work and shaped me into a better thinker. I am especially indebted to Andrea G. Arai, Moonim Baek, Chris Berry, Heekyoung Cho, Michelle Cho, Steve Choe, Youngmin

Choe, Jinhee Choi, Kyeong-Hee Choi, Hye Seung Chung, Steven Chung, David Scott Diffrient, Henry Em, Chris Hanscom, Todd Henry, Theodore Hughes, Kelly Jeong, Kyoung Lae Kang, Christina Klein, Immanuel Kim, Jina Kim, Kyu Hyun Kim, Kyung Hyun Kim, SohYoun Kim, Su Yun Kim, Nayoung Aimee Kwon, Helen J. S. Lee, Lee Jeong-ha, Jin-kyung Lee, Namhee Lee, Sangjoon Lee, Robert Oppenheim, Hyun Seon Park, Sunyoung Park, Young-a Park, Janet Poole, Youngju Ryu, Jiwon Shin, Josie Sohn, Clark W. Sorenson, Travis Workman, Hyun Joo Yoo, Theodore Jun Yoo, Mitsuhiro Yoshimoto, and Dafna Zur. I have been extremely fortunate to develop a close friendship with the colleagues I met in the spring of 2008 as a visiting professor at UC Berkeley. Christine Ahn, Christine Hong, Jodi Kim, Deann Borshay Liem, and Paul Liem taught me the virtue of socially committed scholarship. Their intellectual integrity taught me to think critically about issues surrounding Korean society and culture.

I have been privileged to receive abundant support and encouragement from my colleagues in Korea while conducting research for this book. I owe special thanks to Cho Sung-taek, Choe Yong-chul, Choi Seung-youn, Hara Yusuke, Jung Byungwook, Kong Young-min, Kwon Bodurae, Lee Bong-Bum, Lee Hwajin, Lee Seung-Hee, Lee Sun Mi, Park Heon-Ho, Park Yu-hee, and Yi Youngjae. I look forward to many more years of scholarly exchange and collaboration with them. Research into obscure films on the colonial past was made possible by the professional support of the Korean Film Archive. Cho Junhyoung, Chung Chong-hwa, and Oh Sungji have helped me with their deep knowledge of Korean film history and their archivist prowess.

I am honored to have also received the generous support of the Townsend Center Fellowship, the Humanities Research Fellowship, and TUSA grants at the Institute of East Asian Studies at UC Berkeley, which enabled me to carry out the extended research for the book. The Visiting Scholar Program at the Research Institute of Korean Studies of Korea University offered me the most productive environment for research and writing. I am also grateful for financial support from Yonsei University's Future-Leading Research Initiative of 2015 (2016–22–0118).

Grateful acknowledgment is given to the following publications for segments of this book that were published in different versions: *China Review* 10, no. 2 (2010) for "The Ambivalence of the Nationalist Struggle in Deterritorialized Space: The Case of South Korea's Manchurian Action Film," and *positions* 23, no. 4 (2015) for "War as Business in South Korea's Manchurian Action Films."

I wish to thank Vicki Austin for her editorial work in the early stages of this manuscript, and Kathy Ragsdale for her close editorial supervision. I am also grateful to the anonymous reviewers who offered astute comments and constructive feedback for the revision process.

I would also like to thank my extended family in California and Seoul for their many years of support and love. I want to express my gratitude to my in-laws in Seoul, who made my research stay in Korea all the more accommodating and enjoyable. In particular, I want to thank my father-in-law Lee Yongwoo and my late mother-in-law Kim Chunghee for their indefatigable support. My brother Kenneth An showed me the most enthusiastic support and help for this project. My dear parents Seung Kyun An and Kae Soon An have sustained me with their unwavering love and faith. I would also like to convey my gratitude to my aunt Son Sun Inouye and my cousin Ginger and her family for heartwarming support. Finally, I remain profoundly grateful to my wife Lee Soonjin, who has sustained me with her remarkable patience and love.

Korean names and terms have been transliterated according to the McCune-Reischauer Romanization system, except for words and names that are more commonly known by other accepted spellings. Any errors or shortcomings of this book are entirely mine.

This publication project was supported by the Academy of Korean Studies' Core University Program for Korean Studies (Grant # AKS-2012-BAA-2102).

Introduction

The career of South Korean filmmaker Im Kwont'aek spans over fifty years and one hundred films. His 1978 film *The Genealogy* (*Chokpo*) marks an important point in that career, for it shows a departure from the type of films he made throughout the 1960s and 1970s.[1] Based on a novella by the Japanese writer Kajiyama Toshiyuki, the film reflects Im's self-conscious and serious efforts to move away from the production of low-budget genre films.[2] *The Genealogy* is one of his most thematically coherent and stylistically mature works of the 1970s, foreshadowing the preoccupation with national culture and tradition that would later be a prominent theme in his oeuvre. The film is set in the late colonial period, when the Japanese colonial government was increasing its pressure on Koreans to comply with the cultural assimilation policy aimed at converting Koreans into loyal imperial subjects. Its narrative focuses on Tani, a young Japanese government official who is assigned to convince the Korean patriarch Sŏl Chinyŏng to obey the new policy (*ch'angssigaemyŏng* in Korean) under which Koreans would adopt Japanese names. The film offers a complex narrative of Korean cultural resistance to colonial rule as shown from Tani's conflicted perspective, which is both colonialist and sympathetic to the Korean opposition.[3] In addition, the film's exquisite mise-en-scène both features and manifests the themes of Korean tradition and cultural nationalism in visual terms.[4]

But one image conspicuously deviates from the film's overall realistic visual style. It appears early in the film, when Tani confronts his boss's criticism of his lackluster performance at work. Dejected, Tani walks off to a corner of the office, stands by the window, and lights a cigarette. Through the window we see the Government-General Building of Korea—but not the actual building, for it is

1

FIGURE 1. Tani stands by the window against the backdrop of the distant Government-General Building in *The Genealogy*. Courtesy of the Korean Film Archive.

neither cinematographically captured nor photographically rendered. Instead, it appears as a flat painted image whose artificiality is visible in the poorly rendered details, blurry contours, and overexposed color, creating an odd but momentary distanciation for viewers. Furthermore, the slanted angle is improperly aligned with the angle of the window frame and with Tani in the foreground, leading to a perceptual disarray comparable to a failed trompe l'oeil.

The odd image of the building is in sharp contrast to the rest of the film, which largely adheres to the formal conventions of popular narrative film.[5] A question is then: What do we make of a building image that is out of sync with the film's meticulous visualization of Korean tradition and custom set in opposition to an oppressive colonial regime? To be sure, either Im's authorial intent or his filmmaking circumstances might account for the staging of such an image.[6] Yet the building's "exceptional" appearance raises questions about the history of the colonial period with which it is forever associated in Koreans' memories.[7]

Completed in 1926, the neoclassical building of the Government-General of Korea served as the massive headquarters of the Japanese colonial administration. It stood on the cleared space where the central palace of the Chosŏn dynasty, Kyŏngbok Palace, had once stood, and it subsequently became the icon of Japanese colonial rule in Korea. After Korea's liberation in 1945, the same landmark turned into the headquarters of the American military occupation (1945–48) and later became the central government building of South Korea. Renamed Capitol Hall (Chungangchŏng), it was the seat of almost every major historic event and political ceremony in the modern history of South Korea.[8] Then came the controversies and reversals of the new civilian government–led "national spirit restoration" campaign in the mid-1990s. Eradication of the colonial landmark was proposed to revive the symbolic geography of the palace that colonial spatial politics had effectively displaced and erased.[9] The building was finally demolished in 1995, on the fiftieth anniversary of Korea's liberation from Japan, and since then the original palace has been partially reconstructed.[10]

At stake in the controversy were competing viewpoints and memories of the building's historical associations and symbolic meanings. As a "communicative device," the building became a site where these discursive claims and political and historical views intersected at particular moments in South Korean history.[11] Implicit in the discourses surrounding the building was a naturalized way of seeing that the postcolonial society had cumulatively constructed toward the remnants of the colonial past: not outright repudiation, as in the more usual stance of oppositional nationalist politics, but a more subtle form of disavowal carried out by strategies of reworking, recontextualizing, and erasing the ideas and symbols of past colonial power.[12]

The interjection of the artificial image of the building in *The Genealogy* alludes to this kind of disavowal.[13] The image causes an inconsistency in the visual field, offering a kind of refracted view of the building that would otherwise signal historical continuity between the former colonial regime and the present postcolonial regime. While the image remains perceptible, its flat artificial surface de-frames the building from its historical aura and context and thereby weakens them. Its artificiality is not, therefore, a defect of style but a self-conscious aesthetic choice in the larger chain of significations that South Korean cinema constructed in its inculcation of anticolonial nationalism.[14] In postcolonial cinema, the concept of disavowal illuminates understated but persistent strategies, norms, or rationales for representing the colonial period.[15] Ways of seeing or imagining the past furthermore contributed to the knowledge production that was integral to the formation of a South Korean national subjectivity uniquely influenced by the bipolar order of the Cold War.

My purpose in this book is to bring attention to the configuration of the colonial past in South Korean cinema from 1945 through the 1970s supplemented by a few from later decades.[16] The representation of colonialism is related not only to the stubborn legacies of nationalism in South Korea but also to the nation's appraisal of the colonial past under the intensifying bipolarization of politics that led to Korea's prolonged partition.

I first seek to cast light on how postcolonial cinema transcoded the dominant, that is, nationalist, view of history into accessible narrative and imagery for Korean film viewers. As I will illustrate, the postcolonial rendition of anticolonial nationalism involves more than simply showing Korean people collectively resisting colonial violence and domination.[17] A variety of formal choices and considerations, including new narrative tropes and visual imagery, generic elements and conventions, and spatial configurations, came into play to enhance and further the stories of individuals and groups in struggle. Institutional forces and social factors also intervened. For instance, state policies and regulations, commercial interests of the film industry, transcultural film exchanges, and ideas of national culture all intersected with filmmaking practices. Both filmic representation and discursive and industrial practices therefore receive attention in this book.

Since its liberation in 1945, South Korea has produced over two hundred films that are set in the colonial era (1910–45). Not only is that number impressive, but a breakdown by decade shows a pattern of consistent production output: there has been no discernible drop in production of colonial-themed films.[18] This consistency over time suggests that the anticolonial nationalist impulse is an ideological constant in South Korea's cultural production and that nationalist ideology is embedded in postcolonial society.[19] Such an impression is generally supported by scholars of modern Korean history, who remind us of the structural significance of the colonial experience to the subsequent formation of postcolonial national culture in South Korea. The idea of the nation and its experience is based on the nationalist ethos that was formed in opposition to colonialism, and in film that ethos has served as the grand thematic matrix for individual treatments of widely differing subjects and issues. Consequently, one might imagine that films depicting the colonial experience would have enjoyed critical accolades in South Korea.[20]

Yet the critical appraisal presents a different picture. First, colonial-themed films are largely missing from lists of the film canon of South Korea.[21] Scholars have been slow to examine the subject of colonial representation in films, and only a few films have received their attention. The overall critical lack of interest may be due to a perception that these films are propagandistic.[22] Whatever their actual shortcomings, films on the colonial past have clearly not been regarded as the best examples of Korean cinema. Instead, they have been dismissed as middlebrow cultural productions that have functioned to organize the larger precepts of political ideology in understandable terms.[23] The problem of critical indifference also evidences a peculiar vacuity at the core of postcolonial cultural criticism of colonialism itself.

This vacuity, according to Heonik Kwon, is postcolonial criticism's tendency to neglect the close connection between the postcolonial appraisal of colonialism and the political history of the Cold War. Whereas postcolonial criticism divided colonialism into two schemas—the official demise of the institutional order and the lingering presence of colonial cultural imaginaries—it failed to include the greater ramifications of the Cold War order for ex-colonial societies and cultures.[24] Taking a cue from Kwon, I approach the representation of colonialism in South Korean films as a site of inflection that the new Cold War bipolarity imposed upon postcolonial culture.[25] The semantic struggle over the colonial experience may appear tangential to the existing Cold War discourse and culture. However, I argue that it is integral to the larger politics of knowledge production and cultural meaning making that sustained the liberal capitalist vision of the world and the

US-dominated bipolar ordering. This means that the films that uphold an oppositional view toward colonial rule can be interpreted not only as outlets for nationalist fervor but also as repositories for the refracted signifiers of Cold War optics,
as exemplified in the building image of *The Genealogy*. They refer to the ongoing
negotiation and depoliticization of the local (i.e., colonial) issues that occurred
under the bipolar order that the United States imposed on a global scale. To properly historicize postcolonial cultural productions, one needs to read beyond the
surface signs of anticolonialism. This work hence brings attention to the lacunae
and aporia of "overcoming colonialism" that South Korean cinema has rendered
visible in diverse ways.

A BRIEF HISTORY OF COLONIAL KOREAN CINEMA

The arrival of cinema in Korea dates back to the early twentieth century, when the
country entered a series of tumultuous and prolonged crises that resulted in its
annexation by Japan in 1910. The first film exhibition took place in 1903 in Seoul
as part of a promotional campaign by an American electric company. Most films
shown to Korean audiences at the time were of foreign origin, and they offered
the viewing public access to foreign, modern, and exotic worlds outside Korea.
Politically, the Japanese colonization of Korea (1910–45) led to seismic and violent
changes in nearly all aspects of Korean life. The colonial administration placed
rigid disciplinary measures upon the Korean populace to construct a subjectivity
in accordance with the colonialist logic of domination and control. Under the ban-
ner of civilization and enlightenment, various cultural policy measures were introduced to regulate Korean social activities and cultural productions. Filmmaking
was no exception.

Though Korean cinema slowly grew to become a formidable popular medium,
it consistently faced institutional hurdles and challenges on many fronts. A lack of
domestic funding sources, an insufficient infrastructure for a distribution network,
and a shortage of exhibition spaces hindered the development of domestic commercial filmmaking in the early years. The first Korean film arrived in the form
of a kino-drama called *Righteous Revenge* (*Uirijŏk kuto*) in 1919. It was a hybrid
film used as a short vignette for backstage imagery in theatrical stage productions.
Then, in 1922, Korea witnessed the release of the first commercial feature film,
Ch'unhyangjŏn, which was based on popular folklore. A silent film boom soon
ensued, and over seventy domestic films were released in the late 1920s, all vying
for audiences in the expanding film business. In particular, Na Ungyu's *Arirang*
(1926) galvanized public enthusiasm for Korean cinema, as the film tapped into
the nationalist sentiment of the populace. The success of Korean film in the 1920s
and early 1930s was due to several factors: talented filmmakers, shrewd business
leaders, and the overall expansion of the film industry. Film exhibition showed

conspicuous growth as movie theaters opened and thrived in major cities. The colonial cultural policy also helped create a boom, though only a brief one, for the film industry.[26]

The conversion to talkie films posed a major challenge for Korean filmmakers, for this new type of film demanded substantial capital investment and technological expertise as well as a new sensibility regarding the audiovisual synthesis of filmmaking. Politically, Japan's full-scale invasion of China in the late 1930s triggered a drive for wartime mobilization in Korea, including the colonial government's implementation of various and complex forms of control over cultural productions. A series of decrees made Korean filmmakers highly conscious of the government control and censorship of filmed materials. In the early 1940s, the government cut back on the showing of popular films from the West in Korea and subsequently consolidated Korean film production and distribution companies into a single encompassing propaganda machine. The state administration and agencies worked in tandem to promote films with explicit propaganda messages, such as justifications of the colonial policy of cultural assimilation known as *naisen ittai* ("Japan and Korea as one body," *naesŏn ilche* in Korean). The situation forced Korean filmmakers to navigate and negotiate complex pressures inside and outside the official control of the state.[28] Consequently, Korean cinema became a political tool of the Japanese state from 1936 to 1945, as most films valorized colonial policies that aimed at the total assimilation of Koreans into the Japanese imperial body.

The late colonial "collaborationist" films from this period in particular bring into sharp relief the political, but also formal, orientation of postcolonial cinema. On the surface, these films illustrate the theme of conversion, depicting the participation of Koreans in the war effort as necessary and noble acts for the empire.[29] Making these films involved the consideration of many factors, as filmmakers had to operate under the tightening grip of the colonial administration.[30] The interpretive tendency has been to point out how signs of ambivalence or melancholia, typically inscribed on the bodies of colonized male Korean characters, escape the Japanese administration's pressure on the film industry to uphold and naturalize a policy of assimilation and total mobilization.[31] For example, the ailing body of the Korean male protagonist in Yi Pyŏngil's *Spring of the Korean Peninsula* (*Pando-ŭi Pom*, 1941) alludes to the troubled split condition of the colonial nation forced to take part in the making of *naisen ittai* rhetoric.[32]

My interest here does not lie so much with the elaboration of the gray zone of ambivalence that Korean characters embody and register in relation to the wartime mobilization.[33] Rather, I want to shift focus to the spatialized pattern of mobilization that brings together two different registers of meaning: the inner psychic state of Koreans and the external world of empire. The melancholic or exhausted body has often been interpreted as the troubled, if not resistant, Korean national under the duress of political indoctrination. Such figures function as placeholders in a space that is bound to be filled with "positive" values. This trope then anticipates the gradual development or advent of a change of heart, culminating in the national's decisive entry into the project of empire building. Procedural in nature, these films portray the inner torment of Koreans who are ambivalent and hesitant toward this project as a *necessary* step to underscore their destined gravitation toward the larger system of meanings, namely, empire.[34] Hence, late colonial collaborationist films achieve something unprecedented in Korean film history: they make visible the interiority of the colonized as a sphere of transformation.[35] Korean interiority, in other words, effectively turns into an object of access as it is rendered flexible, plastic, and *ultimately* compatible with the ideological drive of the empire.[36]

The Japanese Empire is represented in these works as the center of an expanding network of progress and movement to which the Korean ethnic body lends its meaning as an important dynamic element. The empire as space offers the promise of opportunity and potential, so the Korean people are no longer constricted either by ethnic difference or by geographical marginality. Instead, they are on board perpetually moving vessels, traversing along the lines and arteries of empire.[37] To become an imperial subject, according to this dominant cinematic discourse, is to take part in an imperial project that guarantees the total meaning of existence. Cinematic representations thus typically highlight a moment of decision when a Korean individual has the privilege of attaining the grand meaning of his or her life. The Korean character—initially portrayed as hesitant—undergoes radical transformation and emerges as a figure determined and shaped by the colonial machinery of assimilation. That said, colonial cinema highlights the efficient and "positive" workings of a Japanese-Korean interface that promises a connection between the parochially defined Korean population and the plenitude of affirmative meanings called "the empire."[38]

COLONIAL SPACE IN POSTCOLONIAL CINEMA

[handwritten marginalia: postcolonial cinema very antreotorial as expected]

In contrast, postcolonial cinema expresses a political ideology of anticolonial nationalism, repudiating the spatial aura, ambiance, and imagery associated with the empire.[39] Just as the question of imperial ideology is closely tied to the particular spatialization of Korea and Korean subjects in colonial cinema, the oppositional politics of postcolonial cinema can be conceptualized by recourse to the aesthetics of the colonial space. Postcolonial cinema's nationalist orientation rests on the systemic rendition of Korea as an occupied but porous space where Koreans can carve out sites of resistance and integrity. In other words, postcolonial cinema negates the greater reach of the colonial power, that is, its infiltration into the "minds" of the Koreans, by setting up a countervailing way of looking that reorganizes colonial space for Korean alterity. For instance, whereas late colonial cinema employed a positive aura of luminosity to render natural the imperial ideology of integration and union, postcolonial films are characterized by a heavy atmosphere of pessimism and darkness that envelops the colonial space.[40]

The Japanese occupation of Korea is shown as pervasive, continuous, and total, while the Korean resistance is shown to be sporadic, yet ubiquitous. This portrayal of occupation and resistance signifies a resistant attitude toward the positive discourse of domination propagated by the colonial government. In particular, it depicts the structural misalignment between the colonizer Japan's rhetoric of benevolence and Koreans' own pessimistic sense of reality. South Korean films on the colonial past constitute a conscious endeavor to challenge a colonial power defined in terms of panoptic vigilance. National authenticity as they narrate it, for instance, is grounded particularly in acts of disruption or disturbance in the supposed field of control and occupation. In this context, such disruption means more than political resistance: it refers to an intraethnic practice of viewing and understanding that films prompt and naturalize to mark the essential difference of Koreans, as a collectivity, from the Japanese. This dialectic between the permeating presence of power and a porous and ever-protean type of resistance forms the important thematic axis around which many postcolonial film narratives revolve.[41] In other words, the visualization of colonial space as the contentious site of both domination and incessant challenges to that domination informs the most enduring postcolonial imaginary of colonialism onscreen.

According to Partha Chatterjee, in anticolonial nationalism it is the inner, psychic domain that holds the unchanging "essential marks of cultural identity."[42] Postcolonial cinema shows adherence to the binary opposition that Chatterjee elucidates but further complicates the discursive picture of nationalism. As noted above, colonial cinema brought its focus to and thereby preempted the "inner domain" of the Korean subject as the foundation of allegiance to the empire. In contrast, postcolonial cinema reconfigures the coordinates of interiority and exteriority to thwart that aggressive construction of Korean psychic interiority. It effectively counters the presupposed access to the minds of Korean people as placeholders for the collective essence. Gestures of loyalty are perfunctory and often complemented by a subservient demeanor, typifying the activities of Koreans exposed to the surveillance of the colonial power. This facade or appearance of allegiance is a guileful tactic that aims to deceive the Japanese onlooker. Concurrently, the capacity of Korean people to recognize acts of duplicity on the part of other Koreans becomes an important component in the postcolonial depiction of the colonial past. The "intention to deceive" the anonymous colonial scopic power hence is integral to the fabric of the postcolonial imagination of the Korean collective. Whereas late colonial films obsessively feature the appearance of the Korean imperial subject as a true register of his or her interior state, postcolonial cinema presupposes the split between outer comportment and inner feeling as necessary for the colonized to maintain their integrity. That said, the postcolonial representation of colonialism rests on the premise of guileful subjects and their collective recognition of each other's true inclinations. The space of Koreans dispossessed by colonial domination is defined simultaneously by the colonial gaze of surveillance and patrol and by the capacity of the colonized to deflect the efficacy of the scopic intrusion.

The convoluted or distorted visual fields of postcolonial cinema become evident when we draw attention to the way colonial urban space is depicted in visual terms. What to include and exclude from the visual and spatial register already predetermines the parameters of action, issues, and problematics. One of the most conspicuous features of representation in these films is the systematic exclusion of Japanese signage and language from the cityscapes of colonial Korea. After liberation—and until recent years—the Japanese language, either in spoken form or in literal signs, was almost completely absent from the Korean film screen.[43] The excision of Japanese signage from view may at first appear elemental and incidental, but the logic behind it has significant implications for the representation of the colonial space. The underlying assumption is that Japanese signage does not simply depict the Japanese cultural presence in colonial Korea. It exemplifies the larger visual matrix associated with the colonial modernization that Japan implemented in Korea. It represents the powerful network of linguistic groups and communities in operation, and signals its deep penetration into the daily lives of the Korean people under colonial domination. Postcolonial censorship practices often blocked the visibility of Japanese signage to suppress reminders of that larger colonial network.

At the same time, postcolonial films that depict colonial urban space often show Koreans' willful lack of interest in the urban modernity introduced by the colonial power. Missing in renditions of colonial Seoul is the fascinated gaze of Koreans upon the modern technological innovations that are central to cultural discourses of the colonial urban experience.[44] Transportation, communication, and information, all of which signal the compression of time and space, rarely occupy the center of attention. South Korean films therefore are out of keeping with the conventional optics of urban modernity that popular cinema habitually thematizes. Early modern cinema, to borrow Kristin Whissel's term, was part of "a broader network of multiple forms of traffic," as it reflected and contributed to "networks and grids that linked individual technologies into expanding systems."[45] Prior to the 2000s, South Korean colonial-themed films did not engage meaningfully with this aspect of colonial development—that of a broader network and its traffic, which necessarily implies the expanding domination of colonial power.[46]

A "negative space" of austerity filled the consequent gap in the representation of colonial urban space. This negative space reflected a recurring sensibility with regard to the depiction of colonial space that transcended individual genres and film cycles. Specifically, it refers to such places as dark passages, back alleys, underground meeting places, and abandoned houses, all of which appear as the backdrop for Korean individual or group action in films set in colonial Seoul.

Presented in a manner that underscores their darkness and emptiness, these places are temporary destinations for Koreans who are scattering and fleeing rather than sites where they can gather for ordinary social interactions.[47] In contradistinction to the traffic-ridden "boulevard" space, they presuppose a sense of disconnection and alienation that informs the complex psychological attitudes of Koreans toward the empire.[48] These films have not merely rendered darkness metaphorically in tandem with nationalist descriptions of history of the colonial period as a "dark time." Rather, the spatial aura suggests ways in which the colonial subject carved out a sphere of alterity within.[49]

One must account for an additional feature that complements the evasion of colonial power that is possible in negative space. These films portray Koreans as capable of staging cunning deceptions against the colonial authorities. Central to their performative gestures is the relay of an intraethnic gaze of recognition that reinforces the hidden Korean alterity and insulates it from external intrusion. This feature is particularly salient when placed against the backdrop of colonial cityscapes. The austere texture of colonial urban space is not designed to show the interior psyche of any particular Korean individual. It lacks the kind of psychologization one may find in the dark urban space of American film noir. Instead, it refers to the general condition of Korea under the supposed colonial surveillance (hence lethargic, defeated, bleak, and intimidating). That space then serves as the ground for staging the self-consciously oppositional actions of the Korean collective. The Korean characters recognize each other's deceptive tactics in demonstrating the required subjection to the colonial authority, and this recognition anchors their intraethnic affinity and trust. Whereas late colonial collaborationist films give the interior space of the Korean national full complexity, postcolonial films project a "superficial" colonial world, devoid of any interior substance. By rendering the colonial space as affectively blank, the films underscore the narrative's focus on Korean subjects' guileful tactics of dissimulation. Hence, the negative space of austerity is an aesthetic precept in postcolonial cinema: it limits the scope of the intense and aggressive colonial gaze in late colonial cinema by refashioning the set of relations that made up the social existence of Koreans under the colonial authority.

THE 1960s: NORMALIZATION AND THE COLD WAR

This type of refashioning becomes particularly salient in the films made around or after the 1965 normalization treaty with Japan. With the exception of the first chapter—on the biopic genre—I organize the chapters of this book around this event and its aftermath to bring into focus the various and evolving conventions of colonial representation onscreen. The treaty formally brought together the former colonizer and the colonized on an equal plane in Cold War geopolitics and facilitated political alliance and economic partnership between the two states under the leadership of the United States. This historic event had a far-reaching impact on South Korean society, as there was fervent protest against rapprochement. It also inspired new cultural productions that revisited the colonial past and the mandate of decolonization by imagining and visualizing Japan as the colonizer in new ways onscreen. But it was the rendition of colonial space in particular that attained a new level of complexity, as it reorganized the parameters of disavowal toward Japan as simultaneously the former enemy and the contemporaneous strategic partner.

A crisis of representation of colonialism in the 1960s resulted from the rupturing of an anticolonial imaginary that, in the previous decade, had sustained a rather facile scenario of opposition. South Korea's refiguration of the former enemy can be traced in part to the shift in focus toward new privileged sites that, while adhering to the aforementioned negative dynamics, entailed reflection upon the perplexing development of new, neighborly exchanges with Japan. Another area of change was genre. Since genre presupposes a unique yet understandable semantic field of action, reaction, and resolution, the emergence of new genres supposed an amalgamation of discursive views and attitudes in the making of the colonial imaginary. Above all else, the genre and genre-like films of the 1960s produced familiar and conventional sites with established meanings and associations that referred to the repressed visual culture of the colonial era. My reading hence moves progressively toward the question of a historical divide before and after normalization and the repression that increasingly came to the fore in film in the aftermath of the normalization treaty and South Korea's assignment of a position in the Cold War world order. *really dealing w/ how Cold War normalization treaty effected 'colonial' films*

ROADMAP FOR THIS BOOK

In film, the original political dictate of overcoming Japanese colonialism resulted in a complex and diffused visual rendition that simultaneously projected various terms of engagement with the former colonizer. However limited or problematic in its effect, this popular new cinematic imagining of the colonial therefore constituted a fertile cultural site in which global pressures and local responses entailed creative and complex terms of dialogue and negotiation. "Japanese color," or the intrusion of Japanese imagery, culture, and language into Korean life through Japanese, Korean, and even US films and other cultural productions, was banned to varying degrees in the postcolonial Korean state and was the subject of prolonged controversy. Relations of postcolonial Koreans to their colonial past have been complicated and emotionally fraught. I follow these relations through discourse of the postcolonial period and relate them to a reading of three main genres of the decade: Manchurian action films, *kisaeng* and gangster films, and revenge horror films. As my analysis of the 1960s' volatile cultural discourse and films will indicate, a general crisis concerning the representation of colonialism also led to prolonged debate on the national and cultural identity of South Korean cinema.

Chapter 1 focuses on the hero narrative of two nationalist films from two distinct eras: the liberation period and the postwar period. The primary films under analysis are Ch'oe In'gyu's *Hurrah! For Freedom* (1946) and Shin Sangok's *The Independence Association and Young Syngman Rhee* (1959). My exegesis draws attention to these works' shared themes as well as the lacunae of the official anticolonial history of South Korea. These films introduce and conventionalize the dominant narrative of resistance, struggle, and sacrifice by contrasting the alternative space for populist nationalism and political activism to the downtrodden and enclosed realm of the failing dynastic authority. In tandem with an enlightenment discourse of progress, the rise of a public sphere in these films informs the spatial practice of nationalism and casts a definitive shadow on the subsequent configuration of colonial space in South Korean cinema.

Chapter 2 moves on to the topic of the crisis of national culture and cinema in the 1960s by focusing on the incursions of Japanese culture and film into South Korea. This section draws close attention to discourses and censorship cases that relate to both the importation of Japanese films and the appearance of "Japanese color" in Hollywood and South Korean films. The April Revolution of 1960 ushered in bifurcating interests with regard to Japan. The chapter chronicles the complex and convoluted passage toward the formation of a rapprochement with Japan and its cultural ramifications. Through readings of the era's controversies in film, I illustrate how the suppressed legacies of colonial visual culture emerged in this period, complicating decolonization in South Korea as the nation became deeply entangled in the intensifying bipolar politics of the Cold War.

The subsequent chapters focus closely on specific cinematic representations. Chapter 3, on the Manchurian action film, examines the shifting logic of the anticolonial struggle in the 1960s. First, I introduce and explicate the popular appeal of this adventure narrative, akin to the American western film, which offers the fantasy of individual freedom and service to a national authority in exile. The advent of the Manchurian action film hence might seem to mark an effort to stage the old straightforward form of anticolonial nationalism. Yet excessive moments of loss and despair inform a profound equivocation on the efficacy of the nationalist endeavor. The second part of the chapter interrogates the persistent theme of political economy that dominates the adventure narrative, namely the pursuit of war funds as the sole goal of the nationalist armed struggle. I approach the Manchurian action film as a unique form of war narrative movie in which the capitalist logic of primitive accumulation, state authority formation, and the structuring of desire all converge and intensify.

Chapter 4 examines popular tropes of two key types of socially marginal bodies in the colonial imagination: the *kisaeng* courtesan and the gangster boss. The film cycles that featured these characters emerged after South Korea's 1965 normalization with Japan. As such, they proceed through an alternate matrix of social interaction and conflict between Koreans and Japanese, typically set in an urban center of culture, commerce, and leisure. The chapter draws particular attention to the legendary gangster boss and folk hero Kim Tuhan, whose exploits in widely popular hagiographical narratives inspired numerous film series. My reading of the films traces the displacement of larger political tensions onto a compressed zone of proximity where the Japanese could be checked and restrained from encroaching on the autonomy of Korean commerce and business.

The issue of marginal sites leads to the final chapter's inquiry into stories of vengeance and an exploration of the troubling remnants, or splintered logic, of colonial imagination. Stories of vengeful figures and their return—often in the form of a female specter—trouble the dominant imaginary of the colonial experience that other groups of films have promulgated. The two films under discussion, *Yeraishang* and *Epitaph,* both feature a return of the repressed from the colonial past that scandalously exposes aspects of that past. In doing so, they implicitly critique the developmentalist logic of the Cold War, which, aiming at moving forward with Japan as an ally and trade partner, suppressed attempts to reflect on the colonial legacy and right the wrongs of colonial violence. This treatise thus concludes with these films' divergent histories of the nation that constitute a heretical but productive contribution of national cinema to Korean society.

Under the Banner of Nationalism

The Changing Imagery of Anticolonial Leadership

Scramble for a nt'l identity
after liberation from Japan]

Japan → USA

✝

Liberation from Japanese colonial rule in 1945 galvanized on an unprecedented scale a new fervor for a uniquely national culture in Korea. In the social euphoria of liberation, intellectuals and cultural critics advocated the need to overcome Japanese domination in the broadest sense. Yet the effort to forge a new national culture soon faced a complex set of challenges deriving from the political confusion of the time and factional rivalries, as well as the pressure of the new occupying force. The US Army Military Government in Korea (USAMGIK) that replaced the former colonial regime introduced new measures of control and regulation over cultural activities to block the spread of leftist ideologies subversive to its political objectives in Korea.[1] Often, USAMGIK reemployed the agents and mechanisms of the former colonial regime to oversee social activity and cultural production in Korea, provoking the ire and discontent of Koreans.

Film production, distribution, and exhibition, in particular, faced stringent constraints from the neocolonial authority.[2] Film production, which had been hampered by the vicissitudes of Japanese wartime mobilization, was in need of the material and institutional support of the occupation force.[3] Concurrently, the new authority imposed strict censorship over film content to inhibit anything deemed subversive to its domination in Korea.[4] In fact, the lack of resources for commercial filmmaking, such as shortages of production funds, raw film stock, production equipment, and postproduction facilities, delayed the resumption of full film production in the immediate liberation period.[5] Film distribution and exhibition sectors also faced challenges of their own under the control of USAMGIK.

The formative years of liberation under the US occupation (from 1945 to 1948) hence were marked by new tensions. How to narrate the colonial experience became entangled with the neocolonial interests of the United States from the beginning, contributing to a highly convoluted view of the colonial experience.[6] Decolonization efforts, moreover, become mired in the polarizing Cold War politics that led to Korea's political unrest, partition in 1948, and devastating civil war in 1950. The incipient but growing ideological conflicts were an important backdrop to the cinematic construction of the collective memory of the past.

The films under analysis here are Ch'oe In'gyu's *Hurrah! For Freedom* (Chayu Manse, 1946; hereafter *Hurrah!*) and Shin Sangok's *The Independence Association and Young Syngman Rhee* (Tongnip Hyŏphoe-wa Chŏngnyŏn Rhee Syngman, 1959; hereafter *Independence Association*). Whereas *Hurrah!* features a fictional account of a nationalist resistance fighter during the last years of colonial rule, *Independence Association* is a biographical film about the early years of Syngman Rhee, president of South Korea from 1948 to 1960. It showcases the rise of Rhee as a young leader at the tumultuous political time of Korea's precipitous downfall and loss of sovereignty. Produced after epochal events, both films express views toward the colonial era at key junctures in the modern history of Korea. As the first feature-length commercial film after the liberation, *Hurrah!* is the earliest cinematic expression of the era's urgent affirmation of anticolonial nationalism as the ideological foundation of Korean cinema. The years that followed it, before *Independence Association* was produced, were filled with seismic events that shaped the course of South Korean history: the Korean War (1950–53), the anticommunist dictates under the National Security Act of 1948, Syngman Rhee's own authoritarian rule, and prolonged economic privation.[7] *Hurrah!* and *Independence Association* thereby represent shifts in cultural attitudes toward the colonial past that were born out of two vastly different historical circumstances: the postliberation period and the post–Korean War era.

On the level of filmmaking practice, the two films mark significant turning points in the careers of their respective filmmakers, Ch'oe In'gyu and Shin Sangok, who had been bound by the master-apprentice system of film training. Ch'oe, who had an illustrious career as the director of such colonial-period films as *Tuition* (Suŏmnyo, 1940) and *Angels on the Streets* (Chibŏmnŭn ch'ŏnsa, 1941), responded to the era's call for nationalist filmmaking after the liberation. *Hurrah!* signified for him a successful career transition from being a filmmaker with tainted pro-Japanese collaborationist credentials to becoming an exemplary artist with a new commitment to nationalist filmmaking in postliberation Korea. His liberation-era films made an indelible impression upon aspiring young filmmaker Shin Sangok, who started his film career as Ch'oe's apprentice and assistant director. After the Korean War, Shin emerged as a major talent on the South Korean film scene by excelling at the sort of popular political filmmaking that his mentor Ch'oe had previously mastered. But Shin went further by introducing a new visual splendor and excess to the depiction of history on screen through his *Independence Association*.

The success and impact of *Independence Association* catapulted Shin's rise as the commanding movie mogul of the ensuing decades.[8]

The two films share a pedagogical ambition to inculcate the political ideal of collective resistance. As my analysis suggests, they do so by exploring the Korean people's loss of sovereignty and prolonged subjugation, while also carving out a space of resistance and highlighting the integrity of Koreans to portray perseverance in a nation under duress. In particular, both films employ the trope of a hero leader who rallies the resistance and emphasizes the righteousness of the cause and the moral authority of the nation under colonial domination. Together, these two films represented major advancements in the cinematic construction of a distinctive historical view toward the colonial past. Their aesthetic effects and narrative features introduced new ways of seeing and understanding the colonial past that strongly influenced subsequent films with colonial themes. They also marked a knowledge production specifically related to the collective memory of the colonial past that was an integral part of the Cold War culture and structure of Korea. In this chapter, I first discuss how these films convey in dramatic and rhetorical terms the unifying force of nationalism and the substance of the anticolonial struggle. I then move beyond the manifest message to explore how these films' portrayal of oppositional politics is embedded in the larger situation of Korea in the Cold War.

HURRAH! FOR FREEDOM AND MOBILIZATION OF PASSION FOR THE PERPETUAL STRUGGLE

Any discussion of South Korea's filmic portrayal of the colonial past must begin with an examination of the "liberation-era film" (*haebang yŏnghwa*). Produced at the height of social euphoria over the nation's independence, postliberation films are the earliest onscreen expressions of anticolonial nationalism. They include works such as Ch'oe In'gyu's *Hurrah!*, Yi Kuyŏng's *The Chronicle of An Chunggŭn* (*An Chunggŭn sa'gi*, 1946), Sŏ Chŏnggyu's *The Immortal Secret Envoy* (*Pummyŏl-ŭi milsa*, 1947), Chŏn Ch'anggŭn's *My Liberated Country* (*Haebangdoen, nae koyang*, 1947), Yi Kuyŏng's *The Chronicle of the March 1st Revolution* (*Samil hyŏngmyŏnggi*, 1947), Yun Pongch'un's *Yun Ponggil, the Martyr* (*Yun Ponggil ŭisa*, 1947), Kim Chŏnghwan's *The Angel Heart* (*Ch'ŏnsa-ŭi maŭm*, 1947), Ch'oe In'gyu's *The Night before Independence Day* (*Tongnip Chŏnya*, 1948) and *An Innocent Criminal* (*Choe-ŏpnŭn choein*, 1948), and Yun Pongch'un's *Yu Kwansun* (1948).[9] As the titles indicate, many are biographical films that showcase those who devoted their lives to the nationalist cause. They illustrate a type of filmmaking that, while commercial in nature, was part of the era's collective effort to forge a national culture and consciousness.[10]

Hurrah! is the earliest and most explicit expression of such nationalist filmmaking and became the archetype for liberation-era film. As the first feature-length commercial film made after liberation, it exemplifies the nationalist fervor that swept Korea at that time.[11] Film critics and historians have acclaimed the film for the historical value of its strong anticolonial message, but this emphasis has led to a short-circuiting of nuanced interpretation.[12] The film's damaged prints are a contributing factor to this critical negligence, for it is difficult for anyone to discern the complete plot.[13] One critic (Yi Hyoin) who deftly reconstructs the film's plot is largely unswayed by its nationalist creed and sees *Hurrah!* merely as an artwork that fails to achieve its promise because of an outmoded style, sentimentality, and a lack of dramatic plausibility.[14] But Yi, like other critics, curiously leaves out analyses of specific narrative details and attendant issues.

While acknowledging critics' insights into the film's historic importance, I want to shift attention to its narrative details in order to show how the theme of militant nationalism garners appeal and legitimacy. Rather than approaching the film as an unmediated conduit for the preestablished doctrine of nationalism, I argue that it uses several key tropes and themes that ground the political ideals of nationalism in visual terms. As Travis Workman has observed, the issues of heterosexual romance, gender, and pro-Japanese collaboration serve a dramatic function as they drive the film narrative and contribute to an aesthetic of liberation.[15] While agreeing with Workman, I also stress that the early cinematic expression of anti-Japanese resistance is not without ambiguity concerning the new possibilities associated with the liberation. This problem of ambiguity is particularly evident toward the end of *Hurrah!,* which shows the tragic fate of the male protagonist, Hanjung. I focus on the timing of his death, as well as the peculiar timelessness of the anticolonial struggle that it entails, as these make the film exceptional among South Korean films about the colonial past.

The film is set in the last days of Japanese colonial rule. Hanjung escapes from prison with his comrade, first taking refuge at his friend's place and later moving to a safe house that a young nurse, Hyeja, and her mother provide. He attends a meeting of elite Korean leaders where he argues for an immediate armed uprising against the colonial power, but he fails to draw the others' support. Later, Hanjung, learning of the arrest of his comrade, attacks the arresting policeman on the streets and rescues his compatriot. The action triggers a police chase, and Hanjung takes refuge at Mihyang's place. Mihyang is a *kisaeng* married to a policeman, Nambu, who is a pro-Japanese collaborator; nevertheless, she develops a romantic passion for Hanjung. She later offers money to Hanjung to support the nationalist cause but inadvertently attracts the attention of the Japanese police. The ensuing shootout between Hanjung and the police results in Mihyang's death and Hanjung's injury and arrest. At the hospital, the young nurse Hyeja attempts to rescue Hanjung. She drugs the guard and leads Hanjung to an escape route. Hanjung, however, is shot and killed on the day of liberation.[16]

The film's emphasis on resistant nationalism centers on the volatile actions of Hanjung. The theme of nationalism as an uncompromising political creed finds its pure realization in this male character, played by the actor Chŏn Ch'anggŭn, whose stoic face and reserved demeanor effectively convey the lofty and serious aura of the struggle. It should be noted, however, that the male protagonist's charisma and authority rely structurally upon the support of other Koreans. For instance, the two main female characters, Mihyang and Hyeja, intervene at crucial moments in the narrative to provide much-needed protection and help for Hanjung, without which he would not be able to sustain his quest.[17]

More specifically, Hanjung's nationalist fervor distinguishes itself from his other personal interests. Female desires rank lower in value than the supremely valued nationalist cause. The two women whose romantic interest Hanjung attracts represent opposite scenarios of Korean femininity. The director, Ch'oe, clearly draws on the popular trope of the love triangle, yet uses it to underscore the priority of the political plot. The narrative shows that two forms of passion, Hanjung's adherence to the nationalist cause and the two women's desire for him, belong to different registers, and a convergence emerges only through the transformation of female desire as it is subsumed under the higher ideal of altruistic devotion.[18] The configuration of women's desire, political involvement, and political conversion hence is central to the political discourse of nationalism in the film.

The film fleshes out this theme by allocating substantial segments of the narrative to two contrasting versions of femininity. Though Mihyang and Hyeja both offer help to Hanjung, the film valorizes Hyeja's contribution while denigrating Mihyang's. In the latter case, this devaluation is made immediately clear by her profession. Since the *kisaeng* is a familiar emblem of colonial Korean femininity that serves the colonizer, Mihyang is marked negatively from the beginning. But it is her suffocating marriage with a pro-Japanese collaborator, not her supposedly debased profession per se, that causes her misery. The film thus draws upon two colonial icons—the *kisaeng* and the policeman—to present a couple who, in their collaboration with the colonial regime, are irredeemable in and fundamentally unassimilable to the film's construction of the national body and imaginary.[19] Mihyang's sentimental and histrionic outpourings illustrate the cardinal logic of colonial social life in postcolonial cinema: a total conflation of the personal and the political. Conjugal relations with a pro-Japanese agent can only lead one to suffer the consequences of a bad marriage. The portrayal of Mihyang's unhappy marriage is part of an overarching strategy that sublimates the personal concerns of romance to the larger political precept of anticolonial struggle that is necessary to construct the nationalist subject.

Mihyang's excessive self-pity is portrayed in thoroughly negative terms, as Hanjung shows no interest in her dilemma. Moreover, it is through his denial of her desire for comfort that Hanjung's nationalist fervor comes into sharp relief. Against the emotional excess of the female character and her narcissistic self-indulgence, his passion for the political struggle contrasts as formidably austere. When he mistakenly assumes that she is untrustworthy in terms of the nationalist struggle, he goes so far as to physically punish her.[20] Hence, while the women in the film initially function as indispensable support for the male protagonist's endeavor, their worth is reassessed through their capacity to embrace the political mandate, which requires the individual to sublimate personal needs to a higher political need. Mihyang's humiliation and subsequent death thus signal the elimination of an undesired femininity. The film approvingly underscores the unwritten code that came to dominate South Korea's filmic depiction of the colonial past: whatever potentially impedes the male protagonist's progress toward fulfilling the larger political purpose must be overcome at any cost.

In contrast, the transformation of Hyeja informs the symbolic economy of female labor and worth that is central to the film's configuration of the nationalist struggle. It is also the distinguishing feature that separates Hyeja from Mihyang. Hyeja is a fresh-faced young nurse, and her religious affiliation, Christianity, speaks volumes about her conservative and righteous moral character.[21] Yet she is also adept at articulating her desire to Hanjung in a subtle and friendly manner. The difference between Hyeja and Mihyang is brought into sharp relief through the domestic spaces that they inhabit. As opposed to Mihyang's gaudy showcase of furniture and objects, Hyeja's abode has an aura of comfort and warmth.[22] Moreover, it is a site of labor and production where her mother constantly works on a sewing machine. Because Hyeja and her mother are alike in their devoted support for Hanjung's clandestine political operation, their labor at home already possesses the positive values relevant to his struggle. The film therefore sets up a clear dichotomy of femininities in order to punish and eradicate the materialistic and self-absorbed while sanctioning and commending the virginal and industrious. From the outset, the liberation film makes clear the value of female labor, both emotional and material, in the service of the nationalist struggle.

In both interactions, Hanjung is not the subject who supposedly knows and empathizes with the plight of the people. Rather, the dynamic operates in reverse. The film portrays him as the rightful *recipient* of the other Korean characters' a priori support for the cause. In fact, the film makes a great effort to establish Hanjung as the leader of the political struggle by making all surrounding figures *presupposedly* recognize him as such. This supposition then leads other Koreans to make efforts and sacrifices for the value he embodies. A construction of proper leadership thereby takes precedence over other concerns in the thematic axis as the film progresses toward its end.[23] The disparity between Hanjung's plan and his action is not depicted as a drawback; rather, it functions as a catalyst that inspires the involvement of other people, which ultimately cements his status as a figure of authority.

The projection of assumed leadership compensates for the narrow, if not myopic, field of vision that the male protagonist maintains in his interaction with other Koreans. Depicted formally as the beneficiary of others' devotion, Hanjung effectively funnels the help of others toward the nationalist struggle. However, his focus on immediate actions is set against the vast sphere and reach of colonial

FIGURE 2. Hanjung and Korean leaders discuss the method for political struggle in *Hurrah! For Freedom*. Courtesy of the Korean Film Archive.

domination. He embodies a nationalist creed that is spatially defensive and reactive in nature, and this becomes a recurring pattern in biographical films of later periods. Postcolonial cinema's typical portrayal of colonial rule as dark, austere, and hostile is a necessary counterpart to the portrayal of an anticolonial struggle that is bounded and narrow in scale. The imaginary projections of both registers— that is, the broad realm of occupation and surveillance on one hand, and the punctured site of resistance and subversion on the other—complement each other in a vast national allegory. The nationalist struggle is shown only as scattered, sporadic "tactical" acts against a permanent system and network of empire. The criticism that a leader like Hanjung does not generate any meaningful chain of actions (as he himself is killed in his escape from hospital) therefore misses the point here. The anticolonial political resistance can be imagined only on a small and myopic scale, in terms of sporadic but continuous disruption of the larger colonial order.

These limitations of this portrayal become conspicuous in the film when Hanjung attempts to advocate nationwide struggle against the Japanese colonial power. This occurs when he has his meeting with the Korean leaders who have gathered in the mountains to discuss the future direction of Korea. The meeting takes place on August 14, a day before Korea's liberation, and the leaders have already been informed of Japan's imminent surrender.[24] Hanjung makes a passionate call for an armed uprising. Given the magnitude of the issue, what he advocates can mean only a military attack on a total, nationwide scale. Other leaders are apprehensive about Hanjung's plan, fearing that such volatile action could lead to unnecessary heavy casualties. Hanjung nevertheless continues to insist, and the difference of opinion leads to an acrimonious exchange of personal attacks for which Hanjung later apologizes.[25] The sequence alludes to an important thematic issue within the nationalist camp that other postcolonial films barely touch upon. It illustrates conflicts and divergences within the group over the direction of the struggle as well as multiple competing views on national affairs and leadership. It also makes clear that Hanjung's advocacy of violent uprising is geared more toward establishing the precept of ceaseless struggle than toward reflecting upon the situation of Korea on the cusp of a new historic development.

Yet the exceptional historic moment of transition also calls into question the efficacy of armed struggle in the first place and makes it difficult to construct a sound argument for the nationalist position. Put simply: Is violent revolt, which may cost Korean lives, justified when the nation's liberation is destined to occur in a foreseeable future? The question challenges the straightforward logic of a nationalism that has been largely defined in opposition to the colonial ruler. When the suffering nation is habitually imagined as stuck in perpetual subjugation to the enemy, Japan, all-out resistance is justifiable. With impending liberation, however, the Korean subject's position can no longer be conceived in a binary anticolonial framework. In fact, the situation is peculiarly open, as national subjectivity can be conceived without necessary reference to the colonial domination that is destined to disappear. Instead, the focus shifts toward the "future" of Korea, where an independent state is the new foreseeable reality. Furthermore, this conception of the Korean nation already possesses an all-encompassing scale in contrast with Hanjung's struggle, which is a reactive, bounded, local, and parochial effort.

In the subsequent sequences, Hanjung's continuing devotion to militant struggle must be considered in terms of the political vacuum and confusion of the postcolonial situation and its impact on the shifting perception of Korean reality. On the surface, the film makes a clear connection between Hanjung's sacrifice and the nation's liberation. However, the apparent prospect of liberation complicates such a facile reading. Though Hanjung's previous actions were reactive in nature, now they are contrarian gestures in the face of the reluctant, if not passive, response of other Korean leaders. With the prospect of liberation on the horizon, the other men have already shifted their focus away from militant anticolonial politics toward the future prospects for Korea and its governance. Hanjung's continuing struggle gains its significance against the expected "transition" of power that will lead to Korea's independence. Read in light of this complex juncture, Hanjung's death at the daybreak of liberation not only signals an individual act of sacrifice but also refers broadly to a larger ideological rationale to affirm persistence and integrity in the new political reality of liberation.[26] The nationalist discourse, as expressed in the film, is not in tandem with the shifting reality of Korea at the time of liberation and instead operates as an unwavering political constant. The film therefore illustrates the atemporal drive of anticolonial politics even at the moment of ultimate fulfillment. That said, Hanjung's altruistic action creates and heightens the symbolic density of the timeless struggle upon which the nation ultimately rests.

Ch'oe's liberation-era films, such as *Hurrah!* and *The Night before Independence Day,* express the hardship of Koreans under Japanese colonial rule, but they do not feature the visual embellishment and realistic depth that Ch'oe brought to his late colonial films. Stylistically, Ch'oe's liberation-era films depict the bare essence of the oppositional gestures and energy that promoted the nation's survival and integrity. The budget constraints and technical limitations of the era are conspicuous onscreen, revealing visible signs of low production values and a technical unevenness. The dim lighting and sparse production design of these films, as well as a general paucity of ambiance, engender an austere aura in the diegetic world. A lack of luminosity and of narrative flourishes renders the films uneven and jumpy at times; the damaged prints compound the problem with their narrative loose ends and lack of character motivation.

Concurrently, these films fail to turn the narrative of crisis into a genre of historical drama on colonialism. It would have been difficult for both the filmmaker and film viewers to secure temporal distance or historical perspective when the colonial experience was still a vivid memory. Furthermore, such films structure their narratives around the event of liberation and thus resolve all problems and tensions as they transmute the characters' suffering and sacrifice into meaningful components of the new reality of Korea. Though they do underscore oppositional rhetoric, the overall effects of such contrarian gestures do not elevate these films to the popular scenarios of anticolonial history that films of the later period realized. Being preoccupied with the immediate reality of liberation, early films lack the larger discursive framework or the self-awareness of grand history that constitutes the larger temporal "stuff" of anticolonial representation. To have a broader perspective on the colonial past and project it onto the screen, Korean films had to wait for an influx of new factors and forces. Shin Sangok in the postwar period soon took the lead in creating a new type of historical film that offered a view of the colonial era as a discrete and distant time period.

HISTORY AND HERO MAKING IN
INDEPENDENCE ASSOCIATION

The biographical films of the 1950s narrate the nation's history by portraying the political turmoil that led to colonial rule and the rise of collective resistance. This new configuration of history involved three contributing factors that made the

1950s films distinct from the films of the preceding liberation period; the adoption of a longer historical view that encompassed times before the colonial era and put the colonial era in a new perspective; industrial change and the effects of its vicis-situdes on genre forms; and an increased self-consciousness about history in gen-eral. By utilizing the decline of the Chosŏn dynasty as their principal backdrop, the 1950s films achieved a unique historical distance that was necessary for the con-struction of a new critical viewpoint toward the political dilemmas of the past. The new productions also achieved an effect of historical verisimilitude as the growing partnership between the state and the film industry made large-scale political film production possible. The 1950s films show increased attention to historical details, which, along with the use of generic tropes, enhances the more serious, if not weighty, ambiance of history. Furthermore, the various textual signs and rhetorical features, as well as the extratextual discourse on film production and unique film exhibition practices, all elevated the status of the 1950s historical drama films close to that of an official discourse of national history.

A discussion of 1950s biopics involves a bit of backtracking because a similar treatment of nationalist heroes began in the earlier postliberation period. The late 1940s witnessed the release of several biopics on patriots whose stories of devotion to the nationalist cause would again be turned into films in the 1950s. Examples of 1940s biopics are *The Chronicle of An Chunggŭn* (*An Chunggŭn sagi;* Yi Kuyŏng, 1946), *The Immortal Secret Envoy* (*Pulmyŏl-ŭi milsa;* Sŏ Chŏnggyu, 1947), *The Chronicle of the March 1st Revolution* (*Samil hyŏngmyŏnggi;* Yi Kuyŏng, 1947), *Yun Ponggil, the Martyr* (*Yun Ponggil ŭisa;* Yun Pongch'un, 1947), and *Yu Kwansun* (Yun Pongch'un, 1948). These works share thematic affinities with staunch nation-alist dramas like *Hurrah!* and both groups of films portray solid anticolonial resis-tance politics against colonial oppression.[27] On the surface, the 1950s biopics seem like repeats of the 1940s biopics that dramatized the heroic tales of anticolonial nationalists. The list of historical figures who were made the subjects of biopics in both decades includes Min Yŏnghwan (1861–1905), Yu Kwansun (1902–20), Yun Ponggil (1908–32), and An Chunggŭn (1879–1910). Repetition is significant here in that the filmmakers of the 1950s, by restaging these individuals' resistance narra-tives, exalted the national history. Through an act akin to palimpsestic inscription, they made the stories of these historical figures an important component of the nationalist imagination directed toward the colonial past.[28]

The drive to produce biopics seems to have been a ritualistic obsession. For instance, the historical figure Yu Kwansun, a female student activist of the his-toric March 1st Movement of 1919, was transformed into an icon of the national-ist resistance by four films honoring her sacrifice.[29] Similarly, three biographical films depicted the life of An Chunggŭn, the nationalist who assassinated Japanese statesman Ito Hirobumi in 1909 as a protest against the Japan-Korea Protectorate Treaty of 1905.[30] The repeated dramatization of select political figures hence served not only the biopics' didactic and memorial functions but also the continuity and predominance of the nationalist historical discourse in the making of Korea's national cinema in the 1940s and '50s.

In the late 1950s, biographical films set in the precolonial and colonial eras reached the pinnacle of their success and popularity. These films—including Chŏn Ch'anggŭn's *King Kojong and Martyr An Chunggŭn* (*Kojong Hwangje-wa ŭisa An Chunggŭn,* 1959), Yun Pongch'un and Nam Hongik's *A Blood Bamboo* (*Hanmal p'ungun-gwa min ch'ungjŏnggong,* 1959), Shin Sangok's *The Independence Association and Young Syngman Rhee* (*Tongnip Hyŏphoe-wa ch'ŏngnyŏn Rhee Syngman,* 1959), Chŏn Ch'anggŭn's *Kim Ku, the Leader* (*Ah! paekpŏm Kim Ku sŏnsaeng,* 1960), and Kim Kangyun's *Nameless Stars* (*Irŭmŏmnŭn pyŏldŭl,* 1959)—represent the mature stage of the genre, offering high production values, a sense of historical grandeur, and a sense of future time as well as historical perspective distinct from those of their antecedents. The new films also were directed by a younger generation of filmmakers who brought a different sensibility, style, and approach to the historical content. One of the most conspicuous features of these films is their pessimistic tone, as the urgent actions of the patriot characters gain their significance against the prolonged enfeeblement of the Korean Empire (Taehan Cheguk, 1897–1910) that ultimately resulted in a complete loss of sovereignty.[31]

These films share the nationalist impulse of the films of the earlier postliberation era but broaden the scope of that nationalism by reframing political concerns in expanded historical terms. Specifically, they interrogate the origins and patterns of the political crisis and explore how the crisis gave rise to the formation of a nationalist consciousness. A particularly salient feature of these films is a visual rendition of radical political activism that chronicles the process through which the patriot leader gains the trust of his fellow Koreans. Depicting the new political leadership, then, is one of the dominant projects of 1950s biopics. The films trace the trajectory of growth or transformation of these patriots. Possessing prescience, courage, and intelligence, they undergo ordeals to emerge as great men and women of history. Stylistically, their unwavering commitment to serve the nation is fashioned in a manner deeply imbued with melodramatic tropes of the Manichaean moral imagination.[32] The authenticity that these heroes represent is a distinctive dramatic effect that also alludes to the ontology of the nation itself. In other words, the concrete stories of great individuals are equated to the abstract notion of nation.

Shin Sangok's 1959 film *Independence Association* marks the most ambitious and comprehensive undertaking of this cinematic experiment. The film chronicles the early years of Syngman Rhee's political career, spanning the late nineteenth and early twentieth centuries. This was the period when Korea tried to change its dynastic political structure, only to lose its grip on sovereignty and independence to the predatory encroachment of foreign powers, particularly Japan. Although the film's time span predates the span of the colonial period (1910–45), it formulates and accentuates several key themes and issues in the historical imaginary of anti-colonial nationalism in the postwar cinema of South Korea.

Before delving into the narrative content, however, I provide a brief production history of *Independence Association,* for it illustrates the close collaboration between the filmmaker and the state in the making of history on the screen in the late '50s. *Independence Association* also represents the clearest use of film as a propaganda tool under the Syngman Rhee administration. In fact, explicit political interests drove the production of the film in the first place. In particular, the mobilization of political networks, financial resources, and coercive measures not only buttressed the film's production financing but also secured special distribution channels and exhibition practices.

The idea for producing a biopic about the sitting president originated from an executive committee meeting of the Liberal Party in early 1960. As a part of a larger scheme to influence the upcoming presidential election in March, the committee members decided to make a film in support of Rhee's bid for reelection. The job was handed over to Im Hwasu, who then resorted to his network and influence to force celebrities and film personnel to participate in or help with the film's production.[33] The Division of Public Information came on board, transferring the seed money drawn from the Liberty Party to Im's film production company, Korea Entertainment Corporation, to initiate the production.[34] Im then ordered all members of the Anti-Communist Artists Association, which was under his direct control, to appear in the film as either actors or extras.[35] In the meantime, the Office of Presidential Security joined in the film's planning and screenwriting. Its involvement in preproduction in particular was widely publicized at the time. Rhee's oral account of his early political activism provided the basic framework for the film's narrative.[36] To facilitate the close collaboration between President Rhee and Shin, Kwak Yŏngju, chief of the Office of Presidential Security, functioned as an intermediary between the two to flesh out biographical details, all of which were faithfully reflected in the film.[37]

With the concerted effort of several government agencies, the film's production proceeded smoothly. Its production budget was 100 million *hwan,* a figure that far exceeded the cost of average film production in the 1950s. It had a cast of 170 actors and additionally mobilized tens of thousands of extras.[38] Palace buildings and other open sets were constructed at Anyang Film Studio in order to increase the sense of historical authenticity and the opulence of the drama.[39] The film was released in twenty-five theaters in ten major cities in December 1959.[40] In addition, hundreds of 16mm prints of the film were distributed to various noncommercial outlets like military units and local cultural centers for free screenings.[41] The traveling roadshow exhibitors who had close ties to Rhee's political machine also joined in, offering people in rural areas unprecedented access to the film. This widespread release was complemented by a prolonged exhibition arrangement. After its initial release in major cities, the film moved to secondary or ancillary chains and stayed in circulation continuously until March 1960. Hence, a combination of resources, talent, and influence was in place to garner public consensus in support of the regime. In short, the film was made with a precise political goal: to glorify incumbent president Rhee and promote his reelection in the following year.[42]

Close collaboration between state machinery and the film business dated back to the colonial period. It continued and intensified into the 1950s under the special circumstances of the Korean War.[43] *Independence Association* was made at the peak of this dynamic whereby members of government agencies and their informal groups of associates used resources and influence to produce films for specific political ends. For the Rhee regime, legitimation was an urgent matter in the late 1950s as it faced the widespread and deepening social problems of corruption, poverty, and malaise that had plagued the country since the devastating civil war.[44] But the discursive effects of the film as an elaborate historical set piece succeeded in doing more than merely valorizing a political leader. They actively promoted to the mass audience a particular view of the past whereby a current statesman was portrayed as the great man of history, the one endowed with a grand view of modern world history itself.

The obsession with the image of a great leader also shows the regime's effort to counteract the similar political trope that dominated the screens in its enemy state, North Korea. Although completely prohibited from circulation, North Korea's cultural productions of the parallel period depicted its leader Kim Il Sung as a figure of inspiration for revolutionary struggle and used this vision to articulate its national cinema. Given that Kim was portrayed almost always as the leader of the uncompromising armed struggle against the colonial power, South Korea's film propaganda needed to create its own trope of political leadership in response. Rather than locating new political capital in the revolt of the oppressed, *Independence Association* showcased the trajectory of a political modernity through which its own version of charismatic leadership gained legitimacy and appeal.

But what, precisely, is the substance and meaning of the leadership that *Independence Association* articulates? Here I want to draw attention to the various moments in the film that relate to the political mode of modernity that undergirds the ascendency of Rhee as the solution to the nation's crisis. The film's elaborate depiction of the failure of Chosŏn Korea reveals a necessary step in the discursive construction of the modern national subject that the leader Rhee cumulatively exemplifies.[45] The making of modern enlightened nationalism represents a progressive notion of history in which there is an ultimate horizon of modernity that Korea is destined to reach. Configured in this fashion, the film's treatment of the national crisis exceeds the temporal parameters of colonialism. Whereas colonialism, as a concept, always signifies various and systemic constraints, the enlightened nationalist thought that Rhee comes to represent is characteristically excessive, expansive, and future-driven as it strives to chart an alternate trajectory of history in which the nation ultimately is triumphant and permanent. The traumatic and [*] prolonged loss of political independence sets in motion the rise of the modern leader whose prescient ideas and actions generate the momentum to inspire and transform Koreans living in a critical phase of history. The film functions as a didactic text precisely because of this higher dimension of moral indoctrination.

The film is also unique for its projection of an epic sense of history with its display of high production values, scale, and mobilization of labor and capital. Vivian Sobchack astutely explains how Hollywood historical epics of the 1950s offered visual plenitude that registered with viewers as a "temporally reflexive and transcendental" notion of time called History.[46] Sobchack's work focuses on the close relations between the genre's popular notion of history and the phenomenological form of temporal existence that shapes the experiential field of an embodied subject. But the insight she offers has conceptual purchase for the expanded and reflexive aura of history that South Korea's biographical films of the 1950s project onto the screen. In particular, *Independence Association*'s exceptionally high production values, drawn from the large-scale mobilization of talents, resources, and props, significantly promote the perception of the staged drama as a serious reenactment of history.[47] The film's casting embellishes the grandeur of the historical time through its self-reflexive rendition of the late Chosŏn period as a crucial historical juncture. The film, moreover, utilized casting for extratextual references particular to the 1950s biographical film. For instance, in the 1959 biopic *A Blood Bamboo,* prominent actor Kim Tongwon played the role of Min Yŏnghwan (1861–1905), the minister of the Korean Empire who committed suicide to protest Japan's annexation of Korea. The actor Kim reappears as the same patriot Min in the film *Independence Association,* released just two months after the opening of *A Blood Bamboo,* creating a clear sense of continuity.[48] The film's casting hence is an aspect of how 1950s biographical films already formed a greater realm of popular history in which one text echoed another.

The main narrative of *Independence Association* captures the vicissitudes of the political crises that brought about the rise of Syngman Rhee as the nation's leader. The film's diegesis chronicles a brief ten-year period (1896–1906) when Rhee, in his twenties, undergoes three major phases of development: from a novice student of Western education, to an active member of the Independence Association, and finally to a renowned leader in national politics. In the aftermath of a series of national crises that include the Kapshin coup (1884), the Tonghak Rebellion (1894), and the First Sino-Japanese War (1894–95), Rhee resolves to acquire new Western knowledge at a modern school, but without abandoning his Confucian beliefs. He makes speedy progress at school, but drastic changes in political circumstances impede his studies. The assassination of the Korean empress Min by Japanese forces prompts Rhee's involvement in protest politics, resulting in his need to seek refuge at a temple to escape political persecution. Rhee returns to Seoul afterward but becomes disillusioned by the stifling situation of Korea under the two competing imperial powers of Russia and Japan. He responds with renewed vigor by becoming active in the campaign of the Independence Association (Tongnip Hyŏphoe) for progressive reforms. In particular, Rhee proves his leadership through editorial service for the newspaper *Tongnip Sinmun* and speeches at public gatherings. His campaign bears fruit as the king acknowledges and reflects upon the popular demand for political reform. However, Rhee soon faces political opposition from the new power group in the royal court and suffers a prolonged imprisonment. When he is finally pardoned, he offers the king his vision for Korea's future but soon leaves the country for education in the United States.

As the above plot summary shows, the film broadly traces Rhee's transformation into a modern subject holding progressive social and political ideals, first through his exposure to Western modes of education and second through his political advocacy for democracy. The first section of the film, however, presents two conflicting values, the Western knowledge of the Enlightenment and traditional Confucian mores, that condition and complicate the course of Rhee's education. Instruction at his new Western school provides Rhee with access to new knowledge but also compels him to establish terms of negotiation by which the Western knowledge he embraces will not overwhelm his Korean identity. The challenge occurs specifically around the idea of personal choice in religion. When he enrolls at Paejae School, the school curriculum includes the subject of religion, and students are expected to learn the history and values of Christianity. When the Caucasian instructor teaches the subject, however, Rhee leaves the classroom in protest. For Rhee, who is entrenched in traditional Confucian teaching, the lessons of Christianity mean more than moral teachings. He perceives them as an outright instance of indoctrination. When his friend remarks on the good virtues expressed in the Bible, Rhee cynically retorts, "Those good virtues are easily found in the teachings of Confucius. What is important for us is English language skills." Rhee's attitude here illustrates his pragmatic approach to the new knowledge and underscores his unchanging affinity with the traditional social and moral values of Korea. His refusal to allow Western learning into the domain of spiritual values indicates in contrarian fashion his affinity with past Confucian values.

The film's domestic sequences are crucial, for they offer Rhee's critical yet pragmatic view on the nature of Western knowledge. His conversation with his father and his father's friends at home offers a good example. When accused of being corrupted by Western influence, Rhee rationalizes his embrace of Western knowledge and civilization as necessary to transform the nation and prevent it from a collapse like that of the Qing Empire. The scene does not stress the collision of two values; rather, it underscores the way by which compromise and understanding can be achieved. Rhee's father and his old friends do not distinguish secular modern knowledge from Western religious doctrine, and Rhee does not attempt to explain the differences to them. Recognizing the legitimacy of their concerns, Rhee instead promises that he will learn only "the knowledge that we do not have from the West, but never abandon the teachings of ancestors." The film consistently stresses Rhee's pragmatic approach as the solution to resolving the inherent conflict between two values. By combining two bifurcating tendencies—honoring "tradition" but also taking part in the universal wave of worldly progress—he exemplifies the very essence of the nationalist mode of history writing.[49]

The moment of compromise is duly noted by Rhee's mother, who secretly observes the conversation. This adjunct imagery of the mother, whose gaze signifies her moral support for Rhee, is significant to the configuration of proper domesticity set against the political turmoil of the time. Rhee's activism is cast against this dimension of passivity associated with the domestic sphere as well as his mother's yearning for his return. Through this additional layer of recognition, the domestic space occupied by his mother appears to be receding from view even as she affirms her moral and spiritual support for the struggle he is about to wage. In other words, the home space remains essentially a site of passivity characterized by all-giving maternal love.[50] The desire of his mother is never fulfilled but functions as a fixed point for Rhee's ever-expanding activism in the sociopolitical realm.[51] As a person who is never able to repay his mother's love or end her yearning, Rhee turns into a larger-than-life figure who sublimates personal concerns to the larger political cause. Service to the nation in this configuration of emotional economy is then charged with moral character: the substance central also to the film's nationalist imagination.

The film then shifts its focus to the international political competition that led to the crisis of Korea's sovereignty and the ascendency of Rhee as a populist leader. Japan's triumph in the First Sino-Japanese War brings major changes to the royal court. With Chinese influence diminished, the king and queen gravitate toward Russian diplomats and associates in the hope of using their political clout to curb the influence of the new power: Japan. Political intrigue, espionage, and counterscheming all ensue in the subsequent sequences, shaping and foregrounding a narrative that highlights Rhee's significance as a leader.

The calamity of the assassination of Queen Min by a Japanese terrorist group, followed by the king's request for asylum in the Russian embassy, leads Rhee to initiate a public protest against Japanese aggression. Yet this episode turns out to be structurally misaligned with the subsequent course of events and political repercussions. Interestingly, the issue of Japan's egregious aggression never enters the frame again, a feature that sets the film at odds with most of the nationalist-themed films set in the colonial period. The film instead changes gears completely to explore the *next* source of foreign interference in the Korean court: Russia. Rhee then becomes the principal activist waging a struggle against the influence of Russia over Korean politics.[52] The elision suggests that the film, though depicting Korean history in a rigidly black-and-white framework, locates culpability differently than later films, which tend to conventionalize an anticolonial nationalist model. As illustrated by the film's favorable treatment of Kim Hongjip, who urged

Korea's adoption of modernizing reforms in Japan, the film portrays political affiliation with an external group as less of a problem than the self-interested benefit
that Koreans might gain from such collusion.[53] Political opportunism and acquisi-
tive greed are, the film stresses, the most deleterious problems in Korean politics,
for they weaken the trust between the king and his officials. Rebuilding trust, consensus, and solidarity becomes an urgent matter, for such values are the source
of the political capital necessary to defend the nation's sovereignty and independence. The film thus depicts Rhee's growth as that of a heroic leader who inspires
the dynamic accumulation of new political resources.

The film's elaborate formal design primarily serves to convey the momentum
and effectiveness of Rhee's campaign effort for political reform and by extension
visualizes his acquisition of political capital. In particular, it portrays Rhee as a
brilliant politician who makes unprecedented utilization of techniques of public
speech and means of modern communication such as print media, thereby establishing a public sphere. Rhee plays a crucial role in acquiring from a Christian
organization the equipment and journalistic know-how for the Independence
Association's publicity campaign. Rhee also assumes the role of editor-in-chief of
the weekly journal to galvanize and steer public opinion toward political reform.
The ensuing montage sequences, accompanied by optimistic music, heighten the
sense of hope and progress that springs from a rising awareness of the importance
of national sovereignty and rights. It is through the overlapping of political discourse for national rights and the use of print media that Rhee's intellectual prowess and organizational skills are proved. The film underscores his speech in an
open public arena as an important moment for his transformation into a national
leader, for he changes a traditional marketplace from a site of mere commodity
exchange into a dynamic public sphere where the communication of political
ideas and ideals shapes consensus and collective action. He later gives additional
speeches in the marketplace in the film, further accentuating his leadership in the
growing populist reform movement.

From the moment of the first speech, the conflict is reframed as occurring
between populist reformers, represented by Rhee, and the Russian camp, which
includes pro-Russian court officials, both of whom compete for the king's attention and action. Yet a communication problem persists between the reformers and
the king. In the meantime, public protest gains momentum to challenge business
as usual in the royal court, and the pro-Russian group presses the king, who must
rely on his advisers for information on the public mood, to take action to suppress Rhee's political activism. The growing tension between Rhee, outside formal
politics, and the pro-Russian group in the court reaches its height in the opening
ceremony of the Independence Gate.[54]

The segment is one of the most spectacular depictions of a historical event
ever staged in 1950s films, with an elaborate mise-en-scène of high production
values and a complex presentation. It visually underscores the large scale of the

FIGURE 3. Rhee delivers his speech to an audience in an open public space in *Independence Association*. Courtesy of the Korean Film Archive.

architecture of the Independence Gate, as well as the mobilization of the large crowd, both of which register the overall presentational grandeur of the ceremony. Against the backdrop of this special historic event, Rhee emerges as the focus of the mise-en-scène when he delivers his passionate speech in front of the gate. The use of a zoom lens distinguishes him as the principal figure of the public event, while the alternating long shots visually portray the historical significance and magnitude of the event and of the turmoil that erupts when thugs hired by the court's pro-Russian faction violently attack the crowd. The film's use of the zoom to valorize Rhee's leadership shows up in a later segment, along with the depiction of an open public space as the ground of new politics and leadership. When the public event ends with draconic suppression, Rhee advocates full-scale resistance, while others argue for a retreat from further suppression by the government.

Rhee orchestrates street protests by transforming public sites into collective spaces of politicization. During his speech at the marketplace, a zoom lens is again used to heighten the sense that his listeners are closely attending to him as their leader. Rhee's ascendency reaches its apex when the king responds to the call of the people by coming out of the palace to meet the group of protesters in person. The king's acknowledgment frames the issues and elevates them to a higher level of communicative politics. As the king properly promises reforms that the people demand, the film underscores his symbolic registration of the political struggle, which ends up reinforcing the monarch's own righteous authority. At this moment, the film resorts to another use of a zoom lens to show the king's appearance and communication with the people. It underscores the authority and leadership of the character in the frame, as it flattens spatial depth by creating a sense of proximity through its myopic focus. As a result, a significant parallel is drawn between Rhee and the king through the repeated use of the zoom lens.

The ensuing sequences show Rhee's active role in the reformist court, but also his entanglement in the oppositional politics that result in his incarceration.[55] His political downfall indicates the volatility of the court's politics, as the king's perception and judgment are easily subject to external influences. However, Rhee's misfortune also brings out an important feature of the reform campaign that has not come into view before: the importance of Rhee to the success of protest and reform. A letter Rhee receives from his friend conveys the vacuum in leadership that Rhee's absence produces within the progressive group and their yearning for his leadership. The pattern of longing for Rhee as the leader repeats from this moment onward. The film's mobilization of progressive politics culminates in the subtle shift of affect and desire from the king toward the new leader. The realignment of the affective trajectory enables the film to resolve the inherent dilemma associated with the leader who is unable to lead because of his arrest.

The depiction of the leader as the passive recipient of mass support reverberates in a later scene. At one point, Rhee escapes with the help of people both outside and inside the prison. When he reaches the marketplace, however, Rhee suddenly becomes disillusioned with his plan as he sees the emptiness of the site. "The reason we escaped prison," he tells his comrades, "is not just for our own safety, but to declare to the people our innocence." Pointing at the deserted public place, Rhee explains, "Look, Heaven has not given us an opportunity yet," and immediately turns himself in. The film has made clear that his populist activities owe their success to his ability to turn conventional places into public sites where he is able to inspire and mobilize people. The scene here renders visible the fundamental limit of such participatory politics. Without the presence of people, Rhee sees no possibility for resistance or mobilization.

After Rhee turns himself in, the film narrative loses its progressive drive. Though Rhee engages in the daily politics of prison, protesting torture and abuse, his rhetoric becomes increasingly abstract, devoid of concrete substance on political issues and concerns. Concurrently, he begins to declare his love for the nation in grand fashion while criticizing others for acting only out of self-interest. These changes coincide with the death penalty he receives for charges of treason.[56] But this absolute nadir also opens the door for a major transformation for Rhee: his conversion to Christianity. The director Shin stresses that this occurrence is an exceptional moment, the turning point for Rhee, through the use of light cast upon

Rhee by a prison window. The serene and ethereal ambiance suddenly dominates the scene where Rhee undergoes his born-again religious experience. Given that Rhee was previously portrayed with a rational understanding of the clear division between Christianity as a foreign religious value and Confucian order as innate to the Korean character, (this instance of conversion signals a drastic change in his values and worldview. Religion and nation become conflated as two supreme values that complement each other here. Consequently, the concept of nation itself becomes more abstract, endowed with religious undertones in Rhee's new conceptualization of values.)

The film then takes viewers into a national crisis. The outbreak of the Russo-Japanese War results in Japan's triumph and the latter's growing control of Korea. The film conveys political urgency by having the king voice an account of the situation. Court official Min advises the king to pardon and use the members of the Independence Association, including Rhee. As events unfold, Rhee reemerges as a central figure. Rhee is released from the prison to an elaborate ritual designed to showcase the aura of dignity attributed to him. He is escorted to a horse-drawn carriage brought by court official Min, who is fully dressed in diplomatic attire as if on a mission to meet a foreign dignitary. The visual splendor of the scene unmistakably emphasizes that Rhee is the anticipated leader of the nation. At the royal court, Rhee confirms the plan that the king and his advisers already have formulated: to appeal to the international community to support Korea's independence and sovereignty.

The film, however, ends with the introduction of a conundrum. The diplomatic strategies for international appeal will prove a failure: as the contemporaneous audience of the film in the late 1950s would know, Korea will become a colony of Japan. The film's last sequence then ironically showcases a gloomy prospect for Rhee's action on behalf of the nation. Rhee is offered an opportunity to study abroad, as opposed to staying in the turmoil of colonial subjugation and decline. The film thus projects a peculiar instance of leadership-making through the mismatch of two developments: the "ineffective" protagonist in ascendency at the moment of the nation's precipitous decline and demise. Rhee's worth is certainly recognized by everyone, but his ineffectuality in the face of insurmountable hardship is equally evident and troubling. The film thus offers a distinctively pessimistic view of history, when future options appear all but foreclosed in a realistic sense, that nevertheless leads to belated recognition of the new leader's knowledge.) The film's narrative moves toward the discovery of the future leader, not the solution for the current crisis. In other words, the film offers a new imagery of the leader, imbued with future possibility, bypassing the wretched phase of history called the colonial period. The agency that Rhee embodies and represents operates precisely against an assessment that the nation is the deeply doomed by the impending colonial subjugation. Rhee is an anticipated leader for the future nation, not the colonized entity, but its successor: postcolonial Korea.

Both *Hurrah!* and *Independence Association* are passionate endeavors to project the nationalist view of history onscreen. Whether they portray the anticipation of the prospective event of liberation in *Hurrah!* or the decline of the Korean polity in *Independence Association,* their sense of national history is pervasive and obvious. They also mark significant points in the development of South Korean cinema. *Hurrah!* is the first feature-length narrative film in the immediate postliberation period that places the political mandate for anticolonial struggle firmly on the screen, while *Independence Association* marks the largest scale of popular film-making in the 1950s and fully realizes the genre form of the biographical drama (the "biopic"). In terms of style, *Hurrah!* exemplifies the aesthetics of urgency in filmmaking through reemployment of narrative and formal properties drawn from late colonial films. *Independence Association* expands the scope of nationalist cinema by offering a distinct spectatorial engagement, pessimistic yet prophetic in turning toward the unrealized future of the nation. The former anticipates the collapse of colonial rule through the subversive operation of the Korean collective, while the latter examines the period leading up to the loss of sovereignty as a necessary precedent to a new chapter in Korea's modern history.

While adhering to the mandate of nationalist historiography, these films also stress the establishment of political authority as the central issue of the new nationalist cinema. How to construct the proper national leader holds the key to the formation of the new national subject in the bipolar order of the Cold War. Both films are significant as they show how such a subjective position can be constructed against the backdrop of the negation of Korean sovereignty and integrity. The heroic leader receives special attention because he embodies the impetus that breaks the double deadlock of an external threat and an internal malaise. Both films instigate scenarios of resistance by offering unique renditions of the heroic leader as the icon of political and moral authority. Political capital also becomes legible and apparent in the visualization of such leadership, shared and recognized by other Koreans.[57]

These works introduce the recurring and entrenched motifs of nationalist imagination in postcolonial South Korean cinema, where political urgency and crisis register not simply pessimism, but also the possibilities of moral certitude and authority that inspire the continuous struggle of the colonized nation. That said, both works are essentially concerned with the question of the relationship between historical time and the nation. Specifically, these films conjure a new imagery of the national collective through a new conception of future time.[58] The supremacy of the nationalist struggle lies in its capacity to project an expanded scope of time beyond the immediate reality of colonial subjugation. These films do not venture into the colonial period, so they do not directly engage with the colonial regime or other attendant issues that raise questions about the Korean self and the Other. The next few chapters will shed light on this dynamic, for the 1965 normalization treaty between Japan and Korea did raise such questions and decidedly shaped colonial representation in subsequent South Korean films.

2

Film and the *Waesaek* ("Japanese Color") Controversies of the 1960s

The 1965 bilateral treaty that brought together South Korea and Japan as regional Cold War partners meant both new opportunities and new hindrances for the local film business and filmmaking in South Korea. Film policy, censorship practices, publicity campaigns, cultural discourses, and film production were newly focused on film exchanges with Japan. Yet entering into cultural dialogue with the former enemy proved to be far more complicated and emotionally fraught than anticipated. It brought up repressed issues of decolonization and highlighted the blind spots of nationalist cultural politics in postcolonial South Korea. As films of the 1960s presented new subjects, themes, and attitudes toward the colonial past, the legacies of colonial popular culture also came to the fore, reshaping the onscreen representation of the colonial period in the ensuing decades.

THE "JAPANESE COLOR" CONTROVERSY

After liberation, South Korea maintained a completely closed-door policy toward Japanese culture and imagery. At times there were signs that the government might relax this policy, but dramatic change proved difficult to achieve. Key to understanding the cultural politics of Korean-Japanese film exchange was the heated and protracted controversy surrounding the concept of "Japanese color" (*waesaek* in Korean), the perceived threat of the encroachment of Japanese popular culture into South Korean society, that persisted throughout the 1960s. The increasing cultural visibility of Japan gave rise to this defensive discourse, which tied directly into South Korea's troubled relationship with its colonial legacy. Further, the repression of postcolonial reflection on colonialism as a cultural system was bound up with a new Cold War order in which South Korea and Japan were allies and partners. Cinema, in particular, was an arena for contestation, for it was where an "acceptance" of Japan challenged the mandate of disavowal or negation that had effectively established discursive parameters on ways of imagining, remembering, and narrating the colonial experience for the people of South Korea.

The visual nature of the new Japanese cultural encroachment placed tremendous pressure not only on how cinematic nationalism would be visualized but also on the unrecognized forces that encouraged such visualization in the first place. I would argue that the crisis of colonial representation provoked by Japanese color in the 1960s explains the advent of such new types of films in the 1960s as the *kisaeng* film and the gangster film. Confrontation with now-visible images of Japan triggered memories of forced assimilation and implied the failure of cultural decolonization. The cultural discourse informed by dread of Japanese cultural infiltration reached its height in the mid-1960s, in response to South Korea's normalization of relations with Japan in 1965. However, it is necessary to return to an earlier period to trace the shift that galvanized the momentum for cultural exchange with the former colonizer.

South Korea's April Revolution of 1960 not only ended the authoritarian regime of Syngman Rhee, but also brought a progressive spirit to all areas of culture, challenging and dismantling various cultural regulations and censorship practices. The revolution was a watershed event in the truest sense. As Kwon Bodurae convincingly argues, the young generation of college students that came to center stage through their decisive participation in the radical events of 1960 threw off the pejorative label of "the silent generation" that they had received earlier and attained a generational "self-validation," opening up a new space of possibility for social and cultural change in postwar Korea.[1]

One of the most conspicuous signs of revolutionary change in South Korean culture was the increased availability of Japanese popular culture, which had been suppressed under the staunchly anti-Japanese Rhee government. The younger generation's eager embrace of hitherto unavailable Japanese culture created an important cultural trend in the early 1960s.[2] Long-established censorship practices and regulations were revised, if not outright ended, during this period. Japanese cultural works quickly gained visibility, with a multivolume translation of Japanese modern literature, in particular, being acclaimed by cultural elites.[3]

The effort to capitalize on the liberal trend of the era was not limited to publishing. The film industry made equally vigorous attempts to cash in on the era's Japanophile frenzy. Less than ten days after the collapse of the Rhee government, the Korean Film Producers Association (hereafter KFPA) filed a petition with the Ministry of Education, the then government branch in charge of supervising film imports, not only to revise film statutes and censorship laws but to consider relaxing the prohibition on Japanese film imports.[4] The ministry responded favorably to the association's appeal for change in censorship practices, which had become stringent and repressive toward the end of the Rhee administration. However, the request to permit Japanese film imports was met with resolute rejection.[5]

The drive to bring in Japanese films intensified by means of a shrewd publicity campaign. The KFPA issued a press release stating that it had collected a list of Korean films that its members wished to export to neighboring countries, including Japan. The report added that the five major Japanese film studios had jointly drafted a letter expressing interest in importing and releasing Korean films in Japan.[6] By publicizing the plan to export Korean films to Japan, the KFPA framed the importation of Japanese films as an act of reciprocity and exchange. The call for the availability of South Korean films in the Japanese film market would mean the reciprocal availability of Japanese films in South Korea, for the mutual benefit of both countries.   *Call for film exchange for both markets*

The impetus for film exchange was fueled in part, by a larger diplomatic drive to integrate culture and film markets across the liberal Pacific region. The annual Asia-Pacific Film Festival, in particular, provided a crucial foundation upon which South Korean film producers could promulgate a permissive, if not liberal, attitude toward Japanese film and work against the current ban. Started in 1954, the Asia-Pacific Film Festival advanced its agenda to integrate the liberal capitalist bloc of the Asia-Pacific region by connecting film markets and facilitating film traffic and coproductions across the Pacific archipelago of US Cold War allies.[7] South Korea won a major award at the seventh festival, held in Tokyo in 1960, opening an avenue for South Korean film attendees, that is, film producers, to begin dialogues with major Japanese film studio personnel to normalize film exchange in the future.

This publicity campaign was part of the KFPA's greater ambition to reshape the structure of the domestic film industry—specifically, to enter and gain control over the lucrative film import business. Its petition on May 27, 1960, illustrates its leaders' business goal quite bluntly. The requests included the reform of film regulations, an overhaul of the film censorship structure and practices, the establishment of public funds for domestic film production, a tax exemption for theater admission fees, tariff relief for film equipment, and a bid to host the Asia-Pacific Film Festival in Seoul. The most controversial item on the list was the appeal that importation and distribution rights to Japanese films be placed solely in the hands of domestic film producers.[8] This "proactive" appeal was designed by the association to procure the future benefits of the Japanese film trade by taking over what had been a separate business sector for film importers and distributors. The organization strategically applied the economic rationale of protectionism: because of the "special (historical) circumstances" of South Korea and Japan, Japanese film imports and distribution should be handled differently to protect the domestic film industry.[9] The KFPA ultimately succeeded in reshaping the domestic industry in the years to come.

The association's use of Japanese cinema as leverage to gain a foothold in the film import sector reflected a growing awareness in the film business of the opportunity to capitalize on the popular interest in Japanese culture. In addition to asserting its claim for involvement in the future of Japanese film importation, the KFPA made official its demand to restrict any foreign films showing Japanese color or themes (such as Hollywood films) until the ban on actual Japanese films was formally abolished. This modest request reiterated in principle the existing cultural policy precept of South Korea: the suppression of onscreen cultural references to Japan, the center of colonial culture and indoctrination. The aesthetics of disavowal that had long dominated the previous era's filmmaking were exemplified by the film policy, and the organization invoked such disavowal for its future business strategy.

When the KFPA made its demand, Japan had already received great attention in film because of the growing use of its imagery in Hollywood films. In the midst of a relaxation of film censorship in the postrevolutionary period, the Hollywood-produced Korean War film *The Bridges at Toko-Ri* (Mark Robson, 1956) was released after the deletion of a four-minute scene that featured American soldiers on a leisurely stay in Tokyo.[11] Film importers read this move as a sign of change in the new era and submitted for review and release additional Hollywood films that featured contemporary images of Japan and close interactions between American and Japanese characters.[12] When the Ministry of Education granted release permission for *The Teahouse of the August Moon* (Daniel Mann, 1956) in the summer of 1960, the KFPA reacted vehemently.[13] It pointed out that films such as *The Teahouse of the August Moon* were not actually "Hollywood" films but coproduction works in which Japanese film companies were deeply involved.[14] According to this line of argument, making these films available to Korean viewers would mean opening the Korean film market to Japanese films. The KFPA also called for strong state leadership that would clear up these contentious issues.

The KFPA's argument illustrates how central the role of the state was to the discursive organization of the cultural politics of nationalism in the 1960s film controversies. The aesthetics of disavowal toward colonial culture led not only to the invisibility of Japan in South Korean films, but also to a particular discursive matrix. Cultural exchanges between Japan and South Korea were structurally difficult, if not impossible, to imagine when the issue was constantly viewed through the *political* prism of anticolonial nationalism. Inherent in the debate over the contemporary image of Japan was a repressed challenge to South Korea: How would it reckon with the colonial culture and its legacy in the present? The call for stronger state intervention as the solution to a problem that was visual and cultural in nature was an apparently counterintuitive impulse given the liberal cultural trend of postrevolutionary society.

The contention over the release of *The Teahouse of the August Moon* was expressed in a series of heated debates in newspapers and magazines that focused on how to protect Korean cinema and culture against the perceived threat of Japanese cultural infiltration. Some critics pointed out the deeper issue at stake:

the problem of the colonial cultural legacy. Yu Hanch'ŏl, for instance, located the root cause of the problem in the unchecked nostalgia of the older, namely, colonial, generation for Japanese culture.[15] In an extensive op-ed, Yu asserted that this troubling historical legacy justified a continuing disengagement from Japanese films and other cultural works. He criticized the film interest group for exploiting the political milieu, arguing that its attempt to bring in Japanese film was a cheap trick to take advantage of the liberal trend of the era.

Though largely adhering to nationalist rhetoric, Yu's article nevertheless was rare in addressing the problem of the colonial legacy and its effects on the Korean people long after the formal demise of colonialism. For him, the problem was not strictly a matter of establishing proper film laws or regulations; rather, it concerned the mental state (*maŭm-ŭi chunbi*) of the contemporary Korean people. Without sound mental preparedness, he predicted, South Korea would suffer the depressing fate of the Taiwanese film market, which according to him had become largely dominated by Japanese films.

[handwritten margin note: colonial legacy of Japan still being felt / relevant]

[handwritten margin note: Seeing it as another takeover / colonization of Japanese film market open]

Overall, Yu's critique resorted to the language and rhetoric of anticolonial nationalism, but also called for rapprochement with the new partner Japan. On the surface, Yu underscored the importance of decolonization in the cultural field and especially in the nation's collective consciousness. There was, however, a short-circuit in his argument that averted more rigorous reflection on the lacunae of cultural decolonization. He emphasized that an anticolonial mentality was essential for sound opposition to the encroaching Japanese culture, and he remained critical of any capricious policy that would permit Hollywood films with Japanese themes and thereby might corrupt the existing film forms, governed by what I call the "aesthetics of disavowal," that postcolonial South Korean cinema had collectively and cumulatively developed. However, at another point, Yu attacked the very principle he was defending for being old-fashioned and pedantic. "The anti-Japaneseness of the past is unreflective, as if it were used as a mere weapon [against the enemy]." He then wrote that contemporary Japan was no longer an enemy state but a partner of cultural exchange in a liberal world.

The bifurcating tendencies in Yu's argument warrant emphasis because the ambivalence he conveyed appeared repeatedly in the articles of other writers in subsequent years. His idea was not simply an expression of an individual view but a statement of the generational anxiety of those who had firsthand experience of colonial culture and indoctrination. This ambivalence originated from the failure to resolve the new challenges brought to the old scenario of anticolonial visuality. The changed circumstances of the early 1960s created a milieu liberal enough to accept cultural works from the former enemy state, bringing the void of representation into sharp relief and effecting a direct critique of the narrow anticolonial visuality of film.

Repeated calls for the suspension of film market liberalization were a desperate attempt to curtail postcolonial questioning that challenged the anticolonial imagining and attempted to fill the void of *critical* decolonization. While what Yu advocated was an understandable response to what he deemed the challenges of Japanese cultural aggression, I would stress that such rhetoric ended up promoting a passive means of managing the crisis of the moment. Like many in cultural fields who imagined the normalization of bilateral relations as somehow happening eventually, Yu sought postponement of a mutual exchange of cultures until the proper time came. His article presupposed the powerlessness of writers like himself by demanding the state's direct action to protect the young or misguided masses who would otherwise be duped by the dangerous lure of Japanese culture. Instead of calling into question the remnants of colonial cultural indoctrination, Yu and his fellow writers directed their elitism toward the Korean people, who might not distinguish "good" art from that which was culturally corrupting. Hence, the only Japanese films that deserved approval for release were films of high artistic merit, educational films, and documentary films.

THE 1960s CENSORSHIP REGIME

The controversy over the release of the Japanese documentary film *The Torch* (*Sŏnghwa*) in 1960 revealed that the notion of culture was, in fact, at the core of the problem concerning filmic images of contemporary Japan. *The Torch,* about the Olympic Games, was petitioned for release as a "culture film," a category that encompassed all films other than feature-length narrative films or newsreels. As a separate film category, a culture film did not need to follow the established protocols and procedures of censorship that applied to narrative films. The film importer had already secured an import license for *The Torch,* but the import division of the Ministry of Commerce sought to block the process. The importer protested the decision on the grounds that the import license guaranteed the release of a non-narrative culture film. A newspaper article featured a critical view of the release of the film, calling it the creation of an "extraterritorial screening space" in South Korea.[16] The Division of Culture within the Ministry of Education, however, defended the film's release, as it was based on the decision of the advisory board, which had approved the importation and release of the documentary for its educational merit. The vice minister, in turn, came forward with a different view. Even if a culture film possessed educational merit, he argued, it still was too early to import Japanese culture films.[17] The Ministry of Education convened a meeting to review *The Torch* and identified its problems. One such problem was that the film featured disproportionate coverage of the Japanese national team and its activities. Moreover, it presented the Japanese national anthem. The ministry ordered the removal of the Japanese national anthem from the soundtrack and allowed the film's limited release thereafter.

The direct censorship of *The Torch* indicates how volatile the circulation of Japanese language was in the cultural politics of South Korea. International sports, the film's focus, was one of the most popular subjects in culture films, and the Korean film audience often flocked to see historic moments of international recognition for Korean athletes' achievements in various events.[18] The sports arena provided a space of interaction and fair competition between countries and thereby fostered a sense of mutual understanding that was rare in any other cultural field. But the Japanese anthem scene in the film posed a direct assault on one of the founding principles of anticolonial nationalism in South Korea: monolingualism and the suppression of the use of the Japanese language and script in public space. For several critics, the strongest objection to the importation of Japanese films was that the films made audible the language of the ex-colonial power. *— even listening to Japanese censored*

As Serk-bae Suh has noted, national bilingualism was completely prohibited in postcolonial Korea. Both North and South Korea adopted measures to suppress the use of the Japanese language in public spaces and to make monolingualism irreversible.[19] It was claimed that the showing of a Japanese-language film would turn a movie theater into a rehearsal site for bilingual education, familiarization with Japanese culture, and the kind of imperial subject formation that many viewers had experienced growing up in the colonial era. Those who had received formal education during the colonial era were especially alarmed because for their generation, a Japanese-language film was not a foreign film but a native one. The producer Han Lim incisively observed that Japanese films would provide a viewing experience distinct from other foreign films, for Korean film viewers would easily understand the Japanese language without the help of subtitles.[20] Screening of a Japanese film would immediately trigger the ideological effect of interpellation, as older Koreans would be called on to react to the Japanese language much as they had done when they were subjects of the colonial era. In the face of this grave situation, one reporter astutely pointed out that what had to be prevented from entering Korea in films was not Japanese color or imagery but the Japanese *language*.[21] *bc of Japanese language involvement in colonization → Japanese film is a different experience*

For the younger generation, who had not received a colonial education in Japanese, falling under the sway of Japanese culture did not seem like a problem or a danger. Yet instead of soul-searching, critics emphasized the harmful effects that Japanese film would have on a naive audience of young people. In addition, after the end of Rhee's regime, a particular elitist view of the Korean film audience emerged in proposals to distinguish culturally worthy artworks from decadent and salacious films.[22] It was the state, these elite writers claimed, that should take an active role in selecting artistic films from Japan when the ban was lifted.[23]

That day grew nearer. Support for opening the Korean film market to Japanese films gained momentum as normalization between the two countries became a foreseeable reality in the mid-1960s. The Park Chung Hee administration, which took power through a military coup in 1961, implemented vigorous efforts to normalize relations with Japan, a reflection of the regime's pursuit of economic incentives as well as its compliance with US demands for greater integration of the anticommunist bloc in the region. The anticipation of normalization translated into an intensification of campaigns to import Japanese films as well as forays into new types of domestic film production, both of which capitalized on a new public interest in Japanese culture and film.

Those who were in favor of liberalizing the domestic film market used the economic rationale of reciprocity to underscore the benefits of trade. As noted, the KFPA worked in tandem with the major Japanese studios to devise and plan future coproductions as part of a business model to benefit both parties. The lifting of the ban on Japanese films would not result in losses to the domestic market. Rather, the quid pro quo of film traffic would create an opportunity for Korean cinema to enter the Japanese market. The prospect of normalization on the horizon helped this discourse gain more support in the film industry. Furthermore, Japanese technological superiority in filmmaking was reason enough for many film producers to push for closer ties with Japan. The disparity was particularly pronounced in the area of the postproduction process. Since the conversion to color film, technological factors had played an important role in a film's overall box office performance. South Korean film producers, who had to send their holiday-targeted films to Japan because of its superiority in handling postproduction work, were eager to learn about Japan's technological advances from close interaction.[24]

The Asia-Pacific Film Festival of 1962 offered a prospect for normalization and stimulated liberal views on film exchange. Held in Seoul, the festival screened Japanese films in Korea for the first time since liberation. Four Japanese films were shown to a select audience, and the Ministry of Information set up an additional screening for Korean filmmakers and personnel. Some of the audience who saw all four films expressed satisfaction but also questioned the current ban on Japanese film, describing it as an "overreaction" to the threat of Japanese culture.[25] It is noteworthy that Shin Sangok's *Sŏng ch'unhyang* was released in Japan just a month before the opening of the film festival, creating the sense of a simultaneity of film exchange across the strait. The film was hailed in the South Korean press as the first wide-screen release in Japan, cementing Shin's reputation as the most influential filmmaker- producer of the era.

Meanwhile, controversies over Japanese imagery spilled over into Korean film production. In an effort to capitalize on the perceived attraction of Japanese imagery, several Korean filmmakers took the bold step of conducting film shoots that captured images of contemporary Japan, which they then used in domestic films. Kim Kiyoung's 1961 film *Over Hyŏnhaet'an Strait* (*Hyŏnhaetanŭn algoitta*) is an early example of this film "smuggling."[26] Kim's film got through censorship because it did not showcase a diegetic event set in the real physical site of Japan. Kim merely used images he took in Japan as insert shots for his film.[27] The filmmakers who attempted actual location shooting in Japan were not so lucky, as the Ministry of Information still upheld the ban on direct references to Japan, its people, and its culture. The filmmakers had to either give up releasing the finished film or suffer the compromise of having the offensive images removed from the film. The same government body, however, reacted very differently to Japanese "color" or themes in Hollywood films, generally giving them more liberal treatment. The obvious inconsistency had a galvanizing effect on the KFPA, which in 1962 made this aspect of film censorship a new target of criticism.[28] *[handwritten: Japanese film censorship inconsistent]*

The challenge posed by films' use of contemporary images of Japan took an unexpected turn in 1963, when the South Korean film *Happy Solitude* (*Haengbokhan kodok*; Shin Kyŏnggyun, 1963) was submitted for a censorship review and release permit. The film's inclusion of location images from Japan provoked ire, adding further confusion about the definition of Japanese color. The film is based on the true story of a Japanese woman who married a Korean man against the opposition of her natal family. She leaves Japan in pursuit of love and settles in Korea with her husband. Given the nature and scope of the narrative, it would have been impossible to meet the stipulation to avoid Japanese elements and images. The film was, after all, the story of a Japanese woman whose troubled interaction with her family was an important part of the whole narrative. Yet the visual references to her Japanese ethnic identity and upbringing, such as her kimono, a Japanese song, and the images of Japan as her natal country, were subject to suppression for violating the established codes of anti-Japanese film aesthetics.[29] To secure the film's release, the film's producer complied with the injunction of the board by removing seven problematic scenes deemed inappropriate.[30]

The miscalculation of the domestic film producer did not occur within a vacuum. Since the advent of the Park administration, the normalization of relations with Japan had been accepted in film circles as a fait accompli, although the terms of such a development remained unclear. This perception, in turn, encouraged the industry to seize the benefits of the anticipated availability of Japanese culture and imagery. The government fueled the anticipation by its liberal handling of Japanese color in Hollywood films. While this elicited vehement criticism from some film and cultural sectors, it also convinced Korean film producers to simultaneously include Japanese color themselves.

Happy Solitude was a bold attempt by the Korean film production company Ihwa Yŏnghwasa to respond to the signs of a change in the times. It also signaled a shift in the approach of Korean film producers, from defensive actions that curtailed the importation of foreign films that included Japanese visual and cultural elements to active filmmaking that featured the interaction of Koreans and Japanese on screen. The treatment of a Japan-related theme in *Happy Solitude* was innovative enough for other film producers to follow suit and underscore the close proximity of the two countries through themes of interethnic romance, understanding, and reconciliation.[31] On the basis of these developments, film critics and industry leaders went so far as to suggest three gradual phases of introducing Japanese color to abet film exchange and market liberalization: the state would allow first the importation of Western films that showed contemporary Japan as the background of a story (or were shot on location in Japan), then films that showed Japanese actors, and finally Japanese films proper.[32]

Such expectations were to prove too hopeful. South Korean filmmakers failed to recognize how protean the definitions of Japanese color would become in subsequent years.[33] *Happy Solitude,* moreover, created a political crisis within the KFPA. The film's supposed promotion of Japanese color gave ample reason for film importers who had been defensive about the issue of Japanese color to wage a publicity campaign against the KFPA. The film represented a filmmaking practice that deviated from the state's official agenda of opposing films of Japanese color, so some members condemned *Happy Solitude* for taking advantage of the current Japanophilia, while others insisted on full support for unrestricted domestic film production. The controversy tarnished the reputation of the KFPA, for it had been vocal about the corrupting influence of Japanese color on the minds of Korean viewers. To many Korean viewers and the censorship bureau, the case of *Happy Solitude* revealed inconsistent, if not contradictory, actions on the part of the KFPA.[34]

The controversy over the film illustrates how even an austere drama that stressed the affirmation of national identity could be subject to censure for violating the established visual protocols of anti-Japanese ideology. The film hence stands for the conundrums that faced the postcolonial film industry in depicting new terms of exchange with Japan. The film's treatment of the interethnic romance deserves particular attention for this reason. Its narrative depicts the female protagonist's conversion from a Japanese to a Korean identity through marriage and thereby reinforces the centrality of the Korean national identity. It is an inversion of the late colonial cultural policy that was geared toward assimilation and conversion of Koreans into docile and faithful subjects of imperial Japan. The film's narrative therefore attempts to "deprogram" this anterior political indoctrination by promoting ethnic harmony and understanding from the privileged viewpoint of the contemporary Korean and having a Japanese woman come to terms with her country's colonial violence through her willing embrace of Korean culture and identity. The state's intervention blocking this postcolonial fantasy scenario of interethnic harmony showed that it was structurally difficult, if not impossible, to faithfully depict a Japanese person—the elementary visual "module," so to speak, necessary for any plausible narrative configuration of the Japanese Other in interaction with the Korean nation in a contemporary setting. Having been deprived of this dimension of visual properties because of the established parameters of the anticolonial mandate, South Korean cinema faced a fundamental and critical crisis of representation concerning Japan. In an effort to sustain the existing masquerade, the government blocked the cultural effort to construct new terms of exchange and relations with Japan onscreen.[35]

It was during this period of experimentation with Japanese themes that South Korean cinema faced yet another charge. Critics began to voice concerns over the pervasive practice in South Korean cinema of copying narrative materials from Japanese film and literature. This disingenuous filmmaking practice, critics argued, was increasing as Korea moved steadily toward normalization with Japan and was a sign of a troubling tendency within the industry to capitalize on the lure and bankability of Japanese culture.[36] Some went so far as to demand that the state take action to curtail outright infringement practices rather than pursue the trifling matter of identifying and eliminating Japanese cultural references in Korean cinema.[37] According to this line of argument, a troubling infiltration of Japanese culture had already occurred. Unchecked, Japanese film sources had been "smuggled" onto the Korean film screen. In particular, the success of "youth films" (*chŏngch'un yŏnghwa*) testified to the phantom presence of Japanese cinema in South Korean culture.[38] *themes in Japanese culture making their way into Korean cinema*

Although the lack of originality in filmmaking identified by critics raised concerns, the dispute was in no way comparable in scope and weight to the controversies over Japanese color. For one thing, the practice of infringement was too pervasive and structurally embedded in the mode of filmmaking of the time. Screenwriter Yu Hanch'ŏl was forthright about the widespread practice. Director Yu Hyŏnmok also acknowledged the prevalence of the problem and noted that it perhaps was too late to correct it on an individual level.[39] South Korea's self-imposed insulation ironically created room for the greater inflow and appropriation of Japanese cultural content into South Korean films.

I would like to complicate the picture of infringement a bit by reflecting on the nature of the disavowal that governed what was Japanese in the mid-1960s. The infringement issue entailed neither lasting debate nor policy repercussions. The serious dilemma of Japanese cultural encroachment was framed almost exclusively in terms of visual and linguistic references. The state required submitted works to be free of any visual or auditory allusion to Japan and suppressed any mention of Japanese sources – disallowing, for instance, the appearance of a Japanese author's name in a film's credits. Ironically, then, any effort by South Korean filmmakers to come clean about the Japanese sources of their narratives was institutionally impossible. Films that passed censorship scrutiny were not mere plagiarisms but translations or adaptations of Japanese originals because of the institutional mandate to sanitize and "indigenize" Japanese narrative sources. *Japan couldn't be seen or heard*

Navigating the demands of the state and the populace was a challenge even for the era's most talented filmmaker. The film director and mogul Shin Sangok jumped on the bandwagon for making Japanese-themed films in 1965. In an effort to reflect the current zeitgeist, he examined the timely subject of South Korea's relationship with Japan through the production of a megahistorical drama, *The Sino-Japanese War and Queen Min the Heroine* (*Chŏngil chŏnjaenggwa yŏgŏl minbi*; Im Wonsik and Na Ponghan, 1965). Set in the declining years of the Chosŏn dynasty, this epic historical drama rehearses the nationalist history lesson of the biographical films of the late 1950s. The film galvanizes anti-Japanese consciousness through detailed presentation of the historical events that led up to the gruesome assassination of Queen Min by Japanese assailants. Unlike other South Korean films that tried to tap into the perceived attraction of contemporary Japanese culture, Shin brought the old politics of anti-Japanese nationalism back to the screen.[40] The film proved to be the year's most prestigious work, winning four major prizes at the annual Grand Bell Awards.

Censorship records reveal, however, that the film had to undergo tortuous steps of review and compromise to earn the final approval of the ministry. In this case, the controversies did not center on a favorable portrayal of Japanese culture. Instead, the film's outright contrarian politics of anti-Japanese nationalism were the cause for concern. In fact, the censorship body in the ministry cited violation of the clause in the new film law that prohibited negative portrayal of foreign countries with which South Korea was about to develop diplomatic relations. For a regime that faced the opposition of the masses to prospective normalization with Japan, the prestigious historical epic represented the type of dangerous filmmaking that could potentially incite dissenting views. Shin's move to incorporate a strand of oppositional politics into his film thus was not so successful. The stringent application of the film law showed how difficult it was, even for a seasoned filmmaker like Shin, to produce films with a strongly anti-Japanese imaginary.

THE NEW ERA OF NORMALIZATION

When the momentous 1965 normalization treaty did come to pass, one direct result for South Korean filmmaking was the opportunity, finally, to pursue coproductions. Normalization promulgated a discourse of an equal partnership between South Korea and Japan in virtually all areas of interaction. Under the aegis of the United States, this new geopolitical integration facilitated production of various imaginaries that were in the service of the two countries' equal and reciprocal relationship. The anterior aesthetic precept of negation and disavowal entered a new phase of adjustment, if not transformation, for the circumstances required cultural productions to align with the expected view of the new partnership. The move toward coproduction gained momentum and support within the film industry, as it was understood by many as the safest and most viable form of filmmaking that would also comply with the new spirit of diplomacy.

The coproduction effort, however, encountered disarray and mishaps despite the measured steps taken by production companies. The story of the production of *Daughter of the Governor General* (*Ch'ongdok-ŭi ttal*; Cho Kŭngha, 1965) is an example.[41] The production company, Segi Sangsa, entered into an informal business partnership with Toei and planned to barter an in-house actor for future

FIGURE 4. Poster for *Daughter of the Governor General*. Courtesy of the Korean Film Archive.

films. *Daughter of the Governor General* was the first instance of such an arrangement. In exchange for the appearance of the Japanese actress Michi Kanako in the film, the South Korean actress Kim Hyejŏng was to appear in an upcoming Toei feature film.[42] Segi Sangsa took the initiative to bring the Japanese actress to Korea to shoot the main segments of the film before it received formal approval for production from the Ministry of Public Information. Coproduction by means of actor exchange appeared to many to be a reasonable strategy and encouraged more directors to plan coproductions.

On July 13, 1965, a month after the normalization treaty, the Ministry of Public Information announced a plan to allow film exchanges with Japan. It would have four phases: (1) permission to include location images of Japan in South Korean cinema, (2) the exchange of actors between South Korea and Japan, (3) coproduction, and (4) the direct importation of Japanese films. Because *Daughter of the Governor General* jumped straight to phase 2 and used a Japanese actress, the ministry blocked the film's release.

While the makers of *Daughter of the Governor General* were prematurely optimistic about the prospects of film exchange, phase 1 was implemented and location shots of Japan immediately proliferated in South Korean films. The director Kim Suyong benefited most from this policy change. Kim made four films in 1966 that prominently showed urban locales of modern Japan: *Affection* (*Yujŏng*), *Nostalgia* (*Manghyang*), *Love Detective* (*Yŏnae t'amjŏng*), and *Goodbye Japan* (*Charigŏra Ilbonttang*).

Many Korean film critics were provoked by what they saw as an excessive use of Japanese urban space in films and claimed that Japanese urban location imagery was being introduced primarily to cater to the tourist gaze of the film spectator.[45] Some critics complained about the prevalence of flat postcard-like imagery that served no dramatic purpose other than providing viewers a virtual form of tourist sightseeing in Japan.[46] Concurrent with increased imagery of Japan was the hiring of actors who were Zainichi (i.e., ethnic Korean permanent residents in Japan) for the roles of Japanese characters. Film producers resorted to this as a method of circumventing the ministry's ban on hiring Japanese actors (since this remained a principal form of censorship restriction). Kong Midori, an actress who first appeared as a Japanese woman in *Over Hyŏnhaet'an Strait* in 1960, played virtually the same role of an ethnic Japanese in two more films: *The Bridge over Hyŏnhaet'an Strait* (*Hyŏnhaet'an-ŭi kurŭmdari*; Chang Ilho, 1963) and *Goodbye Japan* (*Charitkŏra Ilbonttang*; Kim Suyong, 1966).[47] These attempts to evade the stringent restrictions did not garner commercial success or critical acclaim in the end. Yet they illustrate the South Korean filmmakers' difficulties in using and handling visual references of Japan without raising the concerns of the censorship agency.

The burgeoning filmic imagery and references to Japan in the mid-1960s continued to draw criticism, but this criticism began to reflect changes in perceptions of and attitudes toward Japanese cinema. When South Korean and Japanese film producers began their informal meetings at Asia-Pacific Film Festivals in the early 1960s, Korean filmmakers had sought the benefits of film exchange in part to emulate the critical and commercial success of Japanese art films on the international film circuit.[48] Major film auteurs such as Akira Kurosawa and Mizoguchi Kenji had enjoyed phenomenal success in the late 1950s, and the high reputation of Japanese film continued into the early 1960s. In the mid-1960s, however, Korean film critics began to recognize a decline of the Japanese film boom overseas as well as domestically. The rise of youth films and other types of films in Japan that prominently featured sexual subjects and social problems were interpreted as a sign of the decline of Japanese cinema.[49]

Indeed, the salacious treatment of sexuality led to the demand by critics and film personnel that the state should protect Korean audiences from exposure to exploitative Japanese films. The argument that the state should exercise an active role in distinguishing good Japanese film imports from low entertainments gained the support of intellectuals. If coproduction with Japan relied on a rhetoric of exchange and reciprocity for the benefit of South Korea to catch up with Japan and its advanced cinema, growing worries over the decadent aspect of Japanese cinema led to recommendations that only high art or enlightening films should be permitted for import and screening in South Korea. I argue that this division of Japanese cinema into high art and low entertainment, along with the highly elusive notion of Japanese color and continued deferral of proposed changes, gave the government excuses to keep Japanese film at bay until the late 1990s. By acknowledging and incorporating these critical concerns into film policy, the state was able to claim a role as the sole protector of Korean culture against the corrupting influence of foreign culture.

Confusion over the parameters of permissible cultural exchanges with Japan reached its height when the government ordered the suspension of the production of *Lonesome Goose* (*Koan*) in late 1966. The film was based on the popular TV drama *Tokyo Vagabond* (*Tongkyŏng nagŭne*), written by the era's most prolific popular media writer, Cho Namsa. The story presents a romance between a young Korean shipbuilding engineer and a Japanese girl from a noble background. Most of the events take place in Japan, where the Korean protagonist stays to learn engineering skills. Technically, *Lonesome Goose* was not a coproduced film but was planned as a "collaboration project" between two companies: Han'guk Chungang Yŏnghwa Chejak Hoesa of South Korea and Toei of Japan. The level of collaboration was unprecedented, however, as Toei was to be deeply involved in many aspects of the film's production, from its initial planning to the adaptation of the TV drama's screenplay, production design, music, and even partial support for directing. South Korea's Choe Muryong was to direct and play the leading role in the film. After the completion of principal photography in Japan, the film was scheduled for release in both Japan and South Korea in the following year.

Like the producer of *Happy Solitude*, the collaboration team behind *Lonesome Goose* gravely miscalculated the position of the South Korean government regarding rapid moves toward film cooperation.[50] The government's 1965 plan, which had allowed a first phase of film location shooting in Japan to begin in that year, did not lead to further steps. According to the timetable of the plan, the appearance of Japanese actors was also scheduled for 1965, then permission for coproductions in 1966 and full importation of Japanese films in 1967.[51] However, the government reversed itself after it received numerous complaints from various film sectors.

In the meantime, Choe took a proactive step to normalize film exchange with Japan through his de facto coproduction in 1966, an effort that was in line with the original time frame of Korean film market liberalization. The chasm between the enforcement of film policy and film production practice suggests the difficulty in reaching a consensus about the threat of Japanese cinema in South Korea. The government, which promised a lenient approach to the subject of Japanese film, was able to exercise a draconian suppression of filmmaking practices that were deemed inappropriate on the basis of a film law that had been in place since 1962. The government pointed out the disparity between the preproduction plan and the finished film content as being in violation of the existing film law and issued an immediate suspension of production of *Lonesome Goose*.

The fate of *Lonesome Goose* makes clear that the government was able to exercise unquestioned authority over the definition of Japanese color, even though the terms of the definition remained unclear and contradictory. In fact, the Japanese cinema that occupied the minds of Korean cultural elites, filmmakers, critics, and policy makers during this period has a phantom quality. Its presence never materialized, but the discourse surrounding its effects was real enough to forestall and ruin the prospects of two Korean films that ventured into the territory of imagining dialogue with modern Japan.[5] The subject of Japanese color belongs to a peculiar cultural ramification of the Cold War in which the exclusion of contemporary Japan from cultural productions was conceived as the sole approach to dealing with the problem of the colonial legacy and its effects, since it was the approach least likely to disturb South Korea's version of a new partnership with Japan that was required by Cold War politics and economic interests.

During the frenzy of Japanese location shooting in South Korean cinema in 1966, many filmmakers sought to explore themes of cultural exchange and harmony with Japan—and faced frequent censorship hurdles as a result. But the films that represented Japan without any objection from the censors were anticommunist espionage films, which proliferated during this period. Kim Suyong's *Nostalgia* (*Manghyang*) and *Goodbye Japan* are noteworthy for their portrayal of Japanese space as a dangerous ground of communist infiltration and indoctrination.[9] The principal character interaction takes place between a South Korean and a *chŏch'ongryŏn* (a Zainichi Korean) who turns out to be politically affiliated with communist North Korea. These films cultivated one of the most recurring Cold War themes associated with Japan in the ensuing years: the dubious political identity of members of the Korean-Japanese (Zainichi) diaspora and the absence of Japanese political leadership to curtail or suppress the activities of Korean communist subversives. Thus, it was through reemployment of the Cold War trope of international bipolar politics that the imaging of contemporary Japan finally made a full entrance into South Korean cinema. The Japan that existed as the backdrop of espionage films was marked as the Other space, filled with the danger of communist threat and indoctrination, a construction of difference that was indispensable to the continued disguise of all other kinds of integration that were taking place under US hegemony.

Problems with Japanese color also affected the way colonial space was depicted in the films of the late 1960s. As noted earlier, normalization proliferated tropes and discourses of the two countries' future relationship in terms of exchange and equivalency. The normalization treaty of 1965 had encouraged South Korean cultural producers to imagine and pursue collaborations with Japanese partners on an equal footing. Seen from this perspective, it was not just a turning point in Cold War geopolitics. Conceiving the relationship between South Korea and Japan in the framework of equivalence, mutuality, and reciprocity meant that even though South Korea might show signs of underdevelopment in many areas, including filmmaking, it now shared a trajectory of historical progress with Japan and a destiny to defend freedom and fight communism. Japan implicitly represented a model of emulation for South Korea in the area of economic activities, as the two countries were set within the geopolitical structure of a US-dominated bipolar world. Consequently, critical engagement with colonial history and postcolonial reckoning and reflection were regarded as backward-looking resistance to normalization and were criticized as showing a timid reluctance to embrace change and progress.[54]

Given the way Japan had been opposed politically but excluded culturally in the previous visual renditions of the colonial era, the new conceptual framework of equalization was itself a major development. The coproduction efforts within the film industry were a direct application of this new principle. The impulse to bring together two entities with inimical relations created a new zone of proximity in South Korean cinema that, as we will see, gained prominence in films about *kisaeng* and gangster characters.

3

The Manchurian Action Film

A New Anticolonial Imaginary in the Cold War Context

THE ERA OF THE MANCHURIAN ACTION FILM

The Manchurian action film cycle emerged in the mid-1960s, revisiting and refashioning Korea's colonial history. The cycle began with Im Kwon-taek's *Farewell to Tumen River* (*Tuman'ganga chal ikkŏra*) in 1962, peaked from 1963 to 1965, and entered an eclipse in the early 1970s. Along with the 1970s action films that frequently feature Hong Kong as a romantic backdrop for masculine romance and action, Manchurian action films occupy a special place in the constellation of South Korean cinema. They highlight the physical actions of masculine heroes as the principal means by which to figuratively render the colonial past and manage the era's unique social and historical dilemmas.

These films typically present the stories of Korean resistance guerrillas and their heroic struggle against the powerful Japanese military force in Manchuria during the colonial period. Forced into exile, the nationalist warriors engage in guerrilla warfare and eventually defeat the Japanese army in local battles through espionage operations, uncommon valor, and exceptional prowess. The films project the militant struggle of anticolonialism into the multiethnic space of Manchuria and affirm the relevance of a combative anti-Japanese nationalism in the shifting sociocultural landscape of South Korea in the 1960s. The Manchurian action film, in other words, codifies and expands the cinematic vocabulary of nationalism anew by romanticizing and mythologizing the militant nationalist struggle of diaspora Koreans against the Japanese.

While the dream of a unifying nationalism is the most obvious feature of the films' narratives and characterizations, a closer analysis shows the ambivalence these films have about portraying the dark times of the nation's history. In particular, the melodramatic trope of family as an allegory for nation, along with the military aspect of campaigns, brings into question the dire cost of clandestine operations for particular individuals or families. The films also concurrently project a different set of views and discourses on the space of Manchuria. Whereas Manchuria had been crucial to Korean nationalist historiography as an irredentist national space, Manchurian action films distance themselves from such presumptions by framing the actions of anticolonial agents (and criminals) in the language and imagery of war and action genres.

In the second half of the chapter, I make a radical interpretive turn from the critical merit of melodramatic excess in Manchurian action films to the thematic undercurrent that informs the varied ideological dimensions of these films. While the genre captures the oppositional terms of the nationalist struggle, it also reveals a distinct discursive formulation of the nationalist campaign and goals when set against the larger backdrop of war narrative films in South Korean cinema. In particular, the ways in which Manchurian action films invoke the economic aspect of warfare prepare us to approach the genre as a unique instance of war narrative logic in the contemporary Cold War setting. To illustrate the Manchurian action film's location in the war imaginary, however, requires a substantial remapping of South Korea's war narrative films. The long detour is needed to bracket the dominant war narrative films and to distinguish the Manchurian action film's unique yet disruptive ideological operation within the assumed political structure of the time. Hence, the second part of the chapter offers a reading of Manchurian action films against the Korean War films that have provided the dominant war narrative and imagery in South Korea and that have historically overdetermined how war in general has been understood and imagined.

HISTORIOGRAPHY AND THE SOCIAL HISTORY OF KOREAN MANCHURIA

Early in the century, when Korea underwent the turmoil of annexation to Japan, many intellectuals turned to history and history-writing to find solutions to the political crisis. One of the leading intellectuals of this movement was Sin Ch'aeho, who, in publishing his bold treatises on Korea's history in newspapers, forcefully argued for Manchuria's territorial importance to the nation.[2] Sin rejected the peninsula-bound territoriality of conventional history-writing, instead defining the territory of the Korean nation as extending into the land of Manchuria. His irredentist view of the Korean Manchurian connection was meant to forge a particular nationalist history that proclaimed the glory of the ancient dynasties without a constraining notion of territorial sovereignty.[3] According to this view, the nation's success or failure rested on reclaiming the lost northern land.[4] As colonial scholar

Andre Schmid aptly points out, the nation as the subject of history and the territory of Manchuria were inextricably linked in Sin's treatment—Manchuria stood as the ultimate yardstick by which to describe the history of the nation.

Issues of the national border and territorial sovereignty gained strong currency at the turn of the century as newspapers frequently reported the encroachment of foreign forces, incidents of border violations, and territorial controversies.[6] The most notable example was the Sino-Korean contention over Jiandao ("Kando" in Korean), the area north of the Tumen River. For Chang Chiyŏn, a nationalist historian of the colonial period, national geography and borders were particularly crucial to the study of national history. He asserted that the historian's job was to discover and clarify the location of old geographic names.[7] By recasting the premodern account of national space, Chang was able to contextualize earlier premodern texts in strongly nationalist terms, making past knowledge directly relevant to the contemporaneous "Kando" controversy.[8] An empirical study of geopolitical arrangements functioned as a historical anchor for furthering the modern concepts of national rights and sovereignty. The works by Sin and Chang represent a discursive pattern in which Manchuria became a crucial part of Korea's national and historical imaginary in modern times.[9]

It should be noted that Japanese historians had developed their own historical argument on the importance of Manchuria by structurally linking Manchuria and Korea. Japanese historians such as Shiratori Kurakichi used the term *Mansenshi*, which literally means Manchurian-Korean history, to argue for the inseparable connection between the two regions. They then placed the combined history of *Mansenshi* under the rubric of "Toyo" (the East), the new and broad geocultural term in Japan's modern historical narrative that displaced China from centrality and elevated Japan to the dominant position in Asia.[10] In *Mansenshi*, Manchuria and Korea do not signify independent nation-states but precisely a historical lack thereof. They have always been inferior to Japan and in need of Japanese instruction, assistance, and protection.[11]

These diverging theses inform the importance of Manchurian space to both camps. Both imperialist and anticolonial scholars wrote history by claiming Manchuria on their own terms. They also employed the motif of vacancy and emptiness in writing Manchuria, making it a frontier space akin to the West in the history of the United States. This spatial motif was then used as the basis for a call to action to occupy and possess the land. The discursive malleability is an integral part of the representation of Manchuria in various cultural works and ideological treatises. In short, Manchuria became a contested site in opposing historical arguments, which nevertheless were similar in their calls for national action to occupy the "vacant" space.

If Korean historians designated Manchuria as the cradle of the nation, actual migratory history had a different resonance in the social memory of colonialism.

Early Korean migrants to Manchuria were farmers from the northern border who moved to the Jiandao area in pursuit of economic survival. After the Japanese annexation of Korea, Korean nationalists steadily moved to that part of Manchuria to continue their armed campaign for independence. However, migration and settlement often met a hostile response from Chinese residents and officials who were suspicious of Korean people's colonial linkage to the Japanese government. Japanese officials also kept watchful eyes on Korean settlers' activities, alert to anything that might signal an alliance with the independence movement, and responded brutally to suspected Korean involvement in militant nationalist activity. Counterinsurgency campaigns in the 1930s murdered thousands of innocent Koreans.[13] The differing views of Korean settlers' citizenship and political affiliation created enmity and suspicion from both sides, making Koreans' life in Manchuria difficult to navigate.

A sense of loss and hardship, therefore, ran deeply through the nationalist discourses and collective social memory of Manchuria.[14] However passionately Sin Ch'aeho believed in the irredentist dream or Chang Chiyŏn advocated for Korea's territorial rights over Kando, the postcolonial reality of Korea simply did not sustain their arguments. Thus, as much as Manchuria became an important site in the nationalist debate, it subsequently became a space charged with a deep sense of loss and resignation. Migrants' memories of their experiences were infused with the pain of hardships and alienation, recorded by the many guerrilla fighters and farmers who wrote painfully of the trials they had endured to carry out their campaigns for independence and human dignity.[15]

This sentiment of loss is an important dimension in the affective dynamics of Manchurian action films, for it was through the *displacement* of this sense of loss and powerlessness that these films were able to promulgate their codes of masculinity, family, and nation. In particular, the conventions of war narratives carved out space for a new configuration of a manhood that was powerful and resolute. Men in these films do not dwell in resignation over the doomed irredentist dream, nor are they preoccupied with the daily adversities of the immigrant experience. Instead, the films depict Korean men of action who are capable and determined in dealing with crises. Chased by Japanese forces, these men often take refuge in guerrilla hideouts in remote mountain areas, where they analyze military information, train young recruits, and plan new attacks. When they return to urban areas, they are involved in secret covert operations, such as espionage, surveillance, guerrilla attacks, and, most importantly, the procurement of war funds. The masculine discourses of loyalty and comradeship function as significant sources of narrative progression, rendering Manchuria a stage of romantic and self-affirming adventure for Korean men.

The multifaceted generic features of the Manchurian action film deserve close attention and bear some comparison to those of their American counterparts.

According to Robert Burgoyne, the war film, along with the western, is a genre with a long history of articulating images of nation and played a vital role in molding a sense of national identity in the twentieth-century United States.[16] The Manchurian action film is structurally similar to these American film genres in its performance of ideological work. In fact, the two genres—the western and the war film—come together in this South Korean model, making it a distinct cinematic hybrid. Instead of gazing passively on the bygone glory of the past, Manchurian action films project the romantic impulse onto a new geographic space, a quasi-frontier comparable to the West in American cultural myth, where men of action ultimately claim their place. Yet the Korean narrative of Manchuria is also grounded in its colonial history and anticolonial struggle, highlighting guerrilla fighters' armed struggle against the foreign enemy. However short-lived or imaginary, Manchuria thus speaks of the romantic dream of reclamation and repossession of the land that is engrained in the discourse of anti-Japanese nationalism. The Korean film cycle, in other words, demonstrates a way to deflect the trauma of territorial loss by visually specifying the grounds of nationalism anew in Manchuria through perpetual recourse to a generic imagining of military campaigns, espionage activities, and dreams of the frontier.

Despite overcoming the sense of loss, however, these films are permeated by an ideological sense of double removal or impediment. The reality of postcolonial Korea was that the two contending states of North and South Korea could not, in the end, gain control of Manchuria. More importantly, the ideological stance of South Korea during the Cold War made it difficult for its people to engage concretely with the nationalist assessment of the Manchurian experience. Since partition, the two opposing states in Korea have engaged in intense and acrimonious warfare, ideological and actual, to nullify each other. The contending camps have used history as an ideological tool to ground their political legitimacy and popular support, and each state has inculcated its members with its own version of anticolonial history. In the case of South Korea, this has meant locating its anticolonial struggle in the spirit of the March 1st Movement of 1919 and claiming the institutional heritage of the Shanghai Provisional Government in exile.[17] Such a scenario was designed to suppress, in part, the communists' role in anticolonial struggles, particularly those that took place in Manchuria, including the guerrilla activities of Kim Il Sung. Construction of Manchuria as a hotbed of anticolonial activity was a dangerous ground to venture onto in the contentious Cold War atmosphere of 1960s' South Korea. Seen from this ideological perspective, the South Korean cultural productions on Manchuria, such as the films I focus on here, operated through multiple ideological filters in presenting narratives of anticolonial struggle. In other words, the logic of the Cold War imbued the thematic conventions of Manchurian action films—a feature that I explore in depth in the latter part of this chapter.

AMBIVALENT NATIONALISM: THE CASE OF
THE CONTINENT ON FIRE (1965)

Among Manchurian action films, *The Continent on Fire* (*Pulputnŭn taeryuk*; Yi Yongho, 1965) stands out as an exemplar, for it complicates the idea of family as an allegorical stand-in for the nation. It borrows the vengeance motif manifest in predecessors such as *Farewell to Tumen River* to anchor the moral thesis of its narrative. The film rehearses and tests the loyalties of national and familial allegiance through the main character's shifting perception of and attitude toward the militant nationalist campaign. To be sure, the film's narrative development is contingent on the binary polarization of good Koreans versus evil Japanese; however, new themes, including double identity, education, and conversion of allegiance, are introduced to support as well as complicate the dichotomized worldview.

The film's narrative principally concerns the transformation of Kang Chisŏk from a servant of the Japanese military into a born-again guerrilla combatant. It focuses on a series of incidents through which Chisŏk slowly develops a new awareness of his national identity. His changing political affiliation parallels his troublesome yet transformative relationship with his father, who eventually dies in the course of the nationalist struggle. Chisŏk, who works as a spy for the enemy, confronts the familial self he has long set aside and eventually comes to terms with his "righteous" political allegiance and "true" family. The film is thus a narrative of conversion, around which the family's dilemma is staged and resolved, and nation conflated with family. Curiously, however, the film's nationalist preoccupation impedes completion of this familial reunification and thereby leads the narrative to a cliff of ambivalence, despair, and nihilism. The film, in other words, casts significant doubt on its own ideological drive, questioning the feasibility and permanence of the familial restitution and nationalist creed at its close.

The film begins at a train station in Manchuria where the shrewd guerrilla combatant Han Tongmin is following Kim, a pro-Japanese collaborator, who possesses a map of a mineral deposit—information crucial to both sides of the military campaign. Han chases Kim to his house in Seoul, executing him mercilessly and repossessing the map, then heads back to the guerrilla fort. The Japanese military investigates Kim's death, assigning the investigation to Chisŏk, a talented Korean official. Fully committed to Japanese imperialist ideology, Chisŏk begins his mission by tracing Han's whereabouts.

As a typical collaborator, Chisŏk exists in a servile relation to his Japanese superior. His perfectionist work ethic has earned him a speedy promotion and won him praise from his Japanese boss, who permits and supports Chisŏk's courtship with his daughter. This interethnic romance signals Chisŏk's assimilation into the Japanese establishment through marriage.[18] The courtship echoes the complex relations of family name and ethnicity in Japanese colonial law and policy. In 1940, the

Japanese system of family names was introduced to replace Korean surnames in family registers. In addition, the Japanese adoption system, *siyangcha*, was implemented to integrate Japanese and Koreans under the system of Japanese family names. Accordingly, an adopted child could become simultaneously an adopted son and a son-in-law through his marriage with the daughter of the adopting parents.[19] Seen against the backdrop of this controversial legal discourse of family names and adoption, Chisŏk's prospect of marriage to a Japanese woman does not simply mean his upward social mobility. More importantly, it signals, through the new family law and its practice, his complete integration into a Japanese family without any traces of his Korean origins. That is, he can become, through the marriage, an adopted son and a son-in-law of the Japanese family. It is at this juncture, where the Korean man is about to lose all connection to his Korean heritage, that the theme of familial roots returns to alter Chisŏk's destiny.

Opposite to Chisŏk's interethnic consummation is the courtship between Han and Misa'e (the only daughter of the nationalist leader, who also is Chisŏk's stepsister), which promises the ideal heterosexual consummation of two nationalist agents. The latter relationship does not, however, conform to conventional gender relations. Han and Misa'e's relationship takes place outside the domestic domain, a feature that speaks volumes about the nature of conjugal relationships in the nationalist scenario. In fact, the film seems to disapprove of private spaces for any wartime romance, even though Misa'e does express her desire for marriage and settling down when she spends intimate time with Han. Mutual attraction clearly exists between the two; however, they speak and act to sublimate their passion for the larger political cause. The ideal of nationalist struggle functions as a grand substitute for the desire for domestic happiness.

Misa'e's professional activities go beyond expectations of the social roles often associated with conservative gender norms. Instead of being subservient and passive, she has two jobs: she works as a singer in a nightclub by night and as a nurse in the guerrilla fort by day. At the fort she helps her father, a medical doctor devoted to the independence struggle, by tending to battle-injured men. Misa'e works at the nightclub to, in her own words, comfort and console the Korean settlers in Manchuria who have grown homesick for their mother country. Her dual occupations serve the nation by attending to the needs of emotionally and physically injured Korean men in and out of the military.

Yet the nature of her performance and the stage environment do not fit comfortably with her noble motivation. In fact, these factors complicate, if not undermine, her intention and point to the flexible parameters of the nationalist ideology to accommodate diverse tropes of femininity. First of all, the lyrics to her songs are not in accordance with the theme of nostalgia that she articulates. In fact, they stress the contrary, emphasizing the importance of settlement and assimilation into the foreign land. She sings, "If you live long and grow to like the place, it is then your hometown." Although never explicitly political, these lyrics nevertheless have some ideological resonance. They render social messages that can be construed in various political terms, for these words are spoken not only to Koreans but also to other ethnic men in the nightclub. A similar ambiguity is found in Misa'e's stage performance. She veils her Korean ethnic origins and creates an aura of exotic attraction by appearing in Chinese clothing. Her moody song and suggestive gestures then invite the erotic interest of male patrons rather than the tranquil nostalgia she intends to evoke. In fact, her sexual allure is so powerful that it soon incites men; drunken Chinese men approach and harass Misa'e after her performance, which then immediately triggers a brawl at the site. As a nightclub singer, she is closely associated with profane and sexual sensuality rather than the sublime and sober sincerity of nationalism. *again differing forms of femininity*

What is unusual in this figuration of femininity is that Misa'e's self-eroticizing act poses no significant threat or problem to her fiancé Han, through whom her social merit is largely defined. Set right after Han's escape from his dangerous mission in Seoul, the nightclub sequence functions as musical compensation to the male protagonist who has just completed a difficult mission. The romantic communication between Misa'e and Han is introduced and mediated through her stage performance. I would stress that this positive appraisal of the woman's use of her body, here sexualized in the context of night entertainment, is not unusual in Manchurian action films. Indeed, other films communicate a similar sensibility. For instance, Im Kwon-taek's *Farewell to Tumen River* features the noble *kisaeng* courtesan character Yŏnhwa maneuvering and exploiting Japanese military men to help the resistance. Her profession never raises any moral question, nor is there any discriminatory attitude toward it. Contrary to many colonial narratives, which figure *kisaeng* characters as objects of shame and humiliation from a male perspective, Manchurian action films show remarkable tolerance of and lenience toward their sexual(ized) labor.[20] *the genre of film positive portrayals of sexual(ized) women*

What further distinguishes the film from other works is the degree of feminine sexual allure. Misa'e's performance is almost a separate musical number, a brief but self-contained sequence. As the performance progresses, its representational value quickly subsides as the formal apparatus directs close attention to her physical attractions. In other words, the convention of musical presentation distracts, momentarily, from surrounding sociopolitical concerns. It offers, instead, the glamour and magnetism of the female body, which far exceeds the logic and economy of the narrative. The dramatic concern is quickly taken up again as the performance ends. However, the shifting generic feature has created a moment where the woman's sexual allure is not in the service of any purpose other than pure spectacle.[21]

The theme of integration, as rendered in the motif of the usefulness of female labor, functions as an ideological counterpoint to Japan's imperial ideology, exemplified by the incorporation of Chisŏk into the Japanese power circle. For this scenario to work, however, the laboring woman must always be defined in relation to the men who are the agents of the campaign. Misa'e is fully supportive of and devoted to her man's altruistic mission. In this regard, the patriotic man is not just an object of the woman's romantic interest but also the woman's moral anchor; a woman can transgress the boundaries of the conventional feminine role and still retain respect and integrity because of her exclusive relationship with her man. Thus, what matters ultimately in the film is the social utility of Misa'e, which is measured primarily in relation to Han.

This scheme of consummation distinguishes and secures the position of the Korean man against the backdrop of many other ethnic men who are as powerful as the male protagonist in terms of physical strength and political networks. The male protagonist and his mission function to empty out the ambivalence of feminine propriety and sexuality. But, at the same time, the female protagonist sanctions and displays the masculine power of the Korean man through her sexual availability, which is only for Korean men. Misa'e is portrayed as the only sexually attractive woman in this part of Manchuria, and her exclusive romantic interest in Han makes him an exception among the group of men who are without any female partner. This reassessment of Korean femininity is particularly revealing considering the marginal ground that Korean men actually occupied in the social reality of Manchukuo.

This ethnic hierarchy is obvious in the nightclub, where Korean men like Han can occupy only a constrained minority position. As a microcosm of Manchukuo, the nightclub forms a matrix of ethnic relations through its various male patrons. The Chinese constitute the greatest number (here the owner is also Chinese), while the Japanese soldiers and military officials form another group of patrons. Through the work of spies like Chisŏk, the Japanese military employs a secret force to patrol and inspect any activities that might breed subversion. Yet their control over spaces like the nightclub is incomplete and ineffective. In fact, the Japanese military force shows consistent failure to contain the violence that breaks out. Nightclubs in Manchurian action films are generally charged with an air of intimidation and the potential for violence, which largely is derived from miscommunication and hostile contentions. Hence, the nightclub signals a specific "contact zone" where all ethnic groups commingle and interact, only to underscore the espionage prowess of the guileful Korean agent. By contrast, the presence of Japanese military men in the nightclub typically signals the power of surveillance and vigilance over Koreans and other ethnic groups, even while it reveals their inability to distinguish the Korean agent in disguise and to halt the subversive operation in progress.

The issue of allegiance reverberates in the form of recruitment and resocialization at the guerrilla fort, where Chisŏk undergoes a radical transformation. Chisŏk arrives pretending to be a new recruit to the training program. Han, now in charge of instruction, instantly recognizes Chisŏk, who helped him escape from the danger at the nightclub, and thus pays special attention to him. Chisŏk, however, is oblivious of Han's gaze of surveillance and remains committed to his goal of carrying out the espionage mission. Han eventually becomes aware of Chisŏk's secret identity but does not take immediate action. Instead, he quietly observes Chisŏk's actions and awaits Chisŏk's change of heart. Central to Han's decision for discretion are the family tensions, in which he too is implicated, that are closely tied to participation in nationalist fighting. Misa'e alerts Han to her familial relation to Chisŏk and informs him of her stepbrother's secret profession, hinting at Chisŏk's involvement in the failure of the recent campaign. She does *not*, however, inform her father about Chisŏk, perhaps because she fears that such a meeting between her stubborn father and her stepbrother would produce a disastrous outcome. Simultaneously, Chisŏk also learns about his father's whereabouts but never confronts him in person. A complex web of family relations is thus formed, threaded by masquerade as well as ideological enmity.

For the straightforward Han, who is now aware of the infiltration, Chisŏk represents a unique conundrum. Chisŏk's familial connection to Misa'e and her father, whom he not only respects as his future father-in-law but also admires as a political mentor, makes it virtually impossible for Han to resolve the matter quickly by punishing Chisŏk's treachery. Han's predicament—being caught between familial ties and nationalist obligations—illustrates the distinct rift in the familial-national nexus that is the most recurring theme in Manchurian action films. The elements of the familial are typically subordinated to the grand nationalist ideal; however, such conventional conflation does not quite occur here. Han's passivity suggests a certain lacuna in the all-encompassing might of the nationalist ideology, in which serving the nation usually guarantees the personal fulfillment of all those who participate in it.

In *The Continent on Fire,* the moment of reconciliation does not derive from any input from the nationalists at the fort. Instead, Chisŏk's transformation gradually takes place as he assumes a quasi-paternal role to the orphan girl Soryŏ, a child flower vendor. Chisŏk rescues Soryŏ, whose ethnic identity remains ambiguous, when she faces abuse by some drunken men. He takes Soryŏ safely to her house, where he learns of her real plight: her father was killed by the Japanese, and her mother is now bedridden. Later, when he hears that Soryŏ has become an orphan in his absence, he takes her to the barracks at the training camp to care for her. Her alienation and misery have a significant impact on Chisŏk and lead him to make a commitment to take the role of father for this child.

Chisŏk's new paternal role leads to his dawning realization of Japanese brutality as well as his development of a humane perspective on social reality. The episode rehearses, in a displaced form, the deep contradiction that blocks the resumption of a familial relationship between Chisŏk and his father, whose differences in political orientation are irreconcilable. As the film clearly illustrates, Chisŏk's father is a man of impeccable integrity, a true patriot whom everyone admires. Yet privately he is troubled by a serious family problem in the past. As he tells his daughter Misa'e, he abandoned his wife and son in Korea to commit himself fully to the nationalist cause in Manchuria. This decision led him to remarry Misa'e's late mother. The allegorical ties that bind family and nation together are severed in this scenario: the family, Chisŏk and his natal mother, suffered for the nation without a reward. Furthermore, Chisŏk's affiliation with the Japanese illustrates the grave consequence of his father's failure as the head of the family. Han's reluctance to alert Chisŏk's father about his son's identity results from a dilemma far weightier than mere problems of generational conflict, for it could exhume the past and potentially tear down the patriarchal leader's respectable reputation and the moral authority that he holds over the nationalist camp.

Chisŏk's assumed father role to Soryŏ functions as a mode of transference by which Chisŏk, not his father, comes to terms with the hurtful family history. The quasi-parenthood connotes the formation of a new family, composed of two generations who have undergone a similar experience of parental neglect and loss. Soryŏ's ambiguous ethnic background furnishes the additional dimension of the inclusive ideology that the film repeatedly showcases. That is, Chisŏk, who once tried to enter the Japanese circle, now adopts a street girl with an ambiguous ethnic background to form an entirely different social unit that is in accord with the anti-Japanese campaign. The family that he forms is based on choice and affiliation rather than the blood ties that dictate familial relations in normal Korean families. The positive outcome suggests the possibility of a new type of collective that is not biologically determined or ethnically exclusive.

The new type of family is complicated by the imperative of moral retribution against the Japanese enemy. Soryŏ asks Chisŏk to carry out a vendetta against those who killed her parents. Such a plea for vengeance makes Chisŏk's effort to form a family deeply contradictory, for Chisŏk himself is a part of the evil that must be punished and eradicated. In other words, Chisŏk's allegiance to the Japanese is the impediment not only to his relationship with his own father, but also to his connection to his new "daughter." The film hence stresses that one can never be simultaneously a genuine member of a family, however alternatively imagined, while also being affiliated with the Japanese.

It is at this juncture that the film's narrative takes a dramatic turn to resolve the familial entanglement by employing the traumatic death of Chisŏk's father. Pressed to perform his duties by other Japanese spies, Chisŏk finally carries out his mission: stealing the map from the guerrillas. Yet as he runs away from the fort, his father is simultaneously attacked and killed by a Japanese secret agent. The cross-cutting editing suggests the structural linkage between the son's betrayal and the father's death. With his last breath, Chisŏk's father tells Han his dying wish: to see his son in person. Han chases and soon captures Chisŏk and informs him of the death of his father. Moreover, Han delivers the late father's wishes: he had wanted his son to be a warrior for the nation's independence. Engulfed by regret and sadness, Chisŏk rushes to his father's side and breaks down at his deathbed. He realizes that he has forever lost a chance to reconcile with him.

aligning working w/ Japan
to breaking apart the family

The film thus restores a stark moral economy in which serving the enemy Japan and reconciling with a family member are fundamentally incompatible options. That is, as a servant of the colonial power, Chisŏk's treachery eventuates in patricide. And having lost the opportunity to resume relations with his father, Chisŏk suffers from irrecoverable moral damnation and grief. A motif of familial vengeance is then instantiated as Chisŏk vows to commit himself to the nationalist struggle. Chisŏk's endeavor here signifies his moral repentance and resumed responsibility for the nation to which his father has been closely tied. The father's education of his son is fulfilled only belatedly through his death.

What remains *unchallenged,* however, is the centrality of the father's position in relation to his children. Because Chisŏk's father dies suddenly without really resolving his tension with Chisŏk, the question of his parental responsibility is never addressed. Instead, it is the son who disproportionately bears the burden of moral judgment. It is all the son's fault that their relationship could be not healed. This structural disequilibrium then signifies the film's drive to maintain patriarchal power in the narrative of the nation. In other words, the nexus of nation and family demands a strong father figure who is not only a parent to his children but also a paternal figure to the entire nationalist campaign. Consequently, personal concerns, however painful they may be, must be set aside to protect the moral certitude of the patriarchal leader. *strong patriarchal leader >>>*

The film's conclusion, in which Chisŏk proves his valor and dies heroically on the battlefield, conveys another dilemma of the nationalist imagination despite its seemingly propagandistic confidence. His death casts a lingering shadow of moral guilt; although he denounces his past wrongdoing, it ultimately costs him his life. Death seems the only fitting punishment for the initial act of betrayal that he has committed against the nation (and his father). The past haunts the present here to work to the extreme disadvantage of the protagonist. The elimination of the bad seed leads to the formation of another family based on the scenario of vengeance. At his last breath, Chisŏk asks Han and his stepsister Misa'e to take care of Soryŏ, and the couple complies. The three surviving members form a new family where the patriotic parents will raise and educate another warrior for the nationalist cause.

Yet Soryŏ's excessive reaction to Chisŏk's death goes beyond and challenges this easy assessment of family formation. Her grieving over the man who took care of her with genuine love suggests that no one can truly replicate Chisŏk's role as father. Despite the idea of adoption and integration, the sequence thus entails self-doubt concerning the feasibility of perpetual regeneration of the family unit, here visualized specifically to serve the eternal struggle for the nation. The haunting reverberation of Soryŏ's sobs frustrates the happy but fabricated outcome of the nation's permanence and optimism, which appear to be in trouble even as the drumbeat for a continuing campaign is highlighted at the end.

perfect restoration of the family questioned

FIGURE 5. Han carries the body of Chisŏk in *Continent on Fire*. Courtesy of the Korean Film Archive.

MANCHURIAN ACTION FILMS AS
WAR NARRATIVE FILMS

From the 1950s to the present, more than ninety South Korean films, both narrative and documentary, have dealt with the subject of the Korean War, treating the conflict as a historical calamity that had a profound impact on the subsequent development of both Koreas. Yet as an unending war, the Korean War hardly marks a closed historical chapter, as many of these films imply; rather, the war is at the foundation of continuing tensions on the Korean peninsula, where Cold War politics continue to structure reality for people both north and south of the thirty-eighth parallel. Since the formation of North and South Korea as inimical states, both sides have witnessed massive ideological campaigns. Within this ideologically driven context, cinema has performed an effective cultural function by disseminating state ideology to the masses. South Korea's Korean War cinema has sought to establish a negative image of the enemy Other. As Theodore Hughes notes, North Korea in the cultural imaginary of South Korea has over time been increasingly associated with decline and collapse. South Korea itself, in contrast, has been rendered, in overtly visible terms, both present and alive.[23] Through this discursive process in which South Korea is implicitly set against a negative reflection of the counter-regime to its north, the South Korean state, within war narrative films, is represented as the sole rightful Korean nation. Revealing little about South Korea's positive substance but a great deal about its anxieties about legitimacy and security, South Korea's Korean War films have rendered visible and tangible the various scenarios of struggle against the communism that the state has maintained as an immutable political raison d'être.[24]

South Korea's 1960s filmmaking scene is of particular interest and relevance because the period ushered in various new types of war narratives. Certainly, anticommunist Korean War films were a dominant type of war cinema whose

State + national cinema =
anti-communist war
films

THE MANCHURIAN ACTION FILM 65

production dated back to the early days of the Korean War conflict. The South Korean government mobilized film personnel and resources to produce documentary and newsreel films about the nature of the Korean War to inculcate the masses then living under the hardship of total war.[25] In the 1960s, the collaboration between the state and filmmakers reached a zenith, as the state provided a complex form of institutional support for the production of anticommunist Korean War films. At the same time, the success of Yi Manhŭi's *The Marines Who Never Return* (*Toraoji annŭn haebyŏng*, 1963) and Shin Sangok's *Red Muffler* (*Ppalgan mahura*, 1964) proved the commercial viability of the Korean War theme. These works were followed by a slew of Korean War or war-themed films, such as *The Inchon Landing* (*Inch'ŏn sangryuk chakchŏn*; Cho Kŭngha, 1965), *Bloody Kuwol Mountains* (*P'iŏrin Kuwolsan*; Ch'oe Muryong, 1965), *War and the Woman Teacher* (*Chŏnjaenggwa yŏgyosa*; Im Kwont'aek, 1966), *A Journey* (*Yŏro*; Yi Manhŭi', 1968), and *Seven People in the Cellar* (*Chihasilŭi ch'ilin*; Yi Sŏnggu, 1969), which largely adhered to the state's mandate of anticommunism and, in the case of Yi Manhŭi's films, offered critical humanist perspectives on the futility of war. The conspicuous visibility of these films has given rise to an impression among film scholars, however, that Korean War films are the sole type of war narratives that gained recognition in the 1960s, leaving out much-needed discussion on the Cold War as a political structure of war. Korean War films dominate historical memory more than Cold War

It was in the 1960s that Manchurian action films emerged as a different type of war narrative film, accruing a popularity that rivaled that of government-backed anticommunist Korean War films. Unlike the latter, Manchurian action films did not receive any institutional support from the government. Since they dealt with armed exploits of the colonial past, these works often were regarded as a separate film entity, set apart from the contemporaneous concerns of the Cold War politics that Korean War films reflected. As I will illustrate, however, the distinctive critical stance of Manchurian action films affords us an opportunity to engage with the formation and naturalization of South Korea's political discourse of war and experience. They register the perverse logic of Cold War politics in a way that few explicitly framed "war" films do. Although remote in generic, historical, and geographical relation to the Korean War, these films enable us to view how state power is consolidated through the state's involvement in perpetual war as an illicit underground business.

As a category, "Korean War films"—insofar as they are narrowly focused on the war of 1950–53—render the Cold War as largely elusive, if not invisible. Here, it should be recalled that the Cold War, as a geopolitical system, gave rise to a state of war as an ongoing conditioning structure of Korea and its neighboring countries. In the service of US hegemony in the region, this complex system has organized and regulated sociopolitical, economic, security, and cultural relations and operations. In projecting and naturalizing a binary worldview in which the liberal United States and its allies are set against their communist counterparts, the

Cold War system has had a discursive and logical sway that must be theorized and narrated beyond specific instances of military action and engagement.

For this reason, inquiry into Cold War politics in cultural representation needs to go beyond the confines of Korean War stories, which, as a result of the South Korean state's intense ideological programming, offer limited purchase for interrogating state power. As a body of film whose prescriptive parameters have been closely determined by South Korean state regulation and scrutiny, South Korea's Korean War films depict military battles and conflicts, yet they curiously close off the larger matrix of perpetual war that structured the 1950–53 war in the first place. Instead of expanding a critique of war to encompass the protracted nature and ubiquity of the state's military logic and militarized culture, South Korea's Korean War films, including antiwar films, produce the opposite effect: they paradoxically foreclose critical debates on the complexity of war as a structuring imaginary of the Cold War culture of South Korea specifically and of the region as a whole.

Nihilistic in character, South Korean antiwar films critique war and its destruction by highlighting humanistic values. Yet these films are not fundamentally different in kind from state-sanctioned, anticommunist war films insofar as both promote a pessimistic view toward politics without calling into question the structure and practice of state power. Although differences do exist, these can be understood along the lines of an expansion and contraction of narrative focus. Antiwar films include a general critique of the state machinery of war. However, this critical expansion is complemented by an inherently reactive move; instead of problematizing the South Korean state's practice of violence, these films revert to the very framework of liberal humanism that anticommunist war films have developed as an ideological foil to the ostensible depravity and monstrousness of North Korea.

The broadened focus of the antiwar variant of Korean War films, in other words, does not lead to critical analysis of the expanded purview of South Korean state power and authority enabled by the Korean War, much less a reading of it as a sign and symptom of the larger geopolitics of the Cold War. Rather, South Korea's antiwar Korean War films obsessively resort to a nihilistic form of humanism and, in so doing, limit the discursive parameters of inquiry into the relationship of South Korean state violence to the overarching Cold War structure. Enlarged yet paradoxically myopic, the focus of these films may compass a universalizing critique of war violence in the abstract, yet by disavowing the broader structure of the Cold War, Korean War films, classified narrowly as such, remain obscurantist texts. Whether anticommunist or antiwar, South Korea's war films impede critical understanding of the Cold War as a permanent system, effacing the Korean War's geopolitical origins and context. More specifically, they block from view the business side of South Korea's military mobilization—a dimension of the war that has buttressed the South Korean state's role within the coordinates of the Cold War in East Asia.

Korean war films unjust war not how/why or structure that caused it

Just anti-war, not the structure of states power that creates war

ignoring the cold wars role in Korean war

The impulse to foreclose the war and its meanings from the viewpoint of nihil-istic humanism, I thus contend, is constitutive of South Korea's "Korean War films." Central to the reality of the unending Korean War, yet effaced from view in South Korea's ideologically regulated Korean War films, the South Korean state seldom, if ever, surfaces as a meaningful object of perception. Sovereign in its capacity to dictate representation while simultaneously remaining beyond the ambit of representation, South Korean state authority can be understood as a constitutive ideological limit of "Korean War film" as a Cold War cultural text. Hardly passive, South Korean state authority wields its power in its demarcation of interpretive limits. Thus, to explore Korean War discourse—its rationale, mobilization, and logistics—beyond the confines of that body of films conventionally recognized as "Korean War films," I contend that its scope must be expanded to include cul-tural scenarios of the 1931–45 Pacific War, more specifically, the proto-Korean nation-state during the colonial period that waged a military campaign against the Japanese Empire and its colonial apparatus. By directing attention to allegori-cal representations of the unseemly origins of the South Korean state, we are able to challenge how Korean War films can and should be understood.

The structural limitations of Korean War films relative to the perpetual politics of the Cold War raise the question of whether South Korean war narratives are capable of directly addressing the state's Cold War political function. Even as the argument can be advanced that the South Korean state consistently appears in Korean War films as a problematic entity in that it is represented as lacking full political authority or initiative, this depiction nowhere accords with the historical truth: namely, that the South Korean state asserted its dreadful power and violence against its own population before, during, and after the war. Indeed, the authori-tarian state promulgated a developmentalist ideology accompanied by massive programming to control its populace for decades after the 1950–53 war. The incon-sistency between filmic representation and sociopolitical reality compels us to consider whether South Korean cinema is capable of critically reflecting upon the contradictory features of the state as it has functioned within the Cold War system. Are there any filmic texts, in other words, that confront the contentious issue of the state's culpability within the "business" of warmongering?

Manchurian action films furnish a critical opening by way of which the war profiteering of the South Korean state can be scrutinized. In that this body of films imaginatively reflects upon the colonial past, however, the historical connection of these films to the contemporaneous condition of the Cold War—the juncture in which they were produced—is far from self-evident. This lack of obvious con-nection is compounded by the historiographical constraints of South Korea's Cold War culture, in which the colonial past is often myopically conceived as a demarcated time that preceded the emergence of the South Korean state. However, Manchurian action films of the 1960s are remarkably reflective of the capitalist war politics of the Cold War South Korean state and in particular offer insight into the role of state power in rationalizing and maintaining the war as a perpetual business. Though set in the colonial past, these films extend beyond their temporal setting in terms of their significance. They demand analysis relative to the Cold War as a system. Offering crucial insight into the structural dimensions of the Cold War, they assert what most other popular war narratives fail to thematize: the workings of the partitioned capitalistic state in authorizing and managing the prolonged business of war.

Manchurian action films can be read through the conceptual lens of genre even as we attend to the constitutive problematics of genre-based analysis. In examining Manchurian action films as war narratives rather than as action films or westerns, as they are more typically categorized and addressed in existing scholarship, I argue against narrow preconceptions of genres when it comes to cultural narration of the Korean War. By situating the Korean War within the broader political economy of the Cold War, I aim to show how Manchurian action films complicate the generic template and periodized framework of Korean War films. Proceeding from the observation that constant war and military mobilization have structured—indeed produced—a false sense of stability and prosperity in the East Asian region, I argue that Manchurian action films reflect the material contradictions of South Korea's Cold War culture.

FOLLOWING THE MONEY

Growing criticism of Manchurian action films has strongly favored the later-period films at the expense of a close overview of the early works. By *later-period,* I mean the late 1960s and early 1970s films in which the genre's hybrid features were more pronounced and its anti-Japanese nationalism was more ironically represented. Whereas the early Manchurian action films had a strong generic affiliation with war films, the later works began, so to speak, to don western garb. As the critical ascendancy of *Break the Chain* (*Soe sasŭrŭl kkŭnŏra*; Yi Man-hŭi, 1971) illustrates, the generic shift of South Korea's Manchurian action films to the western, the most recognizably transnational genre of the time, facilitated a reading in which the later examples of the genre appear to mark a departure from the dominant state ideology. By valorizing the later films over the earlier ones, film critics, perhaps inadvertently, implied the earlier war narratives of Manchurian action films to be uncritical repositories of state propaganda. As the logic goes, the earlier works show total support for the nation, whereas the later works deviate from such political programming. It thus is widely held that only the later works—that is, the generically western Manchurian action films—deserve critical analysis and retrieval.

Yet such a narrow analytical focus neglects critical features of this hybrid genre's subversive potential. The questions I would like to pose speak to the changing contours of cinematic nationalism, but they also relate directly to how South Korean war narratives engaged the structuring context of the Cold War. In particular, I would like to inquire toward what end male protagonists in war situations, specifically, the armed anticolonial struggle, exert their power and strength. What are the specific gains and rewards of their actions and endeavors? And, how are these actions related to the overarching anticolonial discourse of the nation that seems to dominate this war imaginary? On the surface, the answer is service to the nation and its struggle for independence. However, when examined closely, the answer to these questions is money. By *money,* I am referring to the way money as well as its metaphorical forms and configurations gains structural significance in the war imaginary of Manchurian action films.

Cinematic representations of colonialism prior to the advent of the Manchurian action film depict money or wealth in a purely negative fashion—in the form, more often than not, of ill-gotten gains. This negative depiction of material acquisition enables a dichotomous mapping of the world in which virtuous Koreans are set against treacherous Koreans. Collaborators, for instance, are always associated with material enrichment; their wealth, these filmic narratives make clear, is the direct outcome of their treachery. The binary of seeking money or serving the nation dominates the narrative of films like *Farewell to Tumen River,* an antecedent of Manchurian action films in which Japanese monetary reward for Korean collusion is depicted as pure evil—a system of colonial collaboration that must be eliminated. The imperative of identifying and punishing Korean traitors who receive reward money from the Japanese while exonerating those who are wrongfully accused as collaborators structures South Korea's representations of colonialism in the early postcolonial era.

The role of money changes substantially by the mid-1960s, however. In fact, the advent of the Manchurian action film signaled a radically different conception of money within the anticolonial war imaginary of South Korean film. Money is no longer conceived as a sign of corruption or betrayal—as something, in other words, at odds with the sacred aura of nationalist struggle. Instead, the guerrilla force now needs money desperately to carry out military campaigns. Films like *The Continent on Fire* and *Soviet-Manchurian Border* (*Soman kukkyŏng;* Kang Pŏmgu, 1964) are prime examples of this narrative reconception of money. In these war narratives the procurement, the transfer, and the management of war funds constitute the principal action. In *Soviet-Manchurian Border,* for example, the male protagonist's prolonged suffering and melancholia derive precisely from his failure to complete a business transaction—the delivery of war funds—with the Soviet Army. In the wake of this failure, burdened by guilt and shame, the protagonist is unable to return to the guerrilla headquarters, becoming instead a leader of a local gangster organization. Only with his delivery of lost war funds to the guerrilla force is he morally redeemed by the end of the film.

The narrative of many 1960s Manchurian action films is often structured around the theme of "following the money." The procurement of the war funds by whatever means necessary is featured as central to the struggle against the Japanese, so much so that this economic endeavor is virtually identical to, rather than inconsistent with, upholding the political mantra of nationalism. Here the political creed and the economic agenda of the South Korean state appear to be in total unison. To serve the nation, one must bring money to the table. Patriotism, accordingly, is defined in terms of purloined property or canny resource procurement. This, I argue, is a distinctively capitalist way of imagining the anticolonial struggle particular to South Korea's war narrative films.[26]

It must be noted that war funds never appear as actual banknotes. Instead, they appears in the form of objects, properties, or resources with monetary value: gold bullion, treasure maps, Buddhist statues, jewelry, mineral and ore mine maps, and so forth. Strikingly, identifiably Japanese government notes or banknotes—the actual legal tender of Manchukuo as a Japanese colony—never appear as circulating currency in Manchurian action films. Like Japanese settlers and residents in Korea, who never appear in the nationalist imaginary of colonial Korea, Japanese money is structurally absent in Manchurian action films, even though the genre is thematically preoccupied—indeed obsessed—with money. Manchurian action films, in other words, are largely preoccupied with money in nonmoney forms—in other words, money unmarked as the legal tender of the Japanese Empire.

As I note in other chapters, South Korean films depict Japanese rule over Korea predominantly as a quasi-military occupation. Framing Japanese colonial rule as an unlawful foreign occupation signals the political crisis of a temporary loss of nation. The colonial occupation becomes manageable through the resistance politics of armed struggle. However, depicting the settlement of Japanese residents and the circulation of government notes would engender a different, less recognizably anticolonial nationalist imaginary. Depicting Japanese settler colonialists and the circulation of Japanese *yuan* (yen) would signify the deep penetration of the Japanese colonial power into the economic sphere of Korean people—into arenas of their daily activity. Outright depiction of this penetration could mean, then, the absorption of all Koreans into a system of colonial rule so total that a space of resistance would be difficult to conceive. Any such signifiers of a permanent colonial economy necessarily were omitted from the nationalist imaginary. In Manchurian action films, the male characters, whether villains, good guys, or nationalist fighters, are in competition, forming alliances or committing betrayals to get the prized objects, which are never explicitly Japanese banknotes. Korean nationalists cannot, after all, be seen in pursuit of Japanese currency—such a quest would signal the totality of Japanese colonial hegemony.

Manchurian action films depict the original ownership of properties in intentionally murky terms, yet these filmic narratives are premised on the assumption that the guerrillas *always*, in fact, have rightful ownership. In *Return of the Wanderer* (*Toraon pangrangja*; Kim Hyoch'ŏn, 1970), it is nearly impossible to figure out to whom the gold bullion originally belonged. All the involved characters dispute its history, but the original owner is never verified. The logical disarray over anterior ownership of the property, which produces a series of unintended campy moments, becomes immediately clear once the nationalist guerrillas enter the picture and declare their claim. This conception of guerrilla treasure as the nation's anterior possession is achieved by portraying the nationalist guerrillas as having greater and more precise knowledge of the properties' whereabouts and "true" value. Although the individual guerrillas are often depicted as not initially understanding the true value of the properties, they acquire such information as they are drawn more deeply into their mission. Guided by a higher authority, the desire of the nationalist guerrillas to pursue the property thus appears to be aimed at restoring the rightful order of things.

Not open to questioning, the authority of the nationalist group is tied to its apparently unchallenged ownership claim to the treasure. This rightful lien is matched by the total commitment of the guerrilla agents, who simply follow their orders without reservation. Here the Manchurian action film is explicit in its psychoanalytic figuration of the authority of the nation-state. Although Korea lost its sovereignty to Japan during the historical period described in Manchurian action films, the proto-state nevertheless asserts its authority over its subjects through a dyad of two psychoanalytically drawn subjects, who complementarily constitute the symbolic order of nationalism. On one end of the spectrum is the subject who is supposed to know (the leader of the guerrilla camp), and on the other is the subject who is supposed to believe (guerrilla agents).[27] What sustains the authority of the proto-state, as figured by the all-knowing guerrilla leader, is the leader's knowledge of the specific location of the prized object. The leader, in other words, always already knows the whereabouts and value of the properties; at the same time, the agent unequivocally believes in the leader's knowledge of the properties. The pairing of these two subjects in their shared quest for treasure is indispensable to establishing the symbolic order of the Korean nation and society. Whereas war could easily signify the breakdown of the normal order, war as business, as rendered in the Manchurian action film, serves to solidify the power and authority of the state.

The war funds that structure, define, and regulate militant anticolonial struggle in these early Manchurian action films have an amorphous character. Their depiction clearly echoes the Marxist notion of money as the matrix of social relations. Yet the peculiarly topological aspect of money, devoid of any reference to actually existing Japanese legal tender, encourages us to conceive of war funds in these films in Lacanian psychoanalytic terms as "objet petit a": namely, as that which remains perpetually out of reach but, as a trigger, structures desire, setting it in motion.[28] In this regard, the proto-state, or the subject who is supposed to know all about money, not only commands service to the nation but also tantalizes each individual, compelling the guerrilla into a cycle of action that never reaches final fulfillment. After all, the money that the nationalist guerrilla forces attain ultimately belongs to the state. In this sense, Manchurian action films offer a portrait of a state that regulates not solely through the severity of order and coercion, but also through a powerful scenario of desire.

Not only do Manchurian action films compel a reconsideration of the South Korean proto-nation by figuring it as an anticolonial guerrilla force, and of money by depicting it as ill-gotten gains, they also unveil the seamy underside of war as a profitable state enterprise. Its authority far from righteous, the nation in these films appears as an underground quasi-criminal organization whose main business operations require the liquidation and laundering of stolen goods into money—the conversion, in other words, of plunder into legal tender. In their refusal to figure the nation as a transcendental entity whose legitimacy is beyond question, Manchurian action films perversely identify war profiteering as the motor of the nation. In so doing, South Korea's Manchurian action films offer the possibility of a new interpretation of the Korean War narrative: set within the colonial period yet produced in the decade following the 1950–53 conflict, these films expose the shadowy—indeed, illegitimate—underside of the nation. Founded on ill-gotten gains and perpetuated by the same, the capitalist nation in the throes of war has recourse, in this filmic cycle, to perverse acts of criminal violation and transgression.

The radically ambivalent, primitive setting of Manchurian action films serves to displace the obscenity of the nation's self-sustaining activities by, in effect, relegating and sequestering it to the arena of fiction. In the Manchurian action film, the deeply ideological spatial imaginary of the Hollywood western genre has been grafted onto the making of the South Korean nation. Unable to lay claim to the historic anticolonial revolutionary legacy associated with North Korean leader Kim Il Sung in the region, South Korea's Manchurian action films construct a different lineage—one that borrows from the settler colonial logic of Manifest Destiny in the United States. Indeed, the generic influence of the western, particularly on those films that come later in the Manchurian action film cycle, is unmistakable. Western films generally portray the West as empty, chaotic, and violent but ultimately in the process of becoming part of the nation's sovereign territory. Their narrative simultaneously erases local history and turns the space into a battleground for competing ownership claims.[29] It is a space, essentially, that is up for grabs. Often, the outsider who has no clear historical claim to the space emerges as the proprietor by virtue of being the victor of a violent contest. South Korea's Manchurian action films appropriate this generic configuration of the West as the open, yet-to-be-claimed space. Borrowing their atmosphere of lawlessness from the western genre, Manchurian action films feature westernized spaces in which the guerrillas assume prior ownership of property and resources and legitimize their endless pursuit of the same. Those who know about or discover the valued objects first can claim ownership according to the rationale of "finders keepers."[30]

Yet here the ethics promulgated by spaghetti westerns must be distinguished from those particular to classical westerns, which have little to do with the former's explicit emphasis on personal greed and materialism. Whereas many classical western films are preoccupied with the establishment of law and order in a frontier community, the former are not concerned with such lofty ideals. Instead, the main characters in spaghetti westerns are focused on individual gains and private material rewards. Manchurian action films' persistent emphasis on resource procurement reflects how the narrative logic of individual greed and materialism in the spaghetti western can be incorporated into the particular capitalist logic of South Korea's cinematic nationalist imaginary.

Manchurian action films thus project a distinctively capitalist way of conceiving of anticolonial nationalism and, in doing so, expose the operations of war as a business. They furnish us with a critical opportunity to consider how Cold War bipolar politics and neoliberal logic have deeply permeated South Korea's anticolonial imagination. Here the nation is represented as a political entity that constantly demands individual action to procure money equivalents: namely, objects, properties, and resources that can be transformed into operational resources. The anti-Japanese guerrilla campaign is thus less about logistical specifics—where to fight, how to fight, with whom to fight, with whom to form alliances—than it is about how to secure war funds. According to this logic, bringing money home is the paramount nationalist act. *about money, not the fight*

Produced during the Cold War, Manchurian action films feature war troves comprising sundry material objects, the ambiguity of which, I argue, can be read critically against the historical juncture in which these films were produced. Uneasily recalling the structural amorphousness of the Japanese economic assistance so central to South Korea's economic miracle, the fungibility of funds—and the mystery of their origins—in Manchurian action films must be understood, I argue, against South Korea's historic normalization of relations with Japan in the 1960s. It is no secret that Park Chung Hee's principal reasons for normalizing relations with Japan were economic. And, without question, money from Japan in the form of compensation, grants, and loans was vital to the early stages of Park's development project. Considering this, I would argue that Manchurian action films' persistent conjuration of money allegorizes how the secret of South Korea's financial rise remains hidden from view in South Korean society, much as the concept of "enemy properties" in the postliberation period effectively erased Japanese capital and properties. The fact that the original ownership of the properties is never in question in Manchurian action films is important insofar as it reinforces, in legerdemain fashion, South Korea's social myth of autonomous development and industrialization.

But we must ask: If the basis of the nation is represented as war profiteering, what happens when that nation no longer is associated with war as a business?

FIGURE 6. Three protagonists in *Break the Chain*. Courtesy of the Korean Film Archive.

Put differently, will the profit-seeking individual still fight for and serve the nation when the latter has nothing to offer in material terms? Here, it is worth briefly turning to Yi Manhŭi's 1971 Manchurian action film, *Break the Chain* (*Sesasŭrŭl kkŭnŏra*), in which a decoupling of money and politics occurs. Many critics valorize the film for its seeming resistance to the nationalist call of duty. The film ends with the dispersion of its main protagonists, three men who refuse to join the nationalist campaign, yet I would note that their decision comes after they realize that the object of their pursuit, the Tibetan Buddhist statue, has no monetary value whatsoever; rather, the statue has the names of the guerrilla force inscribed inside—identities that must be protected at all cost. In other words, the statue is important to the guerrillas alone. Upon realizing the purely political value of the pursued object, these men depart. If Yi Manhŭi's film is unusual, it is not because the characters' action signifies a willful rejection of nationalism in its totality. Instead, his film is uncommon because the anticolonial struggle is presented without any promise of material reward: it has emerged as pure politics. The protagonists leave behind the nationalist campaign because it is no longer attractive to them materially. The film's ending then reminds us of the disturbing truth of a state caught in the logic of the Cold War: without monetary objects that it can offer up to compel action, the state is stripped of its authority. The only way to reverse this situation is for the nation-state to assume what is expected under Cold War politics: namely, to maintain war profiteering as its raison d'être.

Set in Manchuria during the colonial period, Manchurian action films are war narratives of a particular kind. These films inherit their nationalist ethos from biographical films of earlier decades that glorified the heroic anticolonial independence struggles of Korean patriots. Manchurian action films, however, replace the didacticism of the earlier nationalist films with a new narrative approach toward colonial history. Instead of highlighting the lives of actual historical figures, these films feature the adventures of armed militants who wage war against the Japanese imperial army. In the late 1960s, these war narrative films incorporated conventions of both the western (hence the hybrid generic term *Manchurian western*) and the martial arts action film, while maintaining the masculine ethos of loyalty particular to earlier nationalist films.

As I have examined, this body of films poses questions about the changing terms of cinematic nationalism during the 1960s. On the surface, Manchurian action films can be read as an attempt to reformulate and reenergize anticolonial and anti-Japanese nationalism during a period when—in response to the pressures of Cold War realpolitik but against the overwhelming opposition of the South Korean people—the South Korean state normalized relations with Japan. Just as the Japanese colonial Other reemerged as the refashioned partner in the bipolar politics of the Cold War, the ways of seeing and imagining the colonial past and space show the deeper repercussions of the historical changes that were under way. The expansive extraterritorial space of Manchuria launched a new imagery of the colonial past filled with masculine adventure and camaraderie for the nation. Yet the promise for the masculine characters was strongly circumscribed by the logic of war and its business, through which the state emerged as the figure of authority and command. It was through this shift in the representation of the political authority from a moral figure to the regulator of materialist desire that South Korea's popular imagination of the colonial past remained under the spell of the authoritarian state.

4

In the Colonial Zone of Contact

Kisaeng *and Gangster Films*

In South Korea, the genre of gangster films first gained popularity in the late 1960s and 1970s.[1] These earlier forms of the Korean gangster film were set against the distinctive historical backdrop of the colonial era.[2] Films such as *Men from Eight Provinces* (*P'aldo sanai*; Kim Hyoch'ŏn, 1969), *A True Story of Kim Tuhan* (*Silŏk Kim Tuhan*; Kim Hyoch'ŏn, 1974), *Righteous Fighter, Kim Tuhan* (*Hyŏpkaek Kim Tuhan*; Kim Hyoch'ŏn, 1975), and *Lynx* (*Sirasoni*; Yi Hyŏksu, 1979) offer historical accounts of the rise of Korean organized crime in 1930s colonial Seoul, with a geographical focus on the market districts of Chongno and Tongdaemun as the principal sites of masculine action. The social themes of violence and order, group hierarchy, and status mobility intersect with colonial questions of Korean identity, culture, and politics. If the colonial questions deal with the inner domain of personal belief and devotion vis-à-vis the idea of nation, the social themes enact in dramatic terms the societal logic of affiliation, loyalty, and entitlement within a subculture of illicit practices and violent crime. The gangster film's presentation of the male protagonist's rise to the top of the gangster organization also mirrors the growing anticipation of confrontation with the Japanese adversary. South Korean gangster films carry an allegorical message of anticolonial struggle and resistance in what is otherwise a fantasy of individual success and social mobility in a hostile, power-driven world.

Typically in gangster films set in the colonial era, the *kisaeng* or female entertainer courtesan complements the righteous masculinity that the male gangster protagonist aspires to represent. The *kisaeng* often functions as the fixed point of the gangster's moral compass; her devotion affirms and inspires his acts of justice in a world of colonial injustice and domination. Yet the scenario of domestic

76

no happy love ending?

happiness almost always remains incomplete in the gangster narrative. The nature of gangster heroics hence intersects with questions of the gendered trope of morality in colonial imaginings.[3]

The character of the *kisaeng* also inspired its own series of colonial-era melodramas in the late 1960s and early 1970s. Films such as *Myŏngwolgwan Lady* (*Myŏngwolgwan assi;* Pak Chongho, 1967), *Blue Light and Red Light* (*Chongdŭng hongdŭng;* Yi Hyŏngp'yo, 1968), *Golden Carriage* (*Hwanggŭm macha;* Kim Kwisŏp, 1968), *A Camellia Blossoms and Falls* (*Tongbaekkot pigo chigo;* Chŏng Chinu, 1970), *A Portrait of Woman* (*Yŏindo;* Kim Yŏnggŏl, 1971), *Warrior Kisaeng* (*Hyŏpki;* Chang Chinwon, 1973), and *Obaekhwa, the Five Renowned Kisaeng of Seoul* (*Changan myŏnggi Obaekhwa;* Im Kwont'aek, 1973) indicate the visibility of *kisaeng* on screen.[4] Although few of these films feature the *kisaeng*'s participation in the anticolonial struggle for independence, the majority underscore the individual plight of the *kisaeng* character buffeted by social prejudice and hostility.[5] The production and popularity of *kisaeng* films show historical overlap with the growing popularity of gangster films, as both genres gained traction in the late 1960s and 1970s.[6] *Kisaeng* were among the most visible and versatile female figures on the late 1960s screen and afforded a popular view of colonial social life.[7] *popular at same time as gangster films*

The generic identifications of "*kisaeng* film" (*kisaeng yŏnghwa*) and "gangster film" (*kkangpae yŏnghwa*) indicate the centrality of these figures in the organization and progression of the film narrative. But these labels also reflect changes, during the postcolonial period of the 1960s and 1970s, in the kinds of characters that represented the colonial experience. These figures focus the viewer's attention on a different type of social interaction and struggle. Consequently, this chapter explores how the narratives of socially marginalized figures like gangsters and *kisaeng* inform a different matrix for portraying colonialism. For instance, the marginal status of these figures introduces and elaborates themes about the hierarchies, divisions, exclusion, and discrimination that operate in, and constitute, social life in colonial Korea. The exploration of these subjects shows these films' very different orientation from earlier films' logic of exclusion and negation. The entangled visibility of *kisaeng* and gangster hence demands a comparison of these two genres' perspectives on social marginality and ethnic interaction as these were incorporated into the changing historical imagination of the 1960s.

Before delving into two key texts—*Kang Myŏnghwa* for the *kisaeng* film and *A True Story of Kim Tuhan* for the gangster film—I would like to examine the larger issue of colonial representation and its logic in the 1960s. The notion of social marginality is salient for this theme; it not only represents a new social perspective but also offers a larger critical window onto how the overall cinematic rendition of colonial space changed in the 1960s. Although much of this chapter focuses on issues of marginality—the dynamics of social mobility and the logic of exclusion and integration—I begin by addressing the seismic shift in the colonial configuration of the 1960s and beyond. I do this in order to address the changing cinematic discourse on colonialism and its historicity within the circumstances of the 1960s.

South Korea's normalization of relations with Japan and, later, its deployment of troops in the Vietnam War caused major changes in how the colonial past was discussed and how it was depicted in film. As the new bipolar vision of the Cold War disrupted the framework of anticolonial discourse and ideology, the repercussions in cinema were visible in several changes in subject matter, thematic focus, and sensibility. Among these were new sociocultural motifs and tropes of social space and cultural activities that reflected the changing construction of Korean identity and its relation to the colonial power. I examine the colonial tropes of socially marginal figures such as the *kisaeng* and the gangster as part and parcel of this crucial representational pattern and its development. These tropes were conceived as a narrative form of response to South Korea's speedy integration into the Cold War bipolar structure and the accompanying renewal of debate and controversy about the cultural heritage of colonialism in South Korean society.

PROBLEMATIZING CULTURE IN THE COLD WAR BIPOLAR GEOPOLITICAL ORDER

To account for the broader implications of this change in attitude toward colonial culture and representation, I draw on Rey Chow's insights into ethnography and the subjective origins of postcolonial visuality. In Chow's formulation, "the binary structure of observer/observed," with its inherent inequality, is central to the construction of the ethnographical fascination with a "primitive" culture, and postcolonially the state of being looked at is internalized as "part of the active manner in which such cultures represent—ethnographize—themselves."[8] Chow brings up this notion to resolve the epistemological deadlock created by the persistence of a Western understanding of ethnography in non-Western intellectual discourse: "We cannot write/think/talk the non-West in the academy without in some sense anthropologizing it, and yet anthropology and ethnography, atrophied in their epistemological foundations, remain 'very much still a one-way street.'" For Chow, a focus on visuality is essential for challenging a particular pattern of knowledge production in anthropology and ethnography, the latter of which can be defined as "a kind of representation with subjective origins," contrary to its claims of scientific objectivity. She asserts that "a new ethnography is possible only when we turn our attention to the subjective origins of ethnography as it is practiced by those who were previously ethnographised and who have, in the postcolonial age, taken up the active task of ethnographising their own cultures."[9]

The condition of possibility that Chow calls "the subjective origins of ethnography" has great relevance for understanding the various forces, conflicts, and inflections that made up the cultural landscape of South Korea in the 1960s.[10] Her insight, in supposing the palimpsestic nature of the postcolonial self-representation of culture, can be used productively to explain the complex film scenes of the 1960s, when the subject of colonialism gained urgency and when debate on the nature of cultural identity in and of South Korean cinema changed. The film aesthetics and discourses of the 1960s that I examine in this and other chapters are located at a crucial historical juncture, a point when colonial imagery and imagining gained new currency, shaping the South Korean film industry in the years to come.

In Chow's formulation, visuality emerges as the organizing field of discourse by which the ex-colonized invent and furnish their own authorial views of the nation's past culture. The new filmic tropes of colonial culture therefore signify the meeting point between two regimes of looking: the historical one that embodies the past colonizer's way of looking at Korea as an object of fascination, and the contemporary postcolonial view that registers new ways of looking at Korea's own culture. As Chow reminds us, the postcolonial view retains troubling traces of the previous, colonial visuality, forming what she calls the "optical unconscious." Chow describes this complex rewriting and reappropriation that the visual narrative medium of cinema performs so effectively for viewers as a process of translation, or a "vast transcription process."[11]

I submit that the 1960s and 1970s mark a particularly conspicuous phase of this kind of translation in South Korean cinema. This epochal process involved not only restaging and revisualizing the unaddressed past, particularly that of the colonial culture, but also actively transcoding the tropes and imagery of that culture to correspond to the political inflection of the era's Cold War bipolar logic. The impetus of this translation process arose not only from indigenous reflection but also from Cold War events: it is crucial to bear in mind these films' relation to the larger context of the geopolitical events and polarization of the 1960s and beyond. The question of the historicity of the cinematic form is tied not only to the vernacularization or transcription of past cultural elements or ideas into a contemporary visual medium, but also to the political inflections and discourse that surround the rise of such new cinematic imagining.

To engage this nexus of the Cold War, I draw insight from scholars of the Cold War who have formulated alternate ways of thinking about its cultural dimension.[12] Heonik Kwon reminds us through an illuminating summary of works by Zaki Laïdi and Christian G. Appy that the Cold War involved a comprehensive meaning-making endeavor that was as important for the global bipolar structure as the domination and regulation of political institutions and relations. A "battle for appropriation of meaning" was central to the competing systems in international politics that saw different scenarios of historical progress and moral superiority.[13] This struggle for words and meaning was not a single totalizing operation; rather, as Christian Appy notes, it encompassed plural and diverse cultural practices that were also perceived and understood in different terms by local people.[14]

I contend that for Korea this meaning-making process included, among other things, a particular visuality or way of imagining and remembering the colonial past that popular cinema dramatized and promulgated. Several scholars have noted the inherent semantic contradictions in the imaginary notion of the Cold War as a period of long peace. Kwon argues that such a belief is inconsistent with local histories and experiences that unfolded when the revolutionary struggle for decolonization collided with the bipolarization of politics. In fact, it was at this contested "historical horizon" that bipolar politics took their most deadly turn in the case of South Korea: the catastrophic civil war that began in 1950 and the ensuing militarization of social relations and culture.[15]

Kwon's conceptualization of the Cold War helps us approach South Korea's cinematic appraisal of the colonial experience as an inflection of the Cold War bipolar mode of thinking. The Cold War, examined from Kwon's perspective, can be read both as the global ordering of bipolar politics *and* as the diverse cultural iteration of local histories and experiences. In the trajectory that I trace with regard to South Korea's *kisaeng* and gangster films, the cinematic configuration of "local" knowledges and imaginaries has been called into question, recalibrated, and appropriated by the dominant bipolar political ordering of the Cold War.[16]

The imagery of cinematic representation informed the negotiated terrain that at first seemed to refer to a bygone era but in practice corresponded to the dilemmas of the present. It was no longer tenable to approach the question of colonialism purely through the prism of national(istic) politics when both former colonizers and colonized states had entered supposedly equalizing diplomatic relations under the Cold War bipolar order. In other words, the anterior principle of nationalist film aesthetics confronted major challenges in the 1960s and changed to accommodate the new geopolitical developments. The political dictate of overcoming Japanese colonialism, as it were, turned into a more complex and diffused visual portrayal of Japanese-Korean relations that envisioned various terms of equivalence and exchange between the two countries.

However limited or problematic in its effect, this new popular cinematic imagining of the colonial therefore constituted a fertile cultural site where global pressure and local responses produced creative and complex terms of dialogue and negotiation.[17] As I previously noted in chapter 2 on the "Japanese color" controversies, the 1960s' heightened sense of urgency over the crisis of representation of the colonial era also led to prolonged debate on the national and cultural identity of South Korean cinema.

Popular memory of the colonial experience was a particular social knowledge that was caught up in the systemic epistemological reordering of values of the Cold War. The ethnographical approaches of Chow and Kwon are useful in exploring the inherent limits of the dominant view of the Cold War and its impact on local expression of the bipolar experience. The ethnographical turn is justified here not simply because it offers a means of considering new small-scale knowledge but

Cold war as a time of peace and the anomaly of the Korean War

Korean war - extension of the Cold War

could no longer be outright anti- ... could blame the ... Korea + Japan in ... partnership also because it allows one to examine the status of national culture vis-à-vis the colonial experience as it took a different position in the matrix of intensified geopolitical ordering.

One result of this shift was an implicit change in Korea's status vis-à-vis Japan. Its autonomy was no longer imagined as national, in terms of an overarching hierarchical order and regulation, but as provincial, in terms of a delimited sovereignty of scattered, porous, island-like discrete areas and places, which would be more appropriately studied by anthropology or ethnography than by history.

IN THE ZONE OF PROPINQUITY:
HARASSMENT, STRATIFICATION, AND THE
SINPA MODE IN *KANG MYŎNGHWA*

When Kang Taejin directed the 1967 film *Kang Myŏnghwa*, which now is considered one of the signal *kisaeng*-themed films of the late 1960s, his reputation as a proficient filmmaker of melodrama underwent a revival. Kang had proven his filmmaking talent early in his career with the commercial and critical success of such classics as *Mr. Park* (*Pak Sŏbang*, 1960) and *The Coachman* (*Mabu*, 1961). He worked steadily during the golden age of South Korean cinema, directing on average three films per year throughout the 1960s. Most of the films he directed belong to the genre of family melodrama, arguably the most popular genre form of the era. Kang subsequently earned a reputation as one of the most reliable and bankable directors in this fast-changing period of the film industry.

His modest auteurist stature reached new prominence in 1967 with a series of major box office hits. This was the period during which the subject of modern Japan and its imagery preoccupied the minds of South Korean filmmakers and audiences alike. Consequently, colonial culture emerged on the South Korean screen with a vengeance, and Kang made a successful attempt to bring the era's cultural issues to box office fruition. Starting with *I Yearn to Go* (*Kagopa*), followed by the even more commercially successful *Youth Theater* (*Chŏngch'un kŭgjang*) and *Kang Myŏnghwa*, Kang emerged as a major director with distinctive skills to open a new popular vista on colonial culture.[18] In particular, Kang's films brought up cultural memories of the colonial past by refashioning and emphasizing social and cultural interactions that had been largely excluded from filmic portrayals of colonialism.

His unique depictions of the colonial era did not go unnoticed by film critics. As one writer observed, Kang's forte lay in the way he expanded the dramatic treatment of colonialism by incorporating humanistic values and a new sensibility into stories while maintaining the necessary critical attitude toward Japanese domination. Another commentator noted that, while Kang's films hardly qualified as artworks of the era, they represented the best examples of "healthy entertainment" or "elegant melodrama." During the Japanese-color frenzy of the 1960s,

Kang Myŏnghwa was noteworthy for inspiring a trend of *kisaeng*-themed melo-drama films, many of them set in the colonial period.[19] Portrayed as icons of tragic love and sacrifice, *kisaeng* characters were typically featured in a culturally deni-grated form of melodrama called *sinpa* in the late 1960s. The Korean film historian Yi Yŏngil criticized these *kisaeng*-themed films and their reactionary *sinpa* senti-ment (*pokkojŏk sinpa chŏngsŏ*), which he regarded as a regressive development in late 1960s film.[20]

Yet *Kang Myŏnghwa*'s favorable critical reception suggests that by the late 1960s the previous decade's treatment of the colonial era had become formulaic and stale. In contrast to heavy-handed nationalist scenarios, Kang's turn to showcasing the *kisaeng* who had previously catered to the colonial gaze signaled not only a change in subject matter and sensibility, but also postcolonial cinema's reappropri-ation of the legacy of colonial-era visual culture in which the figure of the *kisaeng* was the most recognizable icon. To be sure, Kang's sympathetic portrayal of these female entertainers was not unique during this period. Shin Sangok's 1967 literary film adaptation *The Remembered Traces of the Yi Dynasty* (*Ijojanyŏng*) is a serious treatment of *kisaeng* as the embodiment of colonial culture. Drawn from the liter-ary novella by Kajiyama Toshiyuki, the film received enthusiastic accolades from film critics for its presentation of Japanese sympathy and atonement for Korean suffering under colonial domination. Yet the portrayal of *kisaeng* in Shin's film recasts the visual scheme of the colonialist gaze as an impetus to drive the nar-rative forward. What is unique about *The Remembered Traces of the Yi Dynasty* is its violent ending, which registers in allegorical terms the impossibility of true reconciliation between Korea and Japan. Both *The Remembered Traces of the Yi Dynasty* and *Kang Myŏnghwa* raised public interest in the *kisaeng* as a new figure of melodrama and, in doing so, reworked the cultural space of entertainment that her body traverses and makes visual. However, *Kang Myŏnghwa* takes viewers into a different realm of social life barely ventured into by the allegorically oriented *The Remembered Traces of the Yi Dynasty*.

Kang Myŏnghwa engages with, and hence historicizes, the colonial cultural dis-course on the Korean *kisaeng* by framing the narrative around her pursuit of love and its tragic failure. The film projects a set of values and attitudes toward *kisaeng* that overlap with but also diverge from the objectified colonial imagery of *kisaeng*. Through a melodramatic rhetoric of pathos, Kang's film attributes a greater degree of affective intensity. It reworks the cultural memories of the *kisaeng* as it simulta-neously fleshes out and marginalizes her as a new yet outmoded figure caught in the forces of social division and discrimination within colonial Korea. More spe-cifically, it is through the *kisaeng*'s predicament that persistent social problems of discrimination, exclusion, materialism, and marginalization hitherto unaddressed in the colonial imagery of South Korea are brought into view.

The tragic dimension of romantic love in the true story on which the film was based had captured public imagination in the early 1920s. The love suicide of Kang Myŏnghwa was the cause célèbre of 1923, as many newspapers provided full coverage of the incident. According to these newspaper reports, *kisaeng* Kang Myŏnghwa had fallen in love with Chang Pyŏngch'ŏn, but their love soon met fierce opposition from Chang's wealthy family. After a series of tribulations, Kang decided to abandon her *kisaeng* career to prove her fidelity to her love. However, when all her efforts ended in failure, she killed herself by taking rat poison. She died in the arms of her lover, Chang, who soon followed suit by committing suicide out of despair.

In a previous era, Kang's suicide would have remained a mere individual event, but with the proliferation of newspapers in the early 1920s it became the object of the public's enthusiasm for passionate love. According to Kwon Bodurae, the notion of romantic love (*yŏnae* in Korean) attained central significance in social and cultural discourses during this period when Korea was engulfed in a feverish passion for social reform. A new modern discourse of romantic love, Kwon contends, was one of the direct channels through which people could imagine and rationalize the urgency of social reform and enlightenment. It also was a source of personal well-being and happiness and a wellspring of inspiration for new artistic works and experiments.[21] In the new media environment, Kang's story turned into a national headline and Kang's name became a household word that stood for the mythic dimension of tragic love. In 1920s, romantic love coupled up w/ social reform

The story inspired numerous literary fictions and film adaptations. The 1967 film version of *Kang Myŏnghwa* was not simply a direct appropriation of a story of love suicide;[22] it drew heavily from the accumulated narrative elements of popular dime novels of the colonial era, and its screenplay was written by Cho Hŭnp'a, who had previously penned a radio drama version of *Kang Myŏnghwa* that aired on TBC Radio.[23]

Illustrating a growing practice within the film industry since the late 1950s, the 1967 film version of *Kang Myŏnghwa* hence represents story appropriation and adaptation across a variety of media: the print media coverage of the romantic love craze that galvanized the public in the 1920s as well as the cinematic adaptation of a radio drama that had borrowed from dime novel stories and news accounts. Hence, in depicting the colonial culture, the film does not offer a direct view of the past era of sovereignty loss. Rather, it offers interconnected commentaries, references, conventions, and tropes that surround a renowned narrative of the colonial era. Through the complex reuse of the colonial archetype of the tragic *kisaeng* story, the film not only newly imagines the colonial past but also questions what constitutes colonial culture in the visual mise-en-scène of the 1960s postcolonial and Cold War frame.

In addition, the film shares a thematic affinity with the youth film of the mid-1960s, which was the most commercially successful filmmaking trend from roughly 1964 to 1966. In particular, *Kang Myŏnghwa*'s thematic treatment of social hierarchy and the tragic aspect of love suicide resonated strongly with the recurring thematic concerns of youth films, including the quintessential *Barefoot Youth* (*Maenbal-ŭi chŏngch'un*) of 1964. Furthermore, the film is an extension of Kang Taejin's own preoccupation with the youth theme, as in *Youth Theater*, which relates the adventurous heroics of a group of students in the colonial period. The male protagonist Chang in *Kang Myŏnghwa* shares the youthful but naive energy and optimism that is characteristic of the young people in *Youth Theater*. More importantly, actress Yun's portrayal of a *kisaeng* was a new depiction of the old profession, with a novelty value that the film's promotion used to great advantage. The film's connections to literary works, as well as radio drama and youth films, a new film genre from Japan, all made possible the 1960s filmic revision of colonial culture.

From an analytic perspective, one can argue that the new trope of the *kisaeng* afforded a view of the space of interaction between Koreans and Japanese—namely the city streets at night and the *kisaeng* house—that paralleled contemporary attitudes toward the 1965 normalization of relations with Japan. The *kisaeng* house, in particular, gained significance because of the exceptional interaction it introduced and regulated between the two ethnic groups. In this marginal zone, Korean men are portrayed as competing with the colonizer for the attentions of the *kisaeng* and in the process, exemplifying national integrity and moral superiority. Outside this space, where respectful and romantic encounters could take place between the *kisaeng* and Korean men, lay a colonial society where materialist values and rigid rules of hierarchy and discrimination always worked against the aspirations of the *kisaeng* to be included in that society. What typically ensues, as in *Kang Myŏnghwa*, is a conventional narrative of *sinp'a* melodrama in which the female protagonist tries to realize her notion of pure love, only to face ultimate defeat.

The opening sequence of *Kang Myŏnghwa* features a fateful night street encounter between the *kisaeng* Kang and the male student Chang that also introduces colonial tensions in the spatial terms of boundaries and proximity. The film begins with Korean male students strolling through the night alleys of Seoul singing exuberantly with arms around one another. The boisterous mood, enhanced by a backward tracking camera shot, dispels the somber aura of night alleys typical of cinematic treatments of nocturnal colonial Seoul. The group is bar-hopping, but protagonist Chang, played by the 1960s' most sought-after actor, Shin Sŏngil, bids the others goodbye and goes his separate way. His sense of exuberance and freedom that lingers from an enjoyable time with his friends quickly evaporates when he witnesses a Japanese drunkard's harassment of a Korean woman and rushes to her rescue. The ensuing commotion results in his arrest by the colonial police. Chang's chivalrous action does not go unnoticed, however. Kang Myŏnghwa, the Korean *kisaeng* rescued by Chang, had treated to a hidden corner and saw all that occurred. When Chang later visits the *kisaeng* house to be entertained and to socialize with his friends, Kang immediately recognizes her savior. With this scene, the film initiates the momentum that leads to their budding romance.

FIGURE 7. The female protagonist Kang (right), rescued by Chang on a street at night in *Kang Myŏnghwa*. Courtesy of the Korean Film Archive.

The opening sequence utilizes the contrived elements of melodrama, as it introduces the two protagonists through the gendered scenario of the masculine rescue of a damsel in distress. Yet it also includes a view of the social life of an elite group of Koreans. The adult male students' boozing and boisterous socializing bring a sense of freedom to the night alley that stands in sharp contrast to the darkness and emptiness of back alley spaces in previous decades' filmic view of colonialism.[24] The students' clamorous fraternizing also reflects a unique social status and privilege that presupposes society's leniency.

The privileged status of adult male students was hardly new in the colonial imagery of Korean cinema. Such students appear in many literary and other cultural works as the direct recipients of modern education and social progress. The film's portrayal of male students utilizes their complex and often double cultural meanings. On the one hand, it invokes the old cultural imagery of a young social elite whose opportunities for modern education and upward mobility parallel the prospects of the modern nation's progress. Films with this enlightenment theme typically foreground the positive attributes of students.[25] On the other hand, the film portrays street-roaming male students as pleasure seekers who avail themselves of the many leisure options of urban life. The implications of the latter image are particularly important in this and other films of the late 1960s because the sociocultural backdrop that the films presuppose informs the changing cinematic depiction of the colonial social world. The fait accompli of colonialism hence offers something new on the screen: autonomous, albeit scattered and limited, leisure activities for Koreans that thrive under colonial rule.[26]

The recalibration also applies to the portrayal of the Japanese but, even more importantly, to Chang's reaction in the opening sequence. Japanese men's harassment of a Korean woman had been used in earlier films to conceptualize a fundamental Japanese-Korean antagonism and to display the just action of Korean men in defense of Korean women's integrity and chastity. A film such as *Nameless Stars* (*Irŭmŏmnŭn pyŏldŭl*; Kim Kangyun, 1959) is exemplary in its presentation of this line of anticolonial reasoning and action. Based on the 1929 student protest in Kwangju, the film offers a historical view of the collective action of students protesting against colonial forces. Yet whereas the 1959 film frames an incident of harassment as leading to the collective action of the nation, *Kang Myŏnghwa* defines the problem on a limited scale devoid of the political implications of the gendered violence and legal struggles of Koreans. *Kang Myŏnghwa* depicts the incident of harassment as an urban mishap that incites the Korean man's courageous intervention but does not link it to anticolonial politics. The main purpose of the scene is to serve as a motive for Kang to subsequently develop favorable feelings for her savior.

Another convention is the arrival of police on the scene that typically results in the arrest of the Korean man who took action against the Japanese harasser. The film includes this motif, which underscores a key structural feature of colonial domination: discriminatory Japanese police enforcement against Koreans. Again, however, *Kang Myŏnghwa* does not extrapolate political implications; instead, it downplays the problem by shifting it from the political to the social realm. The colonial dilemma is defined in the film specifically as a geographical issue: Koreans occupy the same urban space as the Japanese. The problem of harassment is not presented as the result of structural discrimination against Koreans. Rather, it signifies the unavoidable disruption that results from Koreans and Japanese living side by side. The scene of disturbance that the film features at the beginning shows how the urban streets of Seoul, which previously were the exclusive, though austere domain of Koreans, have become a zone of traffic and encounter between two ethnic groups that the police patrol to prevent disruption. Urban night streets are open and available to both Korean and Japanese men. The scuffle that leads to the colonial police action therefore presupposes an equivalency between the two groups in their overlapping use of the colonial urban streets. Here the Korean is portrayed as being more disciplined in his social behavior than the unruly Japanese, a difference that the inept colonial police fail to perceive and take into account in their patrol actions.

In other words, the colonial problem is clearly reconfigured in spatial terms, conceived now as a matter of equivalency that allows Japanese and Koreans to indulge in the same types of leisure and entertainment. The *kisaeng* is a crucial figure in the zone of equivalency because she functions as the nexus for Koreans and Japanese competition to win attention as equal clients in the entertainment sphere.[27] The *kisaeng* in the late 1960s is not just a figure reminiscent of the colonial legacy, but one who recalibrates the terms of interaction and tension between two ethnic groups rises even as she is always more drawn to the Korean.

The collision of Japanese and Korean individuals that presupposes an urban scene where colonized and colonizer are equal finds its most salient expression in the subsequent standard *kisaeng* scene: a house sequence that typically features the *kisaeng*'s performance of a traditional dance. In *Kang Myŏnghwa* the sequence begins with a clear identification of the renowned *kisaeng* house Myŏngwŏlgwan, and the film cuts to show the *kisaeng* Kang's performance in front of her clients inside the Korean traditional-style living room.[28] In traditional dress, Kang is fully immersed in her dance, accompanied by Korean musicians. The Japanese client, the high government official Tanaka, and his Korean subordinate incessantly applaud her exceptional beauty and exquisite performance skills.

The performance setting utilizes the colonial imagery of *kisaeng*, as Kang is a body made into a spectacle and subjected to the sexual gaze of the Japanese colonial authority. Yet the film also complicates and interrupts the colonial paradigm of looking upon the Korean female body. The editing in the sequence follows the structural convention of shot and countershot: the gaze of the onlooker followed by the ensuing shot of a female body that establishes the lopsided nature of relations between the two. Yet Kang does not always gaze back at the Japanese observer client. Rather, she frequently looks elsewhere, taking satisfaction in her own performance skill.[29] Her averted gaze during the dance sequence suggests the space of contrarian integrity that the marginal *kisaeng* figure maintains at work. Even when she is required to serve and fulfill the fantasy projection of the powerful Japanese man at the *kisaeng* house, she finds a way to avoid meeting his sexually motivated gaze by hiding effectively behind the facade of performance that she puts on for her audience. The subtle sign of disavowal renders legible Kang's gesture of noncompliance and reveals the limit of the totalizing scopic power of the colonial authority at this leisure site.

Kang's noncompliance faces a challenge when Tanaka commands his Korean subordinate to demand more personal service from her. He pressures her to offer to pour liquor into his glass, a ritualistic act that signifies an offering of her sexual services to the client.[30] She refuses, but Tanaka is relentless. Once again, Japanese unruliness appears in the form of harassment of the Korean female entertainer. The colonial power is depicted here as an excessive force that does not take into consideration social propriety and decorum. Just as the pressure mounts unbearably, a waiter in the *kisaeng* house intervenes, breaks the tension, and alerts her of other clients that she is obliged to serve. When she leaves the room, Kang thanks the waiter for coming to the rescue and proceeds to another room to greet the Korean client, Kim Chusa, who awaits her.

This managerial intervention represents the modus operandi of a business that uses the logic of service allotment to protect *kisaeng* performers from Japanese harassment. It also shows how the *kisaeng* house, in effect, establishes equivalency between two ethnic groups by juxtaposing them in an inadvertent competition for the *kisaeng*'s service. The competition itself remains hidden and invisible, as the Koreans and the Japanese occupy separate rooms, which *kisaeng* visit in rotation for entertainment. The *kisaeng* house is the only space in cinematic representation where Japanese comply with the rules of a Korean business site. It thus visualizes the limit of the colonizer's power, which in other instances is assumed to be total and absolute. The spatial division of the *kisaeng* house, which the *kisaeng* is able to cross at will, effectively has a regulating effect on clients who are otherwise prone to form oppositional relations. However limited it may be, this capacity to regulate the demands of both Korean and Japanese clients sets the *kisaeng* house apart from all other colonial spheres of interethnic interactions.

At a *kisaeng* house, the segregation of clients by ethnicity is an implicit rule that inhibits any ethnic enmity. However, in *Kang Myŏnghwa*, a disturbance resulting from the violation of this rule is caused by the excessive demands of the Japanese man, Tanaka, that turn into outright harassment. The conflict with Tanaka leads Kang to flee to the room next door, which Chang and his student friends happen to be occupying for a party. When Kang enters the room and hides behind its folding screen, Chang and the other students understand the situation instantly and act in unison to protect her. Soon the Japanese client and his Korean subordinate enter the room without permission to search for Kang. The students criticize them for the unruly intrusion into their zone of entertainment. Specifically, Chang frames and articulates the expected rules of propriety as the foundation of civilized society. If you are an elite person of integrity, Chang challenges the intruder, you must surely understand how this act of disturbance constitutes an offense against the principles of social decorum and civilization.

Presupposed in this argument is the shared sense of social propriety that the Japanese "neighbor" fails to exercise at the *kisaeng* house. The confidence with which Chang advances his argument catches the Japanese man off guard, and he subsequently withdraws in humiliation from the room full of Korean students. This moment of interethnic conflict soon turns into a moment of camaraderie between the *kisaeng* and the Korean students. The romantic relationship between Chang and Kang emerges out of this second act of valor against Japanese men to secure Kang's safety. Hence, while the ethnically segregated space of the *kisaeng* house may be at moments porous and exposed to transgression and danger, it nevertheless reconstitutes and cements a sense of cohesion among Koreans by means of the rhetoric of civility and decorum. Many *kisaeng*-themed films repeatedly underscore this sense of cohesion between the marginal *kisaeng* and the Korean man from a different social background, paralleling the logic of ethnic segmentation to secure entertainment and a leisure space for Koreans.

Outside the *kisaeng* house, however, the film exposes a set of problems that are deeply rooted in the internal social divisions and segregation among Koreans themselves. The budding romance between Chang and Kang takes place in the form of nighttime strolls along the quiet walled streets of the old palace.[31] Yet these romantic moments introduce a new form of stressful gaze for Kang. After waiting in front of Myŏngwŏlgwan for Kang's departure from work, Chang escorts her to her house. While delighted, Kang expresses her concern that her lowly social status as a *kisaeng* will tarnish Chang's reputation in the eyes of other, anonymous Koreans. Chang is oblivious to the social prejudice directed at the *kisaeng* and regards his visit to the *kisaeng* house as simply an occasion for pleasure. He is largely unaware of the social division, segregation, and prejudice that govern the social lives of Koreans under colonial rule.

Issues arising from this gulf that separates two characters from different social backgrounds recur throughout the film, especially with regard to the subject of money. In fact, much of the tension surrounding their romance has its roots not in a lack of money but rather in its treacherous use-value and its misdirected effects. The affluence of Chang's family is underscored repeatedly throughout the film and has problematic effects on people, particularly Kang's parents. Indeed, the introduction of money as Chang's gift to Kang only complicates his relationship with Kang's parents, on whom his money makes the strongest impression. Chang's money is meant to signal his love toward Kang. The sum he sends to her as a farewell gift on his departure for Japan, however, launches a convoluted series of events. He asks his *kisaeng* friend Ok-sun to deliver the money to Kang, but Ok-sun does not hand it over directly. Instead, she gives it to Kang's greedy mother to convince her how wealthy Kang's suitor is. Not only does Chang's gift of money fail to reach Kang, but its diversion fuels the fierce materialism that dominates Kang's family and friend. In a later scene, Chang offers his tuition to Kang to help alleviate her family's financial hardship, which had led Kang to descend into the *kisaeng* profession in the first place. However, his kind-hearted gesture toward Kang's family backfires as Kang's itinerant father takes possession of the offering and runs off, infuriating Kang's mother. Kang's father then visits Chang's home to blackmail Chang's parents about Chang's "ruination" of his *kisaeng* daughter and her future prospects. Chang's family, who have been misinformed about their son's whereabouts, endure this humiliating encounter and comply with Kang's father's demand. — mis-use of money

The above two sequences illustrate how Chang's use of money, which was intended to cement his relationship with Kang's parents, fails to achieve the desired effect. Instead, the couple's relationship suffers precisely because of the disadvantageous effects of Chang's monetary gifts. Although Kang has a thriving career as a *kisaeng* with an independent spirit, her parents regard her profession as a social disgrace for which they superficially blame themselves. Concurrently, they pressure her to pursue money over all other values, including love and marriage.[32] Chang's frequent offers of money to her parents inflame their materialistic impulses, impeding rather than facilitating the couple's prospects for romance and marriage. The film details the deep mismatches of expectation and value that are organized around money once the couple starts living together. It becomes increasingly clear that Kang's parents regard her as a purely money-making entity. Indeed, Kang's father tells Chang's father that he does not care what they do to his *kisaeng* daughter so long as he gets the money for his gold mine project.

The film's excessive valorization of pure and innocent love is set against a corrupt world where materialism pervades familial relationships. The couple's naïveté lies not in their inexperience in love, but in their inability to comprehend the detrimental effects of money on relations among people. The volatile dynamic of money consumes all who surround the female protagonist. The male protagonist, for his part, shares moral culpability, for he has been the steady supplier of money without a keen understanding of its effects on its recipients. The lack of money that produces so much suffering in the colonial melodramatic imagination is reframed here to underscore opposite, but equally negative, effects. Chang's money does not solve problems; rather, it precipitates a series of actions that make it impossible for the couple to form a proper conjugal relationship.

The film features two sites where the couple escape the exploitative and corrupt social world: the hot springs resort and the metropole of Japan. Chang suggests a trip, a de facto honeymoon, to a hot springs resort to avoid the pressure Kang faces at home. The resort sequence is set in two locales where the couple vow their love for each other in complete privacy: the traditional tower house for a nighttime excursion and a hotel room for the wedding night. The tower house is a serene and quiet setting where Kang, to express her love, offers Chang a precious memento she has prepared for him and Chang in return expresses his unwavering love for her. Sentimental music rises up, heightening the emotional force of the couple's growing passion. Yet the scene also registers a peculiar sense of emptiness, as there is a complete absence of other tourists. This sense continues into the following guest house sequence during which the couple spend the night together. The cinematic properties of low lighting and measured pace, along with continuous sentimental music, create an ambiance of intimacy free of social constraints. It is as if the couple dwell in a completely separate night world of their own.

The film's focused portrayal of the couple's private intimacy is certainly rare in the cinematic rendition of colonialism. But perhaps the more significant contextual factors here are the social discrimination and materialism of the colonial society against which the couple's love and intimacy are oppositionally defined. The film's negative portrayal of social interactions makes their two places of refuge particularly resonant with serenity and sacredness. That said, the film reveals, through the tumultuous narrative of young lovers, a splintered social imaginary of colonial Korea that is very different from the assumed homogeneity of the Korean nation in other political dramas. The colonial reality in Kang Myŏnghwa is one of oppressive rules of social division, hierarchy, and discrimination in tandem with an all-encompassing materialism. It leaves little room to imagine a radical alternative for social change, turning instead toward valorization of "pure" love. The ascendency of sinpa melodrama in the late 1960s, of which the kisaeng narrative Kang Myŏnghwa is a prime example, reflects how the disproportionate power of the fixed social values and order ("the way things are") leads to tragic consequences for the *kisaeng*, who embodies the oppositional value of love ("the way things should be").

This cinematic discourse of individual love involves an overt stylization of love's consummation with an acute sense of ephemerality and fatalism. The conjugal union in a guest house is rendered initially through a silhouette image of the couple cast on a paper window. Chang slowly removes Kang's clothes and the film cuts to show her defloration by cutting to shots from different angles that generate a sense of presentational aura rather than representational transparency. The position of lighting, for instance, does not match with the images cast in the sequence. Aesthetic stylization is evident in the ensuing shot in which coitus is rendered with an image of the clasped hands of the couple in bed, leaving the actual act of lovemaking off screen. However contrived and superficial these images may be in the eyes of the contemporary film viewer, the sequence makes lucid the determined rigor of stylization used to underscore the couple's earnest consummation. The slow but measured pace of action lacks the immediacy of the passion that previously characterized their love affair, and the act of consummation itself seems restrained and even listless, connoting a fatalistic sense of finitude, failure, and even death.³ Yet such contrivance, in conjunction with the stately and serious pace of the act, has a transformative effect, as it gives the consummation the serious aura of ritual practice despite (or because of) its formulaic and performative orientation.

This resort to ritual, which carves out an abstract, alternate space of symbolic condensation, echoes the unique sense of time that the couple share at the moment of lovemaking. Both are keenly aware of Chang's imminent departure for Japan. Being supportive of her man, Kang insists that he leave for Japan even when he expresses a wish to stay. Although they change their minds later and choose to live together instead of parting, the couple dwell deeply in the dejected resignation of the moment. This sense of hopelessness is explicitly expressed in the couple's comments on the caged lovebirds within the guesthouse room. When one bird dies, Kang explains to Chang that the other will soon follow, foreshadowing the future conclusion of their own troubled affair.

In the metropole space of Japan, however, the couple find hope that they can successfully settle down together. The safe abode also provides the most explicit, hence controversial, image of a ritual expression of the couple's pledge of love. Here, the image of Japan as a space for the newlyweds has broad implications for the overall spatial logic of colonial representation in the 1960s. Japan previously was the destination for Chang's higher education, but the couple move to Japan for an ulterior motive: to live in secluded environs for their private moments. Much as the lovers flee to the hot springs resort, they make a rented second-story room in Japan their sanctuary. Unencumbered by social prejudice, Kang is visibly transformed in Japan, as shown by the clothing she wears: no longer traditional dress,

an iconic signifier of *kisaeng* status, but Western attire, a sign of her escape from the social logic of discrimination in Korea.

Metropole Japan offers a space of respite for the couple, whose marriage in practice is filled with blessed moments of love and harmony. The overall ambiance of relief and comfort is evident in their interaction, albeit brief, with the Japanese landlady, who greets them with a friendly demeanor and neighborly understanding. The tension and conflict that typically characterize relations between Koreans and Japanese in the colonial space of proximity are missing here. Instead, the couple blend seamlessly into the daily environs of Japan precisely because this urban retreat imposes none of the constraints of colonial surveillance or social prejudice that they experienced in Korea. Japan signifies a space of possibility for them.[34]

The film challenges and subverts the ethnic bipolarity even more scandalously at the moment of the love pledge scene. On the first night after the couple move into their new home, Kang hears chanting in the distance and inquires about it. Chang explains that it is wish chanting from the Shinto shrine, which comes into the couple's view through the flickering lights that outline the image of a shrine gate in the distance. Impressed by its religious nature, Kang engages Chang in wish-making while pensively gazing at the shrine gate. This moment may be one of the most uncanny in the colonial imagery of South Korean cinema, for it violates the nationalist mandate regarding visualization in which voluntary acceptance of cultural assimilation policies is completely prohibited.

The distant image of the Shinto shrine gate confers on the couple an aura of solemn ritual. While the idea of finding spiritual comfort in such an iconic image may have been offensive to many Koreans at the time, I assert that the Shinto shrine gate stands in as an *abstract* ritual icon that serves a general ceremonial function. Its outline of flickering lights has no realistic substance, curtailing its historical and political implications. Japan here is a localized "foreign" country one can travel to and dwell in with curiosity. In other words, the sense of novelty that Kang experiences in Japan echoes the aesthetic effects of many contemporary South Korean films that featured location images of Japan. The seeming equalization of Japanese and Koreans that characterizes so many aspects of colonial representation in films of the late 1960s presents metropole Japan as an *apolitical tourist site* that Koreans can traverse and dwell in, free from the social constraints of discrimination in Korea. It is a level ground for the colonial elite who find opportunities for their future.[35]

If metropole Japan optimistically stands for the future possibilities for the couple's conjugal life, their forced return to Korea marks the beginning of their tragic downfall and demise. Chang voluntarily changes his profession from student to menial worker in Japan to earn a living, but his absence does not go unnoticed. He receives a letter from his father in Korea, followed by a visit from an old friend, Pang, who criticizes him for continuing a life of disrepute and attempts to persuade him to dissolve his marriage to the *kisaeng*. Chang vehemently refuses, but

Kang, who overhears the conversation, concedes to these demands of others. What follows is a series of events that repeatedly prove Kang's fundamental misconception of the social conventions and constraints of Korea in which her marriage with Chang is challenged and disputed. When Kang decides to return to Korea with her husband, she plans to live a life according to the social norms and proprieties for a respectful daughter-in-law. However, this plan proves gravely miscalculated, as her social integration into Chang's family is completely blocked.

The situations that confront Kang in Korea are characterized by melodramatic turns of betrayal and disappointment. The disparity between her innocent intentions and the immutable barriers of social discrimination constitutes the main theme of the film as a *sinpa* melodrama. Yet the latter, melodrama-saturated portion of the film shows a striking disparity, for Chang, unlike Kang, virtually abdicates responsibility to deal with unfolding events. When the couple return to Korea, they visit Kang's *kisaeng* friend Ok-sun for temporary lodging until they can find a long-term residence. Chang tells Kang that he will visit his home to pay his respects to his parents, but he never follows through on his plan. Instead, Chang stops short as he approaches the house. Aware of the pressure he would face at home, he chooses domestic life with Kang over the resumption of relations with his natal family. For him, the two options do not converge.

His inaction, or failure to communicate with Kang about his decision, sets up a situation in which the relationship spirals downward through misunderstanding. Unaware of Chang's inertia, Kang visits Chang's family's house alone to pay her respects to her parents-in-law, only to face cold rejection. The adamant rebuff is expressed in spatial terms of segmentation and exclusion. From this moment on, Kang acts like a classic melodramatic heroine who behaves contrary to her true desire. Kang returns to working as a *kisaeng* at Myŏngwolgwan, an act consciously designed to infuriate and chase away Chang. She succeeds, as Chang misinterprets her intentions and returns home in disappointment. When he changes his mind and decides to return to Kang, the film shows the futility of his belated action.

The second part of the film, however, does examine another underside of the sanctioned colonial reality. The convoluted narrative of Kang's tragedy points to the remarkable permanence of the social order maintained under colonial rule. Kang's problems derive from her grave misperception of the likelihood of her integration into Chang's wealthy and prestigious family. In other words, the failure of a personal effort to attain upward social mobility also undermines the personal domain of love and marriage. That the film shows a great sympathy for the fallen indicates the resilience of the melodramatic moral reasoning that was the basis of many popular films of the 1950s and 1960s. Yet the film also shows how social mobility and the integration of people from different social strata are blocked in Korean society. Even though the male protagonist Chang kills himself at the end of the story, the film seems to describe the continuation of an unaltered social system of rigid hierarchy. The South Korean gangster film, typically set in the 1930s colonial era, revisits this issue and expands the scope of spatial logic integral to the changing mode of colonial representation on screen.

I want to conclude this section on *kisaeng* film by focusing on *sinpa*, a cultural form inextricably associated with this film cycle of the late 1960s. Critics approached *sinpa* as an old form of melodrama in Korea that dated back to theater productions of the colonial era. Imported from Japan (*shimpa* in Japanese), the term has been explored ad nauseam as a sentimental mode of representation in South Korean cinema with aesthetic limits and failings. Set in contrast to the valorized "social realism," *sinpa* melodrama has often been marked as a regressive form precisely because of its association with the past colonial culture.

The question I raise with regard to *sinpa* is the following: What was the discursive effect of the term *sinpa* in the cultural politics of the late 1960s, when South Korea experienced a major shift in attitudes toward Japan as a partner in Cold War geopolitics? The rise of *sinpa* melodrama, I would argue, was not simply a reuse of the old popular narratives of the colonial era. As the story of Kang Myŏnghwa demonstrates, its affective center lay in the despair and disappointment of a marginalized figure, often a woman, whose yearning to integrate into the larger society was doomed to fail. The repetition here is the mourning for the failure of an individual, but this persistent debacle also signals the shifting cultural logic or view of colonialism from the total negation of and opposition to imperialist politics to the rendition of various levels of equivalency and exchange. The latter development, as I will develop in more detail through an analysis of gangster films, demands identification with the select few Koreans who have the privilege to form an equal mode of exchange with the Japanese. South Korean cinema of the late 1960s moved away from the communitarian ideal of anticolonial justice and politics to an elite culturalist approach to the problem of colonial domination. As colonial imagining became dominated by the actions of social or cultural elites, the *sinpa* melodrama rose to express overwhelming empathy for those who were pushed aside by stringent Korean social norms under colonial rule. The resilience of the *sinpa* form represents a critique of the complacent logic of a colonial imagining that betrayed the communitarian mode of conceiving the anticolonial struggle—a struggle that was waged for the protection of the most vulnerable and disadvantaged.

COLONIAL UPWARD MOBILITY:
HIERARCHY, TERRITORY AND SURVEILLANCE IN
A TRUE STORY OF KIM TUHAN

In this section on gangster film set in the colonial era, I focus on the 1974 film *A True Story of Kim Tuhan* (*Silŏk Kim Tuhan*; Kim Hyochŏn, 1974). As a part of the chapter's larger preoccupation with the colonial space of propinquity as a dominant and recurring thematic trope of 1960s films on colonialism, I bring attention to the various contours of social interactions as well as the cultural values and problems that organize this specific scenario of upward social mobility. First, a brief synopsis is in order. The film begins with revolutionaries' foiled assassination scheme to eliminate a renowned collaborator. Kim Chwachin leads the attack on Song Pyŏngjun but is injured during the operation and chased by the Japanese police. The ensuing sequence shows his retreat into an elderly lady's house, where the lady's daughter, whom he later marries, attends to his recovery. Kim subsequently returns to Manchuria to continue the guerrilla operation. Shortly thereafter his wife visits with his son, Tuhan. When she returns home to Korea, she faces arrest and is ultimately killed. The orphaned Tuhan grows up to be a leader of beggars near the Chongno area, the concentrated Korean business district. He soon becomes entangled in a grand turf war between Korean and Japanese gangsters over control of Chongno. The Korean gang leader Na Kwanjung recognizes Tuhan's talents and recruits and trains him to be his successor. Tuhan embraces the new opportunity and soon shows his allegiance to Na and his organization. When Na is killed in a surprise attack by the Korean gang leader Shinmajŏk, Tuhan reacts decisively and defeats the enemy. The victory secures Tuhan's reputation as the de facto gang leader and leads to an unavoidable confrontation with the Japanese mobs who vie for control over the Korean business district. The latter send assassins to kill Tuhan's *kisaeng* wife and his men. The enraged Tuhan mobilizes a final all-out showdown with the Japanese gangsters. After this triumph, he turns himself in to the Japanese police.

The film's account of the real-life gangster boss Kim Tuhan (1918–72) traces his clear lineage from the esteemed resistance army leader Kim Chwachin (1889–1930), a story of noble origin that is crucial to the construction of Kim Tuhan's authority and leadership. In contrast to the victories of real-life guerrilla leader Kim in Manchuria, the actions of film protagonist Kim in colonial Korea are portrayed as ineffective: at the beginning of the film he barely escapes the police chase, is injured, and hides. It is noteworthy, however, that his weakness is counteracted by the action of an ordinary Korean, who quickly realizes the identity of the person under stress and offers him refuge, thereby not only saving his life but preserving his political role. As in biographical films of the late 1950s as well as the Manchurian action films of the 1960s, an aura of authority is supposed to be an inherent feature of a leader, even when he falls into a predicament due to miscalculation. The refuge scene frames a situation whereby the Korean people find an opportunity to prove political allegiance and self-worth through voluntary interaction with an important leader. Leadership, its construction and naturalization, is one of the central themes that is developed in depth in the subsequent narrative of the general's son.

The large traditional house where General Kim takes refuge is crucial to the film's formulation of his supposed authority. The elderly lady, played with unparalleled charisma and poise by Hwang Chŏngsun, effectively fends off the colonial military force that breaks into the house soon after Kim's arrival. When interrogated, she answers by explaining her nightly ritual: praying for the good health of the Japanese emperor. She also warns the military officer that his unannounced intrusion has already offended the decorum required of a colonial subject such as her to honor the dignity of the emperor. The officer retreats immediately when she implies that she might report his offense to the higher authorities. The brief exchange demonstrates how colonized Koreans could use the very ideological mandate of total loyalty to the emperor to strengthen their position against agents of the colonial power. By feigning complete loyalty to the state ideology, the elderly lady effectively carves out a space of resistance in which she is able to help the cause of nationalist struggle.

Not only her actions in and of themselves, but also their setting is significant. The elderly lady's old house has an aura of safety and security that is similar to that of a *kisaeng* house. It has no male resident, and the absence of a male character typifies in allegorical terms the broken Korean family under colonial rule. Patriarchal authority is missing, but this absence creates a situation in which women are not bound by the traditional precepts of gendered behavior in the household. On their own, they can decide to bring the injured male character into the house for proper medical care. Furthermore, the elderly lady turns out to be a former lady-in-waiting of the defunct Chosŏn dynasty who now attempts to maintain the house in a state befitting its past glory. The historical link between the dynastic court culture and *kisaeng* courtesans was noted frequently in colonial discourse, and some postcolonial films revisit this connection to underscore the special cultural status of *kisaeng* as an embodiment of the fallen beauty of the past dynasty.[36]

In the *kisaeng* house of South Korean cinema, both the colonized and the colonizer are restricted in their scope of action: the colonized must pretend to be subservient to the colonizer, while the colonizer is unable to exert total power because of covert acts of resistance by the colonized. This film's quasi-*kisaeng* house shows similar dynamics. Much as the *kisaeng* protagonist in *Kang Myŏnghwa* puts on a masquerade of servitude to the Japanese client but evades his harassment, the house's elderly lady, through covert resistance, successfully fends off the intrusion of the colonial agents and provides a safe haven for the fugitive Korean resistance fighter. Guerrilla leader Kim and the elderly lady's daughter marry, and soon thereafter Kim moves to Manchuria to continue his nationalist mission, leaving behind his new wife, who subsequently gives birth to their son Tuhan. The house, as if to follow the filmic precepts of colonial representation, never turns into a permanent site of domestic life.

In subsequent scenes, the film makes an explicit material connection between female sacrifice and the nationalist armed struggle. When, after several years, Kim's wife travels with Tuhan to the resistance army headquarters in Manchuria, she learns about the money problems of the resistance and offers her husband the inheritance from her late mother so that he can purchase arms from the Russians. The film uses the same concept of money as the Manchurian action films in which the procurement of war funds is synonymous with the anticolonial struggle itself.[37] What distinguishes *A True Story of Kim Tuhan* from typical Manchurian action films is the follow-up story of Kim's wife. In Manchurian action films, the completion of the money transfer often coincides with the Korean "courier's" unfortunate death, a death that is almost always recognized and mourned, thereby becoming properly registered in the symbolic field of signification.

Such recognition and mourning are not available for the sacrifice and suffering of Kim's wife and child. After Kim's wife delivers the inheritance money to her husband, she returns home to Korea. She soon learns about her husband's military victory at Chŏngsanri. While she is looking at the family photo taken with her husband in Manchuria, the colonial police break in and arrest her, leading ultimately to her death and young Tuhan's orphan life on the street. The film does not show any subsequent communication between General Kim and his family in Korea. Nor does the ensuing narrative pay any attention to General Kim's actions or whereabouts. This is significant because the nationalist leader never acknowledges the heavy price his wife and child have paid for the nationalist cause. The subsequent narrative advances to fill this traumatic rupture in the field of symbolic meanings through Tuhan's growth into maturity and his acquisition of power and stature.

A community of beggars forms the quasi-family unit in which Tuhan grows up to become a respectful and competent young leader. Living under Sup'yo Bridge in the Chongno district, young Tuhan performs the role of eldest brother for other young orphans. Indeed, his sense of duty to protect his "family" drives him into a direct conflict with Japanese gangsters that leads him into the world of organized crime. When a young beggar enters Namsanjŏng, a district heavily populated with Japanese residents, he unfortunately is attacked by a vicious dog provoked by a Japanese thug. Upon hearing of the incident, Tuhan rushes to Namsanjŏng to challenge the Japanese perpetrator, who happens to be a member of the local Japanese gang. After breaking into the man's house and announcing his identity, Tuhan demands a duel and defeats the Japanese gangster.

This incident, which brings out both the physical prowess and the moral integrity of the male protagonist, functions as a turning point in the narrative, catapulting Tuhan into the turbulent currents of interests and conflicts that make up the social and ethnic geography of colonial Seoul. Though socially marginalized, Tuhan possesses a clear sense of human dignity and social justice, dispositions that cause him further trouble down the road.

The sequence also portrays the urban space of Seoul as divided by ethnic and socioeconomic boundaries and stratification. Though Koreans were surely the dominant population in Seoul, in films that are set in the colonial era, some districts such as Honmachi/Ponjŏng and Namsanjŏng are shown as ethnic enclaves reserved for Japanese residents. Beggars usually have an advantage in being able to traverse different regions of the city, but, as the incident indicates, trespassing on

Japanese turf can lead to dire consequences. As portrayed in the opening encounter in *Kang Myŏnghwa*, Korean urban space in gangster films is characterized by the problem of overproximity to the Japanese Other. The social spheres of Koreans and Japanese appear to overlap in the film, a sign of Japanese encroachment into the Korean sphere of activities, with terms of interaction that are highly negative and volatile.

The harassment that the Korean beggar must endure, with only his similarly impoverished fellows to turn to for help, shows the colonial state apparatus of law enforcement and surveillance patrols to be largely absent or ineffective in handling civil disorders that directly affect urban Koreans. Hence, the Japanese colonial regime is portrayed negatively in gangster films not because of its direct political domination but, implicitly, because of its inadequate domestic policing and its incapacity to apply impartial laws and regulations to the problems of Koreans. Villainy therefore is defined in different terms: though it is definitively associated with the Japanese side, it is not solely an aspect of the colonial conquest.

Conflicts among characters in the film likewise are not simple contests between good and bad, for there are undercurrents to every encounter. Tuhan, for example, sternly announces his identity as leader of the beggars upon entering the house of the Japanese who instigated the dog's attack. On a practical level, the resolute self-introduction serves to dispel any misunderstanding that the other party may have about the speaker's true identity and stature. However, this act has a symbolic resonance that no response by the Japanese man can counter.[39] In other words, the sequence presents Tuhan not as an individual with innate personal characteristics, but as a symbolic figure of authority upholding the title of leader with which he fully identifies.

Fights generate meanings greater than the mere physical action in this and other gangster films set in the colonial era. The duel in *A True Story of Kim Tuhan* establishes the Korean Tuhan's aura of authority and power. Having been deprived of this symbolic dimension, the Japanese thug reacts with agitation, launching an attack on Tuhan, only to face an embarrassing defeat. Tuhan's fight proves his physical competence and agility, but his announcement that precedes it highlights something more: it has a ritualistic function, projecting an appearance of confidence that disconcerts the Japanese Other as the latter fails to respond with the same assurance.[40] The sequence's emphasis on appearance is visually embellished by the immaculate Western suit that represents Tuhan's mature masculinity and leadership.

Tuhan's first victory over the Japanese opponent is also significant for its spectatorial effects. Unbeknownst to him, the Korean gang leader Na Kwanjung and his student subordinate happen to witness the fight from a hidden corner.[41] Although Tuhan remains oblivious to the secret spectators, the situation soon leads to the opportunity for Tuhan to receive proper guidance and mentorship. Na's observation of Tuhan's fighting skills anticipates the subsequent master-apprentice

dynamic between the two. Thus the film makes the theme of mentoring and education the principal concern of social activities among Koreans caught in the compressed zone of propinquity with the Japanese Other. Na states, "This is the first
time I have been fascinated by another man's fist [fighting] prowess," and orders
his subordinate to gather more information about Tuhan. Hence, the secret gaze
indicates recognition by the hidden authority/father figure, although official contact for recognition must wait until a later moment.

Na's choice of Tuhan as the heir to his gangster operation alludes to the limit
of colonial representation in the social sphere of Koreans. South Korea's gangster
films of this era are generally preoccupied with the social void that occurred under
colonial rule, and they attempt to fill that void by constructing a social community
that can endure and regenerate itself through selective member recruitment and
leadership training. Na's interest in Tuhan and his subsequent efforts to train and
educate him to a higher rank within the organization create a necessary sense of
group affinity and social cohesion.

The social ideology of gangster film, however, departs substantially from the
cultural nationalist discourse of the colonial era in which the ideal of enlightenment encompassed all people, regardless of social background. The social ideology
of the gangster film does not share this egalitarian belief. Instead of promoting the
all-encompassing utility of education, the film is solely preoccupied with the question of how to select, develop, and train a capable leader.

The film's distrust toward the intellectual approach to the nationalist issue is
evident in a scene where Na spends time with an intellectual friend over a drink in
a tavern. Na himself has an intellectual background; he received a college education in Japan but chose the path of underground business. One of the reasons why
the Japanese gangsters scheme to eliminate Na is his intellectuality, which they
feel could generate subversive ideas. The sequence, however, shows Na as having
a different attitude toward the options of Koreans under colonial rule than his
intellectual friend does. The friend, played by Yi Sunjae, challenges Na's current
illegitimate profession, asking, what good does it do to gather thugs to fight the
Japanese? This criticism is based on the ideas and rhetoric of the enlightenment
mode of social activism that characterized the image of the colonial intellectual in
popular culture. Implicit in his critique is the belief that Na's illicit activities will
corrupt the noble nature of national resistance against unjust colonial domination. Na responds by asserting that during dark times, survival itself is a form of
resistance. To dwell in depression is the real failure. The conversation reaches a
deadlock at this point, and the intellectual friend drops the subject by invoking his
own history. He says, "I understand your frustration. Let us leave the judgment of
our disagreement to the opinion of future historians."

At this point, the film not only effectively captures the friend's dismissive reaction but also brings into sharp relief the two men's reactions to an alluring female
waitress across the room. Whereas the intellectual friend gazes at her body as an

object of fascination as he attempts to drop the topic, Na shows no sign of distraction but looks at his friend and finishes his statement on the failure of Korean intellectuals. What makes him sad, Na claims, is how the intelligentsia becomes corrupted in practice. The cinematic focus on the two men's differing reactions accentuates Na's censure of the friend's empty intellectualism. Although the friend criticizes Na's gang for its betrayal of the enlightenment project of nationalism, his notion of history reaches a dead end in reality and fails to offer any vision of power or agency to bring about change. History is invoked precisely at this moment to cover up the impasse that comes from the malaise of his weak and abstract thoughts. The consequence of this intellectual deadlock is, as the film's focus on his distraction indicates, indulgence in the seductive pleasure of urban entertainment.[42]

The film plainly supports Na's position that survival can be achieved through a reordering of the social hierarchy in which educated people perform a proper support role for the leader's operation. Na's trusted right-hand person crystallizes this conceptualization of the intellectual's role. Always dressed in a college uniform, this student subordinate, played by Paek Ilsŏb, is not a worker who merely follows the boss's orders. Instead, he functions as a managerial supervisor and counsel who offers incisive appraisals of the rapidly changing situation and external threats. In return, Na shows complete confidence in his suggestions. The student subordinate's supplemental role completes the wholeness of Na's authority and control over the organization. It is he who later advises Na to bail out Tuhan, who has been arrested for attacking the Japanese thug in Namsanjŏng. Both men also have prior knowledge of Tuhan's background (i.e., that he is the son of the general Kim Chwachin), and they discuss its symbolic significance when they recruit him into the organization. Indeed, these men later "educate" Tuhan on the meaning of his natal origins, something that Tuhan himself was not able to gauge. The organizational stability and focus that the student subordinate brings to the group illustrate the ideal role for an intellectual. Instead of leading the way toward enlightenment, an intellectual is better equipped, the film seems to suggest, to take the secondary role of counselor and supervisor. His professional position within the Korean gang, moreover, is in sharp contrast to the homogeneity of the Japanese gang, in which no division of labor or specialization exists.

The recruitment of Tuhan into Na's gangster group epitomizes the film's theme of social integration and mobility. But the film has Tuhan enter the gang at an emotionally excessive moment. Dressed in a Western suit, Tuhan tearfully bids farewell to the crying young beggars with whom he has lived most of his life and crosses the empty bridge to join Na and his student subordinate, who await his arrival with enthusiasm. The sequence is exceptional in its overt melodramatic configuration. Mise-en-scène, editing, and music, for instance, construct the moment of his bridge crossing as an excruciating instance of separation, as if he were crossing the Bridge of No Return, the military demarcation line in the Joint

Security Area that separates North and South Korea. The sudden interjection of an image that evokes the Cold War does not add meaningfully to the reading of a film that is primarily concerned with the colonial geography of urban activities and problems, so I am reluctant to follow the historicist impulse to link the parting scene to the Cold War division of the nation. What should be emphasized instead are the critical implications of Tuhan's upward mobility from the lowest stratum to a rank of social privilege and power, a change in affiliation that finds expression through melodramatic excess. The sense of irreversibility that Tuhan's departure signifies does not have anything to do with his later interaction with the beggar group. He is at liberty to visit the beggars later, and they join Tuhan's final showdown with their Japanese rivals. Despite their grief over the loss of a member, the beggars maintain a continuous and close relationship with Tuhan even after he becomes a gang leader.

What is clear, however, and what the sequence attempts to underscore through excess, is the justice of the actions that Tuhan will take from this moment on. If Tuhan's leadership of the beggars was spontaneous and dedicated to protecting the most marginalized Koreans from the abuse of the Japanese, his entrance into the Korean gang changes the nature of his approach to the colonial problem of injustice. As an apprentice, Tuhan is bound to follow the modus operandi of his new group in its competition with the Japanese for business connections to Korean merchants. The film frames his change in association as a necessary step for social mobility. Yet the apparent *sinpa* excess of the sequence allows a metacritical view of the shift in social imagination in which no discernible figure emerges as an agent of larger political action. The lamentation in the bridge scene does not simply depict the beggars' sadness over Tuhan's departure. It also captures and expresses the foreboding sense of closure on the possibility of a populist scenario of nationalism based on calls to address the plight of the socially marginalized. The film affectively registers grief over the impending marginalization of the popular national hero by the mode of equivalency, exchange, and competition that will subsequently make up the cultural logic of colonial imaginings in the 1960s and 1970s.

In general, the gangster film defines negatively the individual act of changing one's affiliation or loyalty. *A True Story of Kim Tuhan* illustrates this tendency by showing the treachery of a rival Korean gang leader, Shinmajŏk, through his submission to and partnership with the Japanese. Yet Tuhan's own shift in association has no such negative implications. To be sure, there is no conflict of interest between the two Korean groups: they are similar in their close and parasitic relations with Korean businesses in the Chongno district. I would stress, however, that the efficient workings of symbolic exchange and the transformation of money cast Tuhan's change in affiliation in a positive light specifically by invoking the nation as the ultimate recipient of all symbolic transactions. Tuhan joins the gang in order to repay the kindness that Na has shown to social subordinates. It was Na who took the dog-bitten young beggar to a hospital for medical treatment and Na who paid bail for Tuhan when he was arrested for creating the disturbance at Namsanjŏng. When Tuhan tells Na that he will repay him for his kind favors, Na asks Tuhan to pay back the favors to the nation instead.

Notions of authority and hierarchy are strengthened by this transfiguration of money into a higher form of symbolic exchange. The gangster film articulates a new conception of authority, one that is structured around the nation as the guarantor of all meaningful social transactions. It is this dimension of symbolic exchange and transfiguration that also differentiates the Korean gang from its Japanese counterpart. The Japanese gangsters seek money and power through violent means of suppression and intimidation. Their use of money is purely negative: it is used to corrupt or compromise individual Korean gangsters to get them to betray their own organization. Monetary transactions are deprived of the elevated symbolic meanings that Na and Tuhan demonstrate.

The film's emphasis on the symbolic values of ritual, decorum, and appearance manifests itself on many levels, illustrating how the Korean gang establishes a stratified group culture superior to that of all competing forces. Such construction of social values and meanings also requires a specific site. The *kisaeng* house, rather than the group's own office space, is crucial as the site of new member initiation. The implication of this setting is clear. To become a new member of the gangster organization is to gain entrance to the adventuresome, if not hedonistic, lifestyle that goes along with having a reputation that garners social respect. *Kisaeng* characters are called upon to provide services and entertainment for the initiation party, but their functions go beyond this. In *A True Story of Kim Tuhan*, the *kisaeng* demonstrate a strong interest in Tuhan, as they already have learned of his heroic acts and reputation. Besides the stated purpose of member initiation, the party effectively serves as a moment for all attendees to affirm and celebrate the entrance of a heroic figure into their world. Tuhan's welcoming and enthusiastic reception is complemented by the romantic match that the attendees arrange for him. When a beautiful young *kisaeng*, Sŏlhwa, played by Yŏm Poksun, is called upon to serve him, everyone at the party expects them to become a couple.[43] The *kisaeng* house in the gangster film is not a multiethnic space but a space of ritual and socialization for the Korean gangster.

It is thus only natural that the first assignment Tuhan performs is the act of espionage that his father failed to accomplish. He and his men sneak into the house of the collaborator Song and force Song to hand over the money he has accumulated from treachery, with the object of sending that money to the Shanghai Provisional Government in exile. Tuhan's act not only completes what his father could not but also displays the dominant mode of conceptualizing and managing money in the Manchurian action films of the mid-1960s. Only by transferring and thereby converting the money gained through corruption into the nation's righteous war funds can the protagonist assume his proper role in society. Here the success of the robbery cements the reputation and leadership of Tuhan.

Surprisingly, Tuhan does not order his subordinates to kill Song. They force Song to drink a liquid that Song assumes to be poison, but it is in fact only a sedative. When Song comes to, he finds a letter addressed to him from Tuhan, censuring him for his treachery but also earnestly asking him to lead a better life. The surprising leniency toward the collaborator indicates the shift in focus of the film's rendition of the nationalist struggle. It is no longer preoccupied with the eradication of the treacherous villain. Rather, it underscores the importance of building consensus for authority and leadership. As long as Tuhan can inherit his father's legacy, which is the major determinant of his place in the new organization, he can afford to extend leniency and understanding toward an enemy of the nation.

The Japanese manipulation and control of the Korean gang leader Shinmajŏk shows a divergence from the Korean mode of symbolic value accumulation in the use of money and the rationale for group relations, as well as in the cultural meanings of ritual and propriety. When Wakejima, a midlevel Japanese gangster boss, and Shinmajŏk, a Korean ringleader in charge of the Tongdaemun district, meet to discuss a business plan, Wakejima outright bribes Shinmajŏk to eliminate Tuhan. Designated solely for the assassination of Na and Tuhan, the Japanese money lacks the symbolic substance that money has within the Korean gang. Ferocious yet primitive forms of viciousness characterize Shinmajŏk's attacks on Na and Tuhan. Na is murdered in a rickshaw after retiring from a night's social gathering. Shinmajŏk's cohorts subsequently carry out a surprise attack at Na's funeral, assaulting Tuhan and other mourners and demolishing the memorial altar in the condolence hall. Shinmajŏk's group are condemned not only for their viciousness but perhaps even more for the complete lack of the sense of propriety that any Korean social group would have. The film depicts the materialistic desires of the gangster collaborator as the cause of the absence of social propriety among his followers. In fact Shinmajŏk is similar to the Japanese gangsters, as both employ heinous methods to defeat Tuhan's organization.

Tuhan's subsequent vengeance involves various preparations and countermeasures, but he never loses the composure that forms the core of his authority and charisma. His equanimity is evident when he makes a public announcement of his challenge to Shinmajŏk. Tuhan, moreover, sends his subordinate to deliver that challenge. The appearance of propriety is unmistakable here, creating a sharp contrast with the callous attack by Shinmajŏk's men. The film continuously underscores the performative importance of ritual, gift giving, decorum, appearance, and dress, all of which make up the social fabric of the Korean gangster world.

A True Story of Kim Tuhan also overcompensates for what is largely missing in the postcolonial imaginary of the colonial era: the social order and cohesion of the Korean people, shown here in a social group living at the margins.

FIGURE 8. The Japanese gangsters' surprise attack on Na's funeral in *A True Story of Kim Tuhan*. Courtesy of the Korean Film Archive.

In the confrontation with Tuhan, Shinmajŏk rationalizes his partnership with the Japanese and the full assault on Na in terms of bringing a singular line of order and hierarchy to Korean gangs. Such a change, however, would benefit only the Japanese gangsters at the top, who then would be able to control the Korean business sphere by means of Korean gangster bosses. Thus, Tuhan responds by accusing Shinmajŏk of betraying fellow Koreans and essentially collaborating with the Japanese occupiers. Tuhan declares that he is about to exact vengeance for his fallen boss. What is noteworthy here is that his motivation is not solely based on the desire for personal revenge. He publicly asserts that he is acting to serve the nation by eliminating traitors. Just as Tuhan's recruitment into the group invokes the nation as the guarantor of personal meaning, his act of revenge has rhetorical recourse to the nationalist ideology to ground its symbolic relevance.

Tuhan's rebuilding of the gang conveys how the small-scale turf war over the Chongno district attains national scope and significance. After Tuhan's victory over Shinmajŏk, men from various provinces volunteer to join his gang. Their entrance brings regional diversity and vigor. Concurrently, their provincial manners emphasize Tuhan's distinct stature and charisma. Presiding over these men who are strongly associated with different regions, Tuhan evidences no trace of lowly social origins. As these men work in harmony for the group, the film projects the image of a unified nation congregated in the space of the *kisaeng* house. The *kisaeng* again performs a significant role in the new formation of collectivity. When Tuhan is asked to give an official speech to new members, he opens the proceedings only to delegate the role of speaker to Sŏlhwa, his *kisaeng* girlfriend, who then articulates the importance of camaraderie and loyalty among gangster members. She also briefly but effectively interjects the rhetoric of nation at the end: "All of you new members are the pillars of this country." The film hence presents an idealized picture of collective harmony that overcomes gender and regional differences, though only after the establishment of a new strong leader and his supreme authority. This leadership does not derive from an active effort of group building. Instead, the circumstances evolve naturally as others recognize and valorize Tuhan's leadership.

Offenses to symbolic values are a key feature of the film's recurring action sequences. After the defeat of the midlevel Japanese gangster boss Wakejima, the Japanese gang leader takes matters into his own hands. His method is strikingly similar to Shinmajŏk's. Sŏngmin has just married Chiyŏn, the supposed sister of Tuhan, and is traveling to the couple's new home outside the city.[45] On the way he is violently assaulted by the Japanese gangsters and returns home to die in Chiyŏn's arms. When Tuhan visits Chiyŏn to inform her of her husband's death, the Japanese assailants kidnap Tuhan's girlfriend, Sŏlhwa. She resists the intimidation of the Japanese boss but is sexually assaulted and then dies.[46] Her corpse is then brought back to Tuhan as he grieves with his sister over Sŏngmin's death. With double deaths, the film exposes the villainy of the Japanese in terms of utter disregard for ritual, custom, and civility. Their incessant attacks leave the grieving Koreans no space for proper mourning.[47] The film has shown that social custom and ritual require suspension of ordinary time and the marking of a moment of "enchanted time" out of the colonial setting. Yet the Japanese attack disturbs this temporality reserved for the symbolic and spiritual order of existence. The Japanese assailants are defined as irreconcilable Others not only because of the pure intensity of their violence but because of their ruthless disregard for even a minimal degree of humanity. Immorality of Japanese characters

What eventuates from this traumatic encounter is all-out revenge on the Japanese. Here the action is not precisely planned to defeat the Japanese opponent. Rather, Tuhan, along with all his subordinates and his beggar friends, takes the initiative and advances into the Japanese business district, a sign that his military campaign is no longer defensive but offensive in nature. Most of the Korean gangsters and fighters under his leadership are dressed in preparation for their walk in unison toward the Japanese turf as if they were making a military march into the enemy's territory. The camaraderie even brings the repentant Shinmajŏk back to join the last battle. His change of heart is evident in his invocation of nation to justify the righteous use of violence against the Japanese: "If we lose this battle, we will forever live as dogs of the Japanese."[48] The lengthy ensuing battle confirms the triumph of Koreans over the Japanese. The fight ends with yet another ritual, this time performed by the Japanese. As the enemy boss accepts his defeat he prepares for honor suicide: hara-kiri. Tuhan helps him in this ritual of suicide by completing the final beheading. The film's last duel ends with a note on the significance of the ritual act that Tuhan himself fully understands. Whereas the two camps have been depicted as irreconcilable opposites, this moment of ritual brings them into the same realm. The film's objective—to fight and defeat the Japanese—also affirms the ending point at which the two entities are involved in the mutual completion of ritual. At the end, Tuhan basically conquers the Japanese district only to face his real punishment. When the Japanese police arrive on the scene, Tuhan proudly faces them but also extends his arms for arrest. Although the film ends rather abruptly at this moment, the implications are clear. When the Japanese colonial force is incompetent to handle domestic policing, the local Korean gangster comes to the rescue, quelling the cause of disturbance and returning order to both ethnic communities. That said, Tuhan's voluntary act can be read both ways. Although it shows signs of resistance and pride, it also conveys the docility of the Korean gangster, who ends up accepting his proper social role within the colonial social matrix.

In *A True Story of Kim Tuhan*, the governing operations of social ritual, decorum, and performance all work to produce unique discursive effects of national allegiance, authority, and leadership. Framing the conflict between the Japanese and the Koreans on the smaller scale of competition over a business district, the film seems to underscore on the surface the economic incentives and interests that the two warring factions share. However, the social dynamics of hierarchy building, leadership education, and performative gestures carve out an autonomous realm for Koreans largely unaffected by the political forces of colonialism. The cinematic strategy of misaligning the nationalist mandate and economic interests finds its channels of expression in gangster films, which also sanction the mode of exchange and equivalence between two starkly differentiated opponents.

[handwritten margin note: Korean gangster providing the police work that Japanese cannot]

5

Horror and Revenge

Return of the Repressed Colonial Violence

The horror genre has often been theorized as a cultural form that dramatizes unsettled but repressed social dilemmas. With respect to the legacy of colonialism, the genre shares with melodrama a recurring structure of return through which past suffering and trauma are confronted. Utilizing the convention of "the unexpected arrival," such films furthermore delineate the problematic relationship between colonial rule and postcolonial reckonings. I here analyze two films that, although separated by several decades, both feature key dimensions of the theme of return that forms an important conceptual component of the postcolonial historical imagination. The 1966 melodrama *Yeraishang* is an obscure "fallen woman" film set against the backdrop of the April Revolution of 1960 and its aftermath.[1] The film's reference to that historic event compels us to pay close attention to the implications of the revolution for the project of decolonization. The 2007 horror film *Epitaph* belongs to a group of recent South Korean films that focus on Koreans' experience of colonial modernity and urban life through the prism of horror. The film is unique for configuring excessive violence and spectral haunting behind the veneer of the rational order of modern medicine. Through its use of the signs of terror, *Epitaph* presents a complex portrayal of colonial subjectivity rare in the South Korean film tradition.[2]

HORROR FILM, TEMPORALITY, AND REPRESENTATIONS OF COLONIALISM

Any discussion of South Korean horror film must include *Public Cemetery under the Moon* (*Wolha-ŭi kongdong myŏji*; Kwon Chŏlhwi, 1967) (hereafter *Public*

Cemetery), which features the tragic death of a virtuous woman.[3] A number of scholars have scrutinized this seminal horror film for its allegorical treatment of colonial history through spectral haunting and violence.[4] Significant for us here is the compressed image that encapsulates the larger problematic that I endeavor to tackle in this chapter. The film begins with a narrative device in which a "prologue character" appears on a nondiegetic stage to provide a brief introduction or warning for the audience about the upcoming drama. However, there is an interesting twist to the film's use of this device. The speaker is an abominable monster who instantly evokes a sense of fear and disgust, the affective response closely associated with the horror genre.[5] The hideous beast-man, who is set against the backdrop of a dark cemetery, acknowledges his own abject condition but also mentions his origins. The man claims that forty years ago he was a handsome *pyŏnsa,* or silent film narrator-commentator. With this statement, the film quickly, through a dissolve effect, transforms him into a poised middle-aged man who begins the *pyŏnsa* narration of the main narrative. The tone of narration is highly stylized and melodramatic, making apparent the *sinpa*-mode staging, the most recognizable melodramatic mode of representation of the colonial era. The film's recourse to a colonial form amplifies the affective power of a drama filled with betrayal, violence, and revenge.[6]

The opening sequence is thus the film's commentary on a past cultural form from the viewpoint of the present. The monstrous deformity of the ex-*pyŏnsa* narrator underscores the thorough marginalization of a mode of film exhibition that was once the most alluring component of colonial urban visual culture: the *pyŏnsa*'s oratory performance at silent film screenings. But what was it about the old form of film presentation that made it subject to such thorough devaluation in 1960s South Korea? I claim that the criticism was not to attack specific features of the *sinpa* genre but rather, as I noted in the previous chapter on the figure of the *kisaeng,* to dislodge the symbols of colonial culture. The denigration of the silent film world (and all its attendant modes, styles, and presentation practices) was part of a larger cultural politics.[7] The impulse derived from a fervent nationalist desire to overcome a cultural form that was imported from Japan and thrived during the colonial period.

The motifs in the sequence also allude to the power of the horror genre to stage complex questions of temporality. The film problematizes the multiple and immiscible temporalities *within* the modern time frame. It advances a peculiar gambit, according to which a certain aspect of popular film culture of the early twentieth century is already considered outmoded, foreclosed, and thereby denigrated. The demonization of the past suggests how the prior years are rendered "out of joint" with the linear, abstract, progressive notion of time in the modern era. Yet the dilapidated past insists on living on as a monstrous figure and even makes a triumphant return to tell the story of the spectral horror. To borrow Bliss Cua Lim's insight, this coeval collocation of the two temporalities—the demonized past in the present time—confirms the immiscible nature of temporalities that is inherent in the horror imaginary.[8]

The treatment of the defunct cultural form alludes to the essential historico-political question of the cultural politics of nationalism: how South Korea is to bracket and engage critically with the colonial legacy. In South Korea's nationalist historiography, the colonial period signifies a unique conceptual conundrum, for it marks a fundamental rupture in the assumed "continuity" of the nation's linear and teleological trajectory of progress. A typical but "efficient" way to manage this dilemma is to portray the colonial period as a time of total injustice, subjugation, and suffering, which is addressed by collective resistance and struggle. But the notion of suffering and injustice invoked in this context is allegorical in nature, as it fundamentally is subsumed by the hegemonic discourse of the nation. The individual's hardship is invoked only to underscore the tenacious survival of the national collective. understood as collective struggle be of hegemonic

One of the peculiar outcomes of this nationalist appraisal of history is that the colonial era turns into a truncated period, removed from the complex realities motivated procative of the postcolonial present. The compartmentalization is an effective way to set aside the ramifications of the colonial legacy and its effects without negating them entirely. Yet this postcolonial production of temporality renders the colonial era devoid of sociopolitical ramifications for the present. It makes the colonial era a peculiarly self-contained period of time despite the obsessive linking of it to nationalist politics within cultural discourses. The mechanical juxtaposition of the colonial period against the postcolonial time frame seldom includes investigation of the complex connections between the two. Given the enduring linkage between the colonial power and the postcolonial social structure of South Korea, the persistent *displacement* of historical perspective and imaginings reflects a distinct but peculiar logic of time that South Korea has produced to render the dilemma of colonialism manageable.

The truncation of the colonial period also entails another recurring formal feature. As if following an unwritten general rule, most South Korean films do not resort to use of the flashback or backward-looking viewpoint to organize stories of the colonial past. Even though South Korea has produced many films since 1945 that relate to the subject of colonialism, there is a dearth of cinematic texts that mobilize the historical investigation of the colonial problem *from* the present viewpoint. Instead, these films often begin and end in the colonial period. Against this backdrop of the historical unconscious of South Korean films, the retrospective tendency of horror and revenge films offers exceptional instances for the investigation of history and memory. The postcolonial subject who suffers from spectral haunting or trauma elucidates how the temporal divide between the colonial and postcolonial is deeply problematic. The figure of the specter (or the figure with a spectral effect) traverses the historical divides that have been central to the discourse of the postcolonial nation. Violent revenge and horror films,

horror genre allows for a negotiation of past & present

ranging from fallen-woman melodramas to ghost horror films, show a sustained critique of the dominant scheme of temporal "ordering" in South Korean cinema. Both *Yeraishang* and *Epitaph* thematize the profound and protracted inflection of unresolved colonial violence and injustice made visible through extreme forms of retribution and social disarray. The temporal span they encompass additionally makes them specific cultural responses to the limitations of the anticolonial nationalist framework for writing history.

THE APRIL REVOLUTION AND
COLONIAL RESENTMENT

The April Revolution of 1960, which toppled the authoritarian regime of Syngman Rhee and created a new political energy directed toward the project of decolonization in South Korea, is the crucial historical context for the narrative of *Yeraishang*. The film begins with the male protagonist's street protest and his injury, which leads to the formation of the romantic couple and their subsequent hardship. Before turning to an analysis of the film's narrative, I would like to introduce a story of the revolution that offers a valuable insight into the thorny issue of the use of violence and the failure of decolonization.

In his account of the April Revolution and its aftermath, historian Bruce Cumings notes how the revolution channeled, albeit momentarily, the populist yearning for decolonization that had been kept at bay in the previous decade. Colonial police officers, many of whom had moved to higher ranks during Syngman Rhee's regime, either had to quit or were fired in the postrevolutionary political environment. However, in several areas the police officers' resignations and retirements were not enough to dispel the populist yearning for justice, as a number of people wanted to settle scores with police officers who had served the Japanese during the colonial period. One incident of vengeful execution of an ex-colonial officer was so shocking and gruesome that only the most violent horror film could possibly render its ghastly image: villagers "boiled a colonial policeman in oil."[9]

Cumings's description is brief, and the details of the incident remain unknown. Yet his laconic account conveys how deeply ingrained yet repressed the popular will to undo past colonial injustices was in the authoritarian political milieu of the 1950s Cold War. Righting the wrongs of colonial violence was an immediate task for the liberated nation in 1945; however, the ensuing political environment of the Cold War systemically repressed that priority, and demands for decolonization were marginalized as mere propaganda slogans of leftist ideology.

While the cruelty of the incident is shocking, such a "horrific" aspect of revolution begs some reflection. I am using the term *horrific* to refer not only to the horror-inducing aspect of the violence itself, but also to the episode's affinity with a crucial thematic motif of the horror genre. It possesses a structure of return, specifically the return of the repressed that is conventionally found in the thematic universe of horror. A monster in a horror film typically signifies the combined projection of repressed desire and the contradictions derived from it. Similarly, the episode's eruption of violence illustrates the explosive revival of long-held resentments, affirming the need to revisit the past colonial dilemma while simultaneously promoting the desire to rectify injustice and the suffering incurred from such injustice. While the April Revolution has typically been labeled an "incomplete" project, one of its historically significant consequences was that it reestablished a social space for reflection in which overcoming the harmful legacies of colonialism was rendered once again an urgent and significant project for South Koreans.[10]

But the radical passion for justice unleashed by the revolution almost necessarily exposed problems that remained repressed under contemporary political conditions. As Cumings's episode illustrates so lucidly, the revolution challenged and changed South Korean politics. At the same time, the passion and awakening that it inspired continued to linger and engender new awareness and motivation for action in a later period. As I explain through the analysis below, the eruption of a passionate zeal for justice and the revolutionary spirit to undo colonial violence reemerged and coalesced most visibly in the mid-1960s, the period when South Korea was forced to confront the dilemmas of its colonial history and legacy on a total sociopolitical scale.

YERAISHANG AND THE MELODRAMATIC RECKONING OF VIOLENCE

The 1966 melodrama *Yeraishang*, directed by Chung Chang Wha, is one of the few Korean films of the era to address the issue of the protracted effects of revolution. *Yeraishang* also, significantly, confronts the colonial past. It is somewhat obscure in the constellation of South Korean melodrama films, and its motif of the "fallen woman" and theme of legal justice have not received much critical attention, presumably because of the film's dramaturgical problems. Moreover, it does not fit too well in Chung's perceived auteurist oeuvre, namely the masculine universe of martial arts and action genre films.[11] The film demonstrates an unusual narrative density that is the result of being a compressed adaptation of an original radio drama.[12] In addition, there is a sudden turnaround in the middle of the narrative, shifting the direction and tone of the narrative to a different thematic orbit and concern: a feature that calls for close analysis precisely because it is so abrupt and radical. The film begins with the event of the April Revolution as a backdrop to the drama, but by its end, it has addressed and thematized the essential passion of revolution: the unquenchable impulse to act out radical justice to undo colonial violence.

The film has a convoluted and compressed narrative. It centers on the tumultuous life of a nightclub hostess, Nanhŭi, whose fateful encounter with college student Seyŏng leads her into a difficult but redemptive romance. The film begins in the turmoil of the revolution when Seyŏng is severely injured while taking part in a street protest and seeks refuge in a stranger's home. This stranger is Nanhŭi, who immediately offers her help to the young man, hiding him in safety and attending to his recovery from the near-fatal injury. Nanhŭi and Seyŏng subsequently fall in love as he recovers. Nanhŭi has previously developed an alcohol dependency problem, but with the help of Seyŏng she is able to overcome this personal demon.

The courtship comes to a halt when Nanhŭi's tainted nightlife profession becomes a humiliating target for those who financially support Seyŏng. After his recovery, Seyŏng finds a job tutoring the children of the wealthy Mr. Park. Park has his eye on Seyŏng as a prospective suitor for his eldest daughter, Chŏngsuk, who subsequently develops a romantic interest in Seyŏng. Home tutoring requires Seyŏng to reside at Park's residence, but he nonetheless makes frequent night visits to Nanhŭi. Suspicious of Seyŏng's nighttime whereabouts, Park orders him followed and learns of his courtship of Nanhŭi, the woman with whom he himself in the past had illicit sexual relations as her patron. Park then, dissembling, asks to be formally introduced to Seyŏng's girlfriend. This meeting turns into a disaster for Nanhŭi, as Park and his cronies maliciously use the opportunity to degrade her before her lover in public. She flees in humiliation and resentment, and Seyŏng expresses his indignation at Park's actions. The film subsequently focuses on Nanhŭi's despair and her relapse into alcoholism. To save her, Seyŏng forcibly hospitalizes her for alcohol rehabilitation. Initially resistant, Nanhŭi becomes convinced of Seyŏng's commitment to their love and slowly recovers from her alcohol dependency.

Up to this point, the film, other than in using revolution as a setting and plot device, shows no discernible departure from conventional melodrama, where the anxieties of love, the distress of misunderstanding, and the recognition of truth, as well as the attainment of redemption, constitute an affective universe of moral righteousness. However, the film careens in a different direction in its second half as new story information is introduced. Suddenly, an old man from Shanghai enters the picture. This man has been searching for Nanhŭi and later informs her of her family history. According to his account, Nanhŭi's father was killed by a pro-Japanese collaborator, an assailant who turns out to be Seyŏng's employer and her former patron, Park. Furthermore, Park sexually assaulted Nanhŭi's mother after her father's death and impregnated her with his child. (Nanhŭi's mother subsequently died in childbirth.) That child is Chŏngsuk, Park's eldest daughter. Upon learning of Park's violence against her parents, Nanhŭi swears her revenge. In the meantime, Park and his allies kill the old man out of fear that he might publicize Park's past collaboration. They also scheme to kill Seyŏng, who begins investigating the mysterious death of the old man. Their plan ultimately is foiled. Nanhŭi, however, is able to kill Park on the nightclub dance floor. She then awaits legal justice for the act of murder.

The film's origin as a popular radio drama series partly explains its excessive story information and complex dramatic turns. But what is nonetheless exceptional about the film's narrative is the sudden injection of the colonial theme via the appearance of the old man from Shanghai. The unforeseen knowledge that he imparts has a totalizing effect on the rest of the film, overdetermining the entire network of character relations and unfolding of events. Once known to Nanhŭi, her family's history of suffering and destruction becomes an overwhelming trauma that completely possesses her. The effort to act out her vengeance preoccupies her so thoroughly that she transforms from a passive woman into a fierce warrior who is no longer defined by her relationship with her man. Here we find the clearest instance of the colonial dilemma as "the return of the repressed," equivalent in structure to the ghastly shock and terror of Cumings's episode. The grand scale of Nanhŭi's past history as well as her thorough transformation also suggests the need to shift the interpretive focus of *Yeraishang* from its melodramatic properties of personal agitation, psychic tension, and the redemptive power of love to its function as an allegory of colonial history, violence, and justice in cultural, that is, cinematic, form.

When exposed, however, the criminal legacy of colonial violence is not represented as a manageable problem in any plausible sense. *Yeraishang* fails to hint at any effective measure of reckoning that is socially acceptable. Instead, the film stresses a personal vendetta, which is inherently transgressive in that it threatens the rule of law, as the only available recourse for the female protagonist to resolve her problem.[13] My emphasis is twofold here. On the level of narrative, the film showcases the colonial legacy as the most serious and grave social problem. Concurrently, it justifies the use of personal violence to rectify the injustice that legal institutions fail to recognize. Although the act of revenge is punished at the end through the female protagonist's trial and imprisonment, the film nevertheless elucidates the moral justification for this personal use of violence to exterminate an evil from the colonial era.

But there is more to the film's excessive dimension of violence. In a strictly formal sense, the return of the repressed triggers a series of actions that make visible the dire consequences of the brutal colonial legacy. The past is revealed through a pattern of representation particular to Korean cinema's way of rendering the colonial past. The film conveys the shock and terror of the female protagonist's family tragedy without recourse to any typical narrative devices such as flashbacks and cross-cut editing. Such devices tend to slow the progression of a narrative by allowing the viewer to comprehend hitherto undisclosed events of the past. Further, a prolonged segment of flashbacks often instills in the contemporary recipient of information in the film a fuller sense of what happened in the past, as he or she is presumed to sit through the duration of the oral account that triggers and accompanies the visualized past history. Such a formal option, however, ironically is absent in the history-focused thematic world of *Yeraishang*. Instead, the film merely shows the old man telling the female protagonist the compressed information about the troubling past.

The absence of formal cinematic techniques to provide past information, I would argue, is indicative of how South Korean cultural works shape and pattern the representational contour of colonial history. By eliminating temporal devices like flashbacks, *Yeraishang* effectively underscores and amplifies the raw impact of the family history on the listener-protagonist Nanhŭi. Nanhŭi is not a reflective subject who develops a distinct viewpoint on the past event; rather, she is a traumatized subject who acts on her own for revenge partly because she has been alienated from developing a clear perspective on history. The fact that the narrator of her family tragedy is killed by the very assailant from the past only intensifies the psychic suffering she endures.

The way the colonial dilemma is rendered comprehensible to her and film viewers alike therefore alludes to representational limits and lacunae. The theme of colonialism almost always entails a certain crisis of cinematic representation that the drama's overt excess then is called on to conceal. While historical representation in general exposes self-reflection as its own mode of figuring the past, *Yeraishang* demonstrates little concern for such patterns of historicizing. Instead, the film resorts to the mode of excess, figured in terms of both the irrepressible pattern of return and the consequential action it instigates, to convey the suffering of the traumatized female protagonist. The setting of the April Revolution is then crucial in this regard because its attendant characteristics of mad passion, suspension of law, ferocious execution of justice, and sociopolitical subversion complement the mode of excess discussed above. It offers a crucial conceptual backdrop for the articulation of traumatic shock as well as unmediated and direct action for justice.

Although the film merely alludes to the April Revolution at the beginning when Seyŏng is injured through his participation in a street demonstration, it has a distinct way of prolonging the revolution's sway and keeping its aura intact: it makes no reference whatsoever to the subsequent military coup of 1961. This is no small matter, for such periodization produces a textual effect distinct from the way the revolution is understood as a historical event. The film deliberately paints the world of diegesis as an uninterrupted and continuous space of revolution and its aftereffects. By decoupling the April Revolution from the May Coup, the film casts aside the historicist reasoning that habitually focuses on the counter-revolutionary event despite its valorization of the revolution. The presupposed decline of the revolution never takes place in the film.[14]

The aura of revolution is perhaps most apparent in the courtship between Seyŏng and Nanhŭi that overcomes the barriers to their romance. Their relationship prevails over large differences in both age and social status: she is an older nightclub waitress, and he is a young, promising college student of law. Reciprocal

FIGURE 9. Nanhŭi exacts her vengeance against Park in *Yeraishang*. Courtesy of the Korean Film Archive.

caregiving forms the strong bond between the two, as Seyŏng receives medical care and treatment from Nanhŭi and, in turn, arranges for her alcohol rehabilitation. The series of medical treatments and recoveries function as a common rite of passage for the couple as they endure ordeals and attain redemption. Through their support for each other in dire conditions caused by larger political events, the couple achieves a fuller unity.[15]

By portraying Park's aggressions, which include both the present assaults and the past violence, essentially as acts related to sexual predation, the film rehearses and extends the nationalist imaginary according to which colonial violence commonly takes a gendered form in many cultural works.[16] Hence, the film's dramatization of the colonial problematic is not limited to politics, or the troubled legacy of colonial collaboration in the present. The film also engages on the level of form with the existing nationalist imaginary—the gendered pattern of colonial violence and struggle—to participate within the larger matrix of cultural representation of the colonial past. *could go deeper w/o the actual gendered violence*

Park also represents the intimate connection between political treachery and materialist benefit that surrounds the act of collaboration. Historically, collaborators have almost always been portrayed as ruthless money seekers in South Korea's cinematic tradition; they would do anything, the scenario goes, to acquire personal material gain, including betrayal of the nation. Park exemplifies this type of materialist collaborator in the "old" nationalist imaginary.[17] However, the film goes further in that it showcases Park as a successful businessman in present-day postcolonial South Korea. In fact, this linkage between colonial collaboration and higher social status in the present is a rare configuration in South Korean cinema, even though such continuity is indubitably clear in the country's postcolonial social history.[18] Whereas in other filmic representations the collaborator is often

*representational of
screen of Japanese
collaborators*

punished for his selfish pursuit of money, Park appears to be running a successful business venture even during the April Revolution. Furthermore, he exemplifies how material accumulation from the colonial period, irrespective of its dubious origins, translated into social prestige and wealth for some in South Korean society.[19] Park thus embodies a peculiar continuity, albeit concealed, from colonial Korea to postcolonial South Korea—one that has received no sustained attention in either nationalist historiography or most South Korean films.

Just as there are complexities in Park's character, so too are there in Seyŏng's. Seyŏng appears as the archetype of a good-natured college student: a promising youth who will most likely become a member of the social elite. The fact that he studies law testifies to his secure path up the social ladder. Park's job offer then signifies not just a mere tutoring opportunity for him but also an entrance to a higher social circle, possibly through romance and marriage with Chŏngsuk. Park of course encourages this plan. What makes this scenario of upward social mobility through marriage potentially convincing is Seyŏng's strange lack of a past. He is a young man with no prior entanglements; he is an orphan with no close friends or associates. When he tries to convince Nanhŭi of his love, he speaks explicitly of the importance of a new start and calls for the urgent need to be unshackled from the burdens of the past. Thus, even though Seyŏng and Park become archenemies, they share a strange commonality as both devalue what is associated with the past. They are both future-oriented men, positioned to enjoy (or about to enjoy, in the case of Seyŏng) higher social status.

Seyŏng's association with prospects for future success stands in sharp relief with Nanhŭi's permanent affiliation with the legacy of the past. It is this chasm, defined in terms of temporal associations, that makes their union as lovers painfully impossible in the end. Here I am not referring simply to Nanhŭi's physical imprisonment. Rather, the conventional narrative logic of courtroom drama films, to which *Yeraishang*'s ending subscribes generically, makes it difficult to conceive of a romantic union as a plausible dramatic possibility. The visiting room sequence shows this dilemma clearly. Seyŏng visits Nanhŭi in prison and they face each other for the first time since her incarceration. The sequence presents the familiar generic imagery of courtroom drama films, where the affective moral truth of the fallen victim is pronounced and valorized, despite the adamancy of the legal system's refusal to acknowledge it. However, while other such films register signs of hope and optimism in the midst of legal pessimism, *Yeraishang* does not offer such a moment of relief. Instead, the prospect of the two lovers reuniting in the future remains murky at best, if not impossible.

Accentuating the pessimistic ending is the forced recognition of newly discovered sibling relations. Although Nanhŭi succeeds in fulfilling her vengeance against Park, she then faces an even more difficult ordeal of family trauma: reconciling with her half-sister, Chŏngsuk, who is the by-product of Park's sexual assault on her mother. The implication of this dilemma is apparent. Even though the agent

legacy of colonial violence remains

of past violence can be eliminated, his legacy in the form of family relations continues to exist. Those who survive are then required to achieve some type of reckoning or reconciliation with this impossible legacy. The two women confront it with ceaseless tears of sorrow and resignation. Complicating their reconciliation is the fact that they both have been romantically attached to the same man, Seyŏng, the future legal professional and social elite. Imprisoned Nanhŭi is painfully aware of her downfall when she meets Chŏngsuk in the visiting room and asks her to resume a relationship with Seyŏng, an offer Chŏngsuk adamantly refuses. But this normative communication of offer and refusal, whereby one is expected to refuse the offer, does not assume the provider's retraction of the offer. Nanhŭi's true misery lies in the fact that she is neither able to give up nor "take back" the offer she has proposed to her new sibling. Her prospect for reuniting with Seyŏng is virtually nil in this configuration of generic and social reasoning.

This brings us to a final appraisal of turmoil, violence, and reconciliation. The outright purge of the colonial collaborator by the long-suffering victim is resoundingly and mercilessly carried out. Justice, in short, is fully served as long as only this part of the story matters. Yet this form of justice, carried out by an abject social member, poses a question that has far-reaching legal and historical implications. That Nanhŭi has to resort to her own means to exact punishment testifies to the thoroughly personal nature of retaliatory violence. The necessary acting out of a personal vendetta paradoxically reveals the limits of the nation-state as the sole sovereign, that is, legal, authority, over its subjects. The point I am trying to make is not that the legal authority of the nation-state is challenged by Nanhŭi's transgressive act, but rather that the truly significant question the film poses is whether the postcolonial nation-state of South Korea is capable of handling the gross injustices committed during the colonial period, the era prior to the establishment of the state as a proper polity. In other words, is colonial violence within the parameters of the historical jurisdiction and legal reasoning of the South Korean state?

I think South Korea's social history informs us that the answer to this question is a resounding "no." The film's pessimistic ending and its attendant reasoning, moreover, have some sobering implications. Although Seyŏng the future lawyer speaks of the possible leniency of the court when he interviews Nanhŭi in prison, his statement remains largely an empty wish; it is not based on concrete legal reasoning. While the film upholds the moral intent behind her retribution, it also makes clear that she will pay a heavy price for her socially disruptive action. The male protagonist who is thoroughly defined in terms of his future prospects and legal profession cannot offer any effective help for the victim/criminal who took matters into her own hands to rectify colonial injustice. The film exposes troubling legal boundaries and the limits of the South Korean nation-state. The permanence of the sovereignty and legal authority that the South Korean state assumes and exercises, the film instructs us, is made possible by its structural and deliberate obliviousness toward the historical problem of colonialism. What *Yeraishang* conveys through the story of a morally righteous female victim is an effort to render the hard lesson of colonial legacy meaningful and relevant against the historical machinery called "the nation-state" that ironically attempts to erase it.

The film's implicit critique of the permanence of the state in the domain of law and justice helps us perceive and understand how the revolutionary spirit expresses itself in cultural form. While the narrative of revolution has mostly been assimilated into the conventional historical account over which the nation presides, here we find a cultural text that deviates from such assimilation. Instead, it preserves the gist of the radical revolutionary spirit *without* giving in to the all-encompassing discourse of the nation. *Yeraishang* is thus a formidably scandalous work of South Korean cinema. It makes the subject of colonialism ultimately unsettling or "out of joint" with the prescribed social reality of postcolonial South Korea. What is so resoundingly unique about *Yeraishang* is its dramatization of a theme that is virtually absent from other South Korean films: the detrimental legacy of colonial violence on the postcolonial lives of the people. While indicting colonial violence, the film simultaneously justifies violence as a proper means to eradicate the lingering evil in the contemporary situation. As in the prologue, the film presents the thorny question of colonial violence and oppression as that which becomes irrepressible and intolerable and ready to explode violently in the present.

EPITAPH: SPECTRAL TERROR AND THE PERVERSE DESIRE FOR EMPIRE

Epitaph, the debut film of the Chŏng Brothers (Chŏng Pŏmsik and Chŏng Sik), was released in the summer of 2007 as seasonal genre fare.[20] *Epitaph* differs from conventional Korean horror films in a number of ways. Reminiscent of *A Tale of Two Sisters* (*Changhwa hongnyŏn*; Kim Jee-woon, 2003), *Epitaph* illustrates how formal properties of cinema, such as mise-en-scène, lighting, sound design, and production design, can be arranged to produce strikingly affective elements of horror.[21] But it is the production design of the set, the modern hospital where all events unfold, that in particular distinguishes the film. The hospital set transmits an eerie aura of uneasiness while expressing a mixture of technological rationalism on the one hand and supernatural terror on the other.

The film is made up of three episodes that take place at Ansaeng Hospital in Seoul in 1942 at the height of Japanese imperial wartime mobilization. But the film's prologue begins in 1979, a year of political turmoil and unrest, when the assassination of South Korea's president Park Chung Hee brought a heightened hope for democracy that provoked countermeasures of authoritarianism. The male protagonist Chŏngnam, an elderly professor in the medical school, learns of the impending demolition of the hospital. The news triggers his memories of the building where he began his career as a young intern, destined to marry the daughter of the Japanese hospital owner. Three ensuing episodes show the inexplicable tragedies that befell him and two other young Korean medical professionals. After chronicling the three events, the film returns to the present time of 1979 and the sole survivor, Chŏngnam, who now confronts the demons of his own past.

In my analysis of the film, I focus on Chŏngnam's story, which makes up the first episode as well as the prologue and the epilogue.[22] The fact that the film begins with his recollection and ends with his demise underscores the significance of Chŏngnam as the principal character as well as the witness of all three incidents. It is through his perception and understanding (or lack thereof) of the supernatural phenomena that we the audience concurrently acquire layers of comprehension of the dreadful events. Because of this narrative design, we develop an emotional affinity with Chŏngnam, who believes he is an innocent victim of bizarre circumstances. This is further accentuated by the fact that he provides voice-over narration, reflecting upon what happened to him and other colleagues in the hospital. In other words, he carries the role of the narrator, framing and guiding the viewer's knowledge of the events depicted in the film.

The synopsis of Chŏngnam's episode is as follows: Chŏngnam is a young intern with an unusual background and status in the hospital, which is owned and run by a Japanese widow. From early on in the film, Chŏngnam is introduced to viewers as the prospective son-in-law of this Japanese owner.[23] When Chŏngnam's parents died in a traffic accident, the widow owner took him in as her son and supported his education. In return, Chŏngnam remained very grateful for her kindness. One odd feature of his prospective marriage is that although he is expected to marry the owner's daughter, Aoi, he has had no recent chance to meet her in person, as she has largely grown up in Japan. Chŏngnam, indeed, does not know what Aoi looks like, for she has not visited her mother in Korea for many years. The hospital owner anxiously waits for her daughter's return, but there is a problem.

Aoi has already fell in love with another man. Instead of following the path that her mother has laid out for her, she chooses to commit double suicide with her partner to escape the arranged marriage. Her dead body is brought to the hospital, where the grief-stricken hospital owner hides the death from her employees, including Chŏngnam. Simultaneously, she assigns Chŏngnam to work in the morgue where her late daughter's body lies. Chŏngnam subsequently becomes enthralled by the beauty of the dead girl. A once-aspiring art student, Chŏngnam starts drawing her image on paper and falls in love with her. Meanwhile, Aoi's mother puts a spell on Chŏngnam with the help of a female Buddhist monk's supernatural powers, a scheme that leads to his fantastic consummation with Aoi.

The fantasy consummation sequence requires careful examination here. It begins with an unknown woman's mourning at a Buddhist-style funeral altar inside the hospital. The creepy yet loud mourning sound reaches everyone, but the mourner's identity is never revealed until the end of the episode. By controlling the identity of the ritual host/mourner, the film maintains the mystery surrounding

FIGURE 10. Chŏngnam's perverse fantasy of interethnic romance is fulfilled in *Epitaph*.

the event. The film underscores the grotesque and uncanny sight of the ritual through various cinematic means, including the amplification of sounds, accentuation of sound-image matches, a high-angle shot to defamiliarize the site, and levitating camera movements that seem to approximate an otherworldly being, all the while blocking the viewer's clear access to the principal host/mourner of the ritual.[24] Toward the end of the episode the film unveils the information, hidden from others, including Chŏngnam, that the faceless mourner is the hospital owner and the mastermind behind the "spirit marriage" ritual. The inaccessibility of the true cause of events, the unknowability of the truth to all involved characters, is a recurring theme through all three episodes of *Epitaph*.[25]

The morgue sequence in Chŏngnam's story that features the spectral terror is most striking for its stupendous idealization of his double transgression: an act of perverse sexuality and defilement (necrophilia) that also breaks the social taboo against interethnic romance. The film introduces Chŏngnam's fascination with the beauty of the dead girl early on, but his infatuation enters a new phase when he comes under the supernatural spell. This moment begins immediately after the ritual arranged by the hospital owner to bind the dead (her daughter Aoi) with the living (Chŏngnam) through "spirit marriage." The unsettling sounds and music that accompany Chŏngnam's exposure to foreboding signs lead to his descent into the nightmarish consummation. He reacts to the strange phenomena—a snail crawling on the morgue rack, followed by the incessant gushing of dirty water from the morgue storage freezer—in a characteristically conventional horror-genre fashion. As if under a spell, he succumbs to his blind curiosity about the irrational occurrences. He opens the freezer and looks at the dark void inside. This moment of suspense is soon accentuated by the crescendoing thumping sound from inside which is the prelude to the sudden attack of the female ghost, who grabs and Chŏngnam and pulls him inside. The door shuts immediately, completing the scene of spectral terror.

But it is the ensuing ethereal sequence that recontextualizes and complicates the meanings of the spectral haunting in the film. The film now transports viewers to a completely different setting charged with the sublime beauty of marriage, consummation, and domestic life. The rendition of this fantasy sequence comprises the following vignettes: formal greetings between Chŏngnam and Aoi, Aoi's pregnancy, the couple's child rearing, and recurring sexual intercourse. In short, the vignettes capture a progression of marriage, procreation, and domestic bliss, all presented against the backdrop of a traditional Japanese home and iconic references to Japan. The use of the sliding door, along with tracking-forward shots, organizes the visual representation of the interethnic marriage. The tracking-forward camera progresses toward the featured characters first, then continues its movement to the sliding doors with opulent images beyond. The door then slides wide open, offering the newly expanded field of vision where the next level of the conjugal relationship is staged. The process repeats until Chŏngnam awakens from the fantasy in terror at the morgue. Catapulted out of erotic kisses with Aoi, he is petrified at the sight he beholds: the corpse of Aoi in defilement, her face infested with snails and her mouth gaping open and releasing dark liquid. The reflected water on the floor shows Chŏngnam in terror but also the image of Aoi, standing behind his shoulder.

The first episode ends with the revelation that the hospital director is the culprit behind the creepy nocturnal ritual that cast a spell on Chŏngnam. It shows Chŏngnam's freakish experience to be the direct effect of the Japanese superior determined to bind her late daughter to him. Yet the ethnic and cultural specificity of Chŏngnam's staged fantasy raises questions. At its core, the sequence stages necrophilia in the displaced form of interethnic romance. But given how the latter social scenario also has been repressed in the postcolonial cultural imaginary and politics of South Korea, the imagery of interethnic romance has an equally compelling power. This is particularly the case when one considers that Chŏngnam was never given a clue that the dead girl was the daughter of the Japanese hospital owner. Nevertheless, Chŏngnam imagines the consummation in thoroughly Japanese style and terms. In other words, the sequence offers a scandalous rendition of *naisen ittai* (the Japanese colonial policy of assimilation, literally "making Japan and Korea into one body") but fantasized by a Korean man in terms of a sexualized liaison and domestic bliss. The allusion to necrophilia hence functions like an effective smokescreen for the more egregious transgression: the Korean man's fantasy to become Japanese through sexual union and marriage with a Japanese woman. No Korean cultural trace is discernible once Chŏngnam sinks deeper into his domestic bliss. The sequence thereby explicitly illustrates what is in fact a cultural taboo in contemporary Korea's nationalist imaginary.[26]

Significantly, this necrophilic fantasy is the result of the imaginary scenario of interethnic consummation that the Japanese hospital owner has arranged for him *in the first place*.[27] Chŏngnam certainly expresses qualms about following the path of prearranged marriage, but his reluctance is rooted in his inability to know more about the event. His wariness is never about who he is going to marry, as the ethnic identity of the bride never becomes an issue for him. Thus his consummation with the Japanese woman, albeit in necrophilic practice, fulfills not only what the hospital owner intended but, more importantly, what he has yearned for at a deeper level. More precisely, it is through this ideal but also defilement-inducing union with the phantom woman that his desire becomes fully realized *and* perpetually suspended at the same time.

As for this suspension of desire, it must be remembered that this kind of unabashed desire for "becoming Japanese" could not be expressed openly in the hospital, where all staff members were Koreans. That is, the ethnic homogeneity among Korean staff workers meant a culture of cooperation that ensured at least some distinction between Korean and Japanese. The male protagonist Chŏngnam is portrayed as a member of this tight Korean ethnic circle. Even though he is destined to become a "Japanese man" through marriage, a social marker separates him from fully acquiring Japanese ethnic membership.[28] Seen in this context, his fantasy of consummation with a Japanese woman is a projection of his desire to earn the recognition of those in power: the Japanese. The problem is that what is pictured as benevolent authority, as embodied in the hospital owner, is already in peril. Her daughter's death does not signify simply a loss for her family; rather, it marks an irreparable dent in the owner's aura of authority that makes it impossible for her to sustain this harmonious and self-contained microcosmic world. The owner's endeavor to keep the secret of her daughter's death thus reflects the far-reaching ramifications of a larger order in trouble.

From Chŏngnam's viewpoint, not knowing the truth of the matter means that he can still believe in the colonial scenario of ethnic integration that he yearns for and has willfully accepted. Although the supernatural spell unleashes his true desire, the fact that this is unknowable to Chŏngnam leads him to develop his own unique scenario of perversion and self-victimization. The moral culpability of the owner recedes from view, and the blame is placed solely on the female specter, Aoi. The film's epilogue is Chŏngnam's effort to construct and complete the scenario of perversion, according to which he is a victim of uncontrollable forces and commands.[29] When Chŏngnam confronts the ghost figure of Aoi at the end, Chŏngnam accuses Aoi of making his a life one of loneliness and misery. Aoi does not answer. Instead, she remains largely silent, creating the sense that she is an unfathomable abyss for Chŏngnam and the audience alike. But Chŏngnam's blame is fundamentally misdirected. On the level of the supernatural plot, Aoi's mother is the one who manipulates Aoi and Chŏngnam through the spirit marriage ritual. Following this logic, one can see Aoi's mother as also responsible for the suffering that the female ghost Aoi had to endure from her captivity to the supernatural spell.

The ambiguity surrounding Aoi illustrates how the film departs from South Korea's horror tradition where the female ghost possesses a considerable degree of agency in her vengeful actions. Often the social injustice that was once inflicted upon a woman becomes the focal point of the dominant ghost revenge narrative. It is the moral economy of vengeance, with the female ghost being able to exact her retribution, that compels us to perceive and understand the meanings of historical violence and justice. In contrast, Aoi lacks such an ability to elicit moral interpretation; instead, she remains in total silence, offering no room for us to read her inner thoughts other than apparent uncanny sorrow. The encounter between Chŏngnam and Aoi illustrates the protracted ramifications of the colonial power, in the form of supernatural ritual, that burden the living and the dead alike. The sign of mutual recognition finally takes place; however, the moment of encounter fails to lead to a proper historical understanding between the two parties. Instead, it features their inability to confront the historical nature of their problems. They reconcile with each other but are not given power or agency to reflect upon the past injustice.[30]

It is thus no surprise that the film ends with another sign of Chŏngnam's perverse tendency: a grand nostalgia for the colonial past. At the beginning of the film, Chŏngnam states in his voice-over narration that he was living in the safe zone during the height of Japanese imperialism. After the demolition of the hospital building, which coincides with Chŏngnam's death from his encounter with Aoi, the film's epilogue takes the viewer to a joyous moment of the past, the prelapsarian phase at the hospital before calamity struck. The moment is the night of a blackout, a power outage that halts all operations at the hospital, forcing everyone to take a break outside the hospital building. Everyone holds candles in apparent joy and relief at escaping the drudgery of work. The last image of the film captures the dark hospital hallway where main characters are slowly evacuating the building. Chŏngnam follows suit but turns around suddenly. As his face is shown to us, his expression freezes, and we hear his final voice-over narration: a remark that back then he and his colleagues thought everything would last forever.

The peculiarity of the narration should not be missed here. As the ultimate statement of the protagonist, this voice-over narration crystallizes the thought long withheld from view. The statement registers the obliviousness of the speaker, but the word *everything* plainly refers to the symbolic order of colonial rule generally. Furthermore, the disembodied and spectral voice returns to the surface to seal off the meaning of the wartime mobilization era. Having failed to grasp the root cause of the violence and suffering in his story, Chŏngnam now declares the colonial past an object of eternal yearning and fulfillment.

The willful ignorance of the historical cause of his suffering and the sentiment of self-pity form the film's historical view on the colonial past. *Epitaph* employs horror conventions and devices to problematize this perverse way of perceiving oneself in history. Perhaps confronting the problem of colonialism is itself an arduous task in South Korea, where the colonial legacy is viewed only through refracted and convoluted prisms.

Yeraishang and *Epitaph* both frame the colonial past and its unresolved trauma as the source of a contemporary aporia of history. The way the repressed past enters the frame of the narrative is extreme, enabling us to examine two otherwise separate films through the same aperture of analysis. The *sinpa* melodrama *Yeraishang* brings a remarkable intelligence and urgency to the question of the long-lasting impact of colonial violence. *Epitaph* makes use of the spectral return of horror to explore the unsettled remnants of the past. Questions of violence, victimhood, and revenge become complicated and entangled in this highly subjective narrative of fantasy. The film utilizes the surprising turns and surprises of the horror genre to depict underlying perverse desires in the psyche of the postcolonial Korean subject. It also puts forth a rare view of a perpetual state of amnesia and its grave consequences for the proper development of historical consciousness and moral agency.[31]

In both films, we find characters who look back or are forced to look back from the present because of spectral haunting or the eruption of past violence. To be sure, these retrospective gestures and returns have limitations of their own. But regardless of whether or not they advance sound critiques and raise proper consciousness toward the colonial past, they use spectral haunting and vengeful passion to explore what other films often do not: the unsettled legacies of the colonial period and the contemporary meanings of such encounters. These films therefore "translate" time, to borrow Bliss Cua Lim's term, to expose and explore the jarring dissonance between different modes of temporalities. They advance a pointed critique of the centrality and permanence of the postcolonial nation state of South Korea by dramatizing the effects of lingering ties to the colonial order.

Coda

After 2000

The 2009 fantasy film *Chŏnuchi*, also known as *The Taoist Wizard* (*Choi Dong-hoon*), presents a feast of the special effects and spectacle common in contemporary Korean blockbuster films. It showcases a plot about a wizardry competition that has been passed down from ancient to modern times. Toward the end, the film provides an interesting view of the way in which contemporary South Korean film reflects the signs and markers of the colonial era. The film's narrative chronicles the struggle between Chŏnuchi and Hwadam, two sorcerers from the dynastic era. Earthly harmony shatters when the evil wizard Hwadam kills Chŏnuchi's sorcery master in order to possess a magic flute from heaven. The enraged apprentice attempts to exact vengeance but fails and becomes imprisoned on the surface of a brush painting. Time then shifts to the present, and Chŏnuchi and Hwadam resume their duel against the backdrop of metropolitan Seoul.

At one point, a sorcery duel takes place near the renovated park along Chŏnggyechŏn creek in the heart of Seoul. Hwadam gains the upper hand in the bout, but Chŏnuchi adroitly conjures up a magic portal and escapes the attack. The attacker quickly gives chase, passing through the portal to arrive at an odd and unexpected site: an empty outdoor movie set. Hwadam's entrance into this built environment brings a brief pause to the relentless action as the two archenemies face each other on a deserted boulevard.[1] It also instigates a shift in the style of the action. The spatial enclosure brings a sense of fatalism to the scene, as the two opponents now take measured steps to realign their course of attack. In the subsequent action, both men demonstrate their magical powers, with each bearing the brunt of his opponent's massive attacks through superhuman fortitude.

FIGURE 11. Showdown of wizards and the artificial movie set in *The Taoist Wizard*.

The surrounding movie set's buildings and properties break and falter under the prolonged and incessant assault.

This sequence distinguishes itself from other segments of the film as it makes an explicit reference to the colonial urban space—but with an interesting twist. The entire span of spectacular action operates against a constructed environment that is intended to approximate the urban milieu of Seoul in the colonial period. The boulevard is populated with familiar icons of the 1930s: trolley cars, Japanese billboard signs, and neoclassical-style buildings signify the urban modernity of colonial Korea. As noted, this ersatz site and its buildings suffer spectacular destruction, gradually revealing the flat and drab location on which the movie set has been constructed. The configuration of the colonial urban space as mere display raises questions about the meaning of colonial imagery in this and other contemporary South Korean films and how this imagery compares with depictions in earlier postcolonial films.

In previous chapters, I showed how attending to various spatial sites, tropes, and preoccupations allows one to problematize the aporias and tensions in the colonial imaginary of postcolonial film narratives. Popular film genres of the 1960s like Manchurian action, *kisaeng*, and gangster films not only showcase a privileged location from which to deliver new narratives of the colonial past, but also feature attitudes and viewpoints strongly influenced by the pressure of the Cold War bipolar order. Concurrently, certain signs in these films allude to disavowals of a colonial legacy that continued to cast a long shadow on South Korea's postcolonial visual culture.

The Taoist Wizard's frivolous treatment of the colonial past as surface image suggests a changed attitude toward colonial popular culture in general. Using the colonial storefront as an expendable movie prop, the film shows a departure from the austere but realistic aura of urban space that was prevalent in films of earlier decades. Although this book has been concerned mainly with the cultural imaginary of the colonial past during the formative postcolonial decades of the 1960s and onward, I conclude here by reflecting on the new ways of seeing and imagining the colonial that recent South Korean cinema demonstrates. My adumbration here is rudimentary and schematic, as the phenomenon is constantly unfolding and evolving. How to explain these changes is beyond the scope of this book. Nevertheless, I would like to offer my observations on some developments that bring into sharp relief the key features of films from earlier decades: that is, the body of works whose historical, political, and cultural meanings I have aimed to illuminate.

An important shift occurred in the 2000s in the area of colonial representation in South Korean films. Along with a growing suspicion of the "meta-narratives of nation," a revisionist impulse became pervasive in the postdemocratic South Korea of the 1990s.[2] The era witnessed a growing revisionist movement within various cultural fields to revisit and rewrite the modern history of the nation. This development is most conspicuous in the films of the Korean New Wave directors of the 1990s, although the tendency continued in the genre-driven filmmaking of the 2000s. The rise of films on the colonial past, in addition, coincided with a discourse on colonial modernity that gained increasing critical and cultural currency from the 1990s onward.

The relaxation of censorship in the popular culture of the time made it possible for films to employ archival visual images of and references to the colonial era that had long been kept out of circulation. Photos of colonial urban culture and settings also became more available thanks to the spread of digital media technology and high-speed Internet distribution. These coalescing factors sparked the interest of a young generation of filmmakers and cultural producers, who then experimented with stories set in the times of colonial modernity. In addition, colonial-era films that had long been thought lost were discovered in various film archives in the region and were "repatriated" to the Korean Film Archive for public exposure and screening. These repatriated works rekindled the interest of not only the filmgoing public but also scholars, who then produced a steady stream of impressive works on colonial cinema. In other words, several dynamic factors contributed to a cultural milieu that was ripe to engender a new interest and approach toward the subject of colonial modernity and culture onscreen.

The comedy sports film *YMCA Baseball Team* (*YMCA Yagudan;* Kim Hyŏnsŏk, 2002) is a particularly significant case in this regard. The film shows a clear departure in the way the colonial past is narrated and understood in cinematic terms. It spearheads major changes in perceptual orientation toward the colonial past that post-2000s films commonly illustrate. The film introduced a new vocabulary and sensibility in relation to colonial space by focusing on various developments in modern culture. In particular, its focus on the cultural impact of modern spectator sports had a lasting effect on later films by rendering a kind of social space and communal interaction unavailable to Koreans in preceding decades.

What makes this and other colonial-themed films of the past decade so unique is the way in which the sociocultural activities of Koreans are drawn against the backdrop of exciting new developments and changes. The urban setting shows shifts in focus toward various modern novelties and their embrace by Koreans under colonial rule—a theme that received little attention, if any, in the films of earlier years. A fascination with the new and modern manifests in films that showcase modern sports, such as baseball in *YMCA Baseball Team,* martial arts and professional wrestling in *Yŏktosan* (*Rikidozan: A Hero Extraordinary;* Song Haesŏng, 2004), marathon running in *My Way* (Kang Jegyu, 2011), aviation skills in *Blue Swallow* (*Chŏngyŏn;* Yun Chongch'an, 2005), broadcasting culture in *Radio Days* (Ha Kiho, 2008), nightclub entertainment in *Modern Boy* (Chŏng Chiu, 2008), medical science in *Epitaph* (*Kidam;* Chŏng Shik, Chŏng Pŏmshik, 2007), and crime investigation in *Once upon a Time* (Chŏng Yonggi, 2008) and *Private Eye* (*Kŭrimja Sarin;* Pak Taemin, 2009).[4]

In these recent films, unlike most of the earlier films that I examined, no protagonists show a clear allegiance to the subversive activities of anticolonial struggle from the outset. Instead, they are initially portrayed as apolitical, with no interest beyond the individual pursuit of happiness, which involves the enjoyment of modern cultural events and phenomena. South Korea's move from the political era of the previous decade is evident in this orientation. However, as these characters are thwarted in their individualistic pursuits, they become increasingly affected by the colonial politics of domination and resistance. Most of these films, by the end, turn to the overarching theme of anticolonial struggle and its moral justification. Hence, the motif of conversion frequently appears, even in the most recent films, highlighting anticolonialism as, ultimately, the fundamental lens through which to view the colonial past.

Yet I stress that these recent films offer a different interpretive possibility with respect to the configuration of colonial space and the meaning of popular culture. They show a clear shift in focus from the sterile negative space of the dark back alley and the secluded *kisaeng* house to the brightly illuminated traffic space of the urban center. This "boulevard" space is densely populated with urban walkers who are in constant movement and flux. The bustling public space signals a network of transportation and communications in operation. Furthermore, many of these films highlight the moment when the novelty of modern networks or infrastructure reaches and captures the scopic attention of Korean residents. This Korean colonial viewing subject, needless to say, is considerably different from the subject featured in late colonial cinema, where the expansion of a modern colonial realm is depicted to allot space for Koreans as the faithful subjects of empire. These recent films strategically bypass the question of colonial development and modernization altogether by showing Koreans' fascination with modernity pre-dominantly in the frame of nascent interactions with its Western forms.

Technological marvels and activities entice the fascinated gaze of Korean urban onlookers, and the boulevard site or marketplace often turn into the modern public sphere of daily interaction and quotidian activities among urban Koreans. The marketplace may typically signify traditional commerce, but its depiction entails more complex social dynamics and characteristics. In the biographical films of the 1950s, for example, the marketplace was significant as a site to forge the modern subject of enlightenment, political consciousness, and authority. Recent films stress it as the site of horizontal social interactions among those drawn by the attractions of the new or modern technology. In *YMCA Baseball Team,* characters from a variety of social backgrounds show a keen interest in the public announcement that a new baseball team is forming and recruiting members. The pervasive impulse to transcend social barriers—a hallmark of modern consciousness and subjecthood—manifests through the people's collective response to new, modern forms of culture and leisure, all of which serve as a stimulus for individual enjoyment and social bonding. Similarly, attentive and disciplined listening to radio programs happens in the marketplace, bringing simultaneous fascination to the listeners in *Radio Days.* Listenership is not a personal habit, but a collective social activity in the film. Overall, the marketplace shows how ordinary Koreans become immediately drawn into new forms of popular culture through leisure and communications media. Often a film's formal properties, like editing and mise-en-scène composition, are utilized to deepen the viewer's emotive identification with the protagonist and his or her fascination with the latest novelties.

These films, however, have to navigate the thorny question of a colonial modernity in which autonomous space for the colonial subject is inherently limited and marginalized. I argue that recent films attempt to resolve the dilemma by resorting to a particular spatial and representational strategy: the reconfiguration of the sports arena as a pivotal public sphere for Koreans. *YMCA Baseball Team* is a pioneering and influential text that exemplifies the new depiction of a public sphere where the lopsided relations between the colonizer and the colonized are staged and challenged. Set in 1905, the year Korea became Japan's protectorate, *YMCA Baseball Team* dramatizes how baseball is introduced, spread, and popularized to urban Koreans as a new form of Western sport. Its portrayal of baseball as a novel form of sport conveys more than the spread of team sports: it provides a series of instances by which the new terms of gender, sexuality, ethnicity, and power are mobilized, regulated, modulated, and normalized. Baseball immediately captures the attention of Korean urban dwellers, whose passion for it transforms them into the most formidable players in the nation. It also brings together players of different social backgrounds and strata, effectively forging a community of horizontal membership. Class enmity and gender discrimination dissipate as cooperation and

FIGURE 12. The advent of spectator sport in *YMCA Baseball Team*.

team play become increasingly serious and important for those who play baseball at the public site. Baseball creates room for the advent of the new modern national subject and for something akin to the powerful horizontal social membership that Benedict Anderson describes for an imagined community.

In *YMCA Baseball Team*, sports competition is significant not only to Korean athletes but also to spectators in the arena for its *presupposition* of a system of impartiality, fairness, and objectivity. In this world of rigid regulations, the Japanese counterparts no longer have the upper hand of domination; instead, they subscribe to the same established rules and regulations. Concurrently, sports competition conjures up an imaginary social space in which the Korean subject can claim prowess and superiority outside the confines of colonial space. More importantly, the film emphasizes the advent of collective spectatorship as the central thematic feature of sports activity. Baseball games are situated specifically within the matrix of the collective and concentrated gaze, around which the formal network of horizontal membership and participation takes shape.

The theme of sports competition also reverberates in such films as *Blue Swallow*, *Yŏktosan*, and *My Way*, although in each of these the team match is largely replaced by individual competition. In each, a Japanese counterpart performs an important role in affirming both the fairness of the rule-governing system and the Korean character's unique place in it. For instance, the Japanese woman aviator in *Blue Swallow*, played by Yu Min, affirms the Korean aviator's superior skills and talent through her gaze of sympathy and respect. Her act of looking, which registers her empathy for the Korean protagonist, cements the validity of the space of rules and fairness that had been threatened by ethnic discrimination against the Korean protagonist in the outside world.

Yet in these films the effort to secure ground for Korean autonomy can go only so far. The Korean subject remains alienated from the network and traffic of colonial modernity despite winning the gaze and recognition of his Japanese counterpart.

This inherent dilemma manifests most clearly in *Modern Boy*, a film that features the ambivalent political conversion of a Korean, pro-Japanese government official. The film's protagonist is an urban playboy who works at the Government General of Korea. He uses his inside knowledge of urban development in Seoul for his material benefit. He is not outside the colonial gaze; rather, he is within the apparatus of the colonial government's control over Koreas' urban sectors. His affinity with the colonial power, however, is disrupted when he becomes mistakenly implicated in a subversive terrorist plot. Moreover, his courtship of a cabaret singer triggers a brutal counterinsurgency action by his old friend who is a Japanese prosecutor. The protagonist's loss of control over his relationship with the Japanese friend and the cabaret singer becomes acutely clear in a sequence where his endeavor to carry out an assassination of Japanese officials results in embarrassing failure. What the film chronicles is the slow undoing of the protagonist's confident sense of being at home in the boulevard spaces of Seoul. The failure forces him to walk into the kind of negative space familiar from so many anticolonial nationalist film – here, the drab underground hideout of the terrorist group. This return signifies the limit of the colonized subject's range in the vast space of colonial Seoul.

A survey of colonial space in recent South Korean cinema is helpful for pondering the odd artificiality of colonial imagery in *The Taoist Wizard*. The shallow ambiance of the movie set does more than expose the environment's constructed nature. The film extends the presupposed artificiality of the urban space that was a central feature of cinematic representations of the colonial past. It effectively draws on some inherently empty aura of colonial urban imagery to further accentuate the spectacle of destruction.

But this reading of the movie set's semantic features takes us only so far. There is another dramatic component in the film's coda that complicates an assessment of the colonial imagery. After the destruction of the movie set, Chŏnuchi returns to the site to showcase the making of an espionage-melodrama film in which Ing'yŏng, now a promising movie actress, stars in a drama set in the colonial era. A brief enacted sequence features a cross-dressed Ing'yŏng, Chŏnuchi's love interest, and her assassination of a Japanese collaborator lover on the boulevard. The ersatz colonial urban space is reconstructed for its proper use here: that is, to render the affirmation of the nationalist spirit in South Korea's cinema.

The assassination of the pro-Japanese collaborator is symbolically crucial in bringing closure to a narrative that occupies several temporalities. The pan-historical story of Korean wizardry seems to arrive at a plausible conclusion that stresses a nationalist cause for action. Curiously, the self-reflexive sequence also entails an undermining of such assurance, for the manner in which this segment is rendered appears too conventional, excessive, and even parodic to register sincere concentric meanings. The coda that follows this dramatic enactment of the nationalist dictate further complicates the film's reflection of the bygone colonial history.

It shows Chŏnuchi and Ing'yŏng on a Southeast Asian resort beach, which they reached through a magic portal in order to evade police questioning on the movie set. On the beach, both are in bewilderment, as they question whether they have been to this place before. The film makes it clear that they indeed visited the same site in the past, during premodern dynastic times. The sequence hence marks a moment of déjà vu for the couple.

The film's coda can be interpreted as a desperate attempt to open up a new space, now an extranational one. But it also alludes allegorically to a certain limit in South Korean cinema's historical imagination. It makes a mockery of the flat imagery of colonial history, but in doing so it ironically ends up exposing the very limit of closure as well. Though successful at transporting themselves to a safe place, the couple quickly become uncertain of place and time. Their spatial disorientation can be read in relation to, and as a premonition of, a historical amnesia of a particular kind. Chŏnuchi has been active and triumphant in his struggle against the archenemy at various faux sites in the colonial space. Yet it remains uncertain whether he is aware of the historical meanings of the colonial imagery and facades that he habitually obliterates. It would be safe to assume instead that his exuberant action is made possible precisely because he remains oblivious to the trauma of colonialism in modern Korean history.

Hence, *The Taoist Wizard* and other recent films seem to have reached a point of exhaustion as they too easily traverse the readily available colonial tropes and imagery. Perhaps this malaise is an unavoidable consequence of a postcolonial filmmaking tradition in which colonial imagery was used and constructed narrowly and selectively—and for too long—for the contrarian goals of negation and opposition. The amnesia that the male protagonist Chŏnuchi demonstrates toward the colonial past hence shows a unique symptom of history. His obliviousness captures the location of colonial imagery in South Korea's visual culture. It inherently alludes to the curtailed view and willful disavowal that for many years conditioned and restricted the imagining of the colonial past during the protracted Cold War.

NOTES

INTRODUCTION

1. In the mid-1970s, Im decided to make "honest" films instead of churning out more popular genre films. In many interviews, Im downplays the artistic integrity of the genre films that he directed in the early years of his film career. Though he debuted in 1962 with *Farewell to Tumen River* (*Tumanganga charigŏra*), he regards *Weed* (*Chapcho*), the 1973 film on which he collaborated with the screenwriter Na Hanbong, as the first of his "honest" films. There nonetheless is continuity between the supposed two phases of his career. His authorial preoccupations with questions of nation, nationalism, and national culture are often manifest in his early genre works. To be sure, his thematic preoccupations changed in the 1970s, but these changes can be read as a gradual shift in focus regarding the issue of national history and culture rather than a wholesale redirection of his thematic concerns. For Im's interview and analysis of *The Genealogy*, see articles in David E. James and Kyung Hyun Kim, eds., *Im Kwon-Taek: The Making of a Korean National Cinema* (Detroit, MI: Wayne State University Press, 2002).

2. The film marks a rare instance in which the adaptation of a Japanese literary source was openly acknowledged. Chapter 2 examines the widespread practice of unacknowledged borrowing from Japanese narrative sources that occurred in the Korean film industry in the 1960s.

3. The film depicts Sŏl undergoing a series of ordeals as the head of the clan, all from the viewpoint of Tani. The relationship Tani develops with Sŏl makes him increasingly dubious about the efficacy of the coercive policy, and his growing sympathy and affinity with Sŏl make clear the film's moral indictment of Japanese colonial domination. As Kyung Hyun Kim points out, Tani's privileged "outsider" position carves out a potential space for mutual understanding between the colonizer and the colonized by portraying the two men's shared appreciation for Korea's tradition and beauty—an appreciation that transcends ethnic

differences. Kyung Hyun Kim, "The Transnational Constitution of Im Kwon-Taek's Minjok Cinema in Chokpo, Sŏp'yŏnje, and Ch'wihwasŏn," *Journal of Korean Studies* 16, no. 2 (2011): 231–48.

4. This aesthetic theme finds its most rigorous visual expression in Sŏl's funeral sequence. It features the funeral procession on a distant hill, with Tani, observing from afar, in the foreground within the frame. The composition frames and organizes the event from his privileged standpoint. The sequence echoes the film's recurring theme of the appreciation for Korean aesthetics that both men share, imbued with a sense of sorrow and fatalism. Tani comes to his fullest understanding of the tragic beauty of Korea through the landscape view, which in turn leads to his resounding indictment of and pessimism regarding Japanese colonial rule. In effect, the sequence uses the spectacle of ritual to visualize and materialize a particular culturalist discourse on colonial Korea.

5. The image also deviates from the meticulous visual design and rigor of Sŏl's grand funeral procession at the end of the film. In that scene, Im adroitly uses the widescreen format to generate a nostalgic sense of the Korean countryside, and Tani's view is framed in such a way that it not only focuses on the funeral procession as object but also "withdraws" (to borrow W. J. T. Mitchell's term) the viewer to see the gestalt of the scene. See Mitchell's *Landscape and Power,* 2nd ed. (Chicago: University of Chicago Press, 2002), vii–viii.

6. According to the director, Im, the artificial appearance of the image was in part the result of an artistic compromise he had to make during the film's production. Using a large photograph as the backdrop of the scene was too costly, so he was forced to resort to a more economical option. To compensate for the uncanny effect of a painting, Im made an effort to add a sense of geographical authenticity to the sequence by locating the viewpoint in the actual government office where Tani would have worked: the historical site of the Kyŏnggi Provincial Office. He constructed the vista from the seat of the old Kyŏnggi Provincial Office, looking at the Government-General Building in the distance. Im Kwont'aek, telephone interview by author, September 9, 2013.

7. By *exceptional,* I refer to the fact that the film's visualization of the building as a site of colonial power is a rare instance in South Korean cinema, however artificial the rendition may be. No other South Korean film, as far as I know, has explicitly shown the building as the icon of colonial rule while it was extant. Its association with colonial rule has been rendered invisible in cinematic production. Instead, South Korean films show the building as the center of South Korea's political authority. Kang Taejin's film *The Coachman (Mabu,* 1961) is a good example. In it, a lower-middle-class family that has undergone a series of troubles and hardships is suddenly on the threshold of great prosperity and upward mobility because the eldest son has passed his bar exam. This moment of jubilation takes place in front of the government building gate where the official announcement of the bar exam results is posted. The building serves as a site of melodramatic upheaval where the personal, familial, and political all coalesce in a moment of euphoria.

8. The major events include the inauguration of the Constitutional Assembly, the establishment of the South Korean state and government, and the first national presidential election and inauguration, as well as the South Korean army's recapture of the capital, Seoul, during the Korean War. One of the most memorable historical moments of South Korea's modern history and of the Korean War in particular is captured in the photo image of two South Korean army soldiers raising the national flag, T'aegukgi, on the flagpole in front

of the building. Later, the building was used from 1986 to 1995 as the National Central Museum, housing over 120,000 archaeological finds and national treasures.

9. The conservationist camp had argued for the building's historical associations and its service as a political symbol of the South Korean government since its establishment in 1948. But by employing the traditional geomantic rhetoric of *p'ungsu* (propitious space) to argue for the building's demolition, the administration promoted a new scenario of nation, departing from old discursive models based on anticommunism and developmentalism. For a detailed survey of the controversies surrounding the building's demolition, as well as its discursive impact on the official narratives of the nation, see Jong-Heon Jin, "Demolishing Colony: The Demolition of the Old Government-General Building of Chosŏn," in *Sitings: Critical Approaches to Korean Geography*, ed. Timothy R. Tangherlini and Sallie Yea, Hawai'i Studies on Korea (Honolulu: University of Hawai'i Press, Center for Korean Studies, 2008).

10. The administration pushed for demolition as a way to symbolically sever its relations not only to the colonial legacy but also implicitly to the authoritarian regimes that had long sustained the troubling legacies of the colonial past. See Kal Hong, *Aesthetic Constructions of Korean Nationalism: Spectacle, Politics, and History*, Asia's Transformations (New York: Routledge, 2011), 102.

11. Jin, "Demolishing Colony," 40.

12. During the colonial period, historic photographs underscored the building's magnitude, molding the public's perception of the building and its historical and political identity. But the new postcolonial photos entailed a unique temporal, that is, historical, density that set them apart from the old colonial-era photos. While the former tend to feature solely the building itself, underscoring its magnitude in colonial Korea, the postcolonial photos principally emphasize historic moments in the narrative of the independent nation-state. Such images were circulated and disseminated through various distribution channels such as newspapers, magazines, government documents, and textbooks. The new images became the visual repository of the nation's official history, and the building's association with national history in turn displaced its anterior link to the colonial grandiose. Parallel to this recontextualization and historicization was the gradual but clear withdrawal of the colonial photos of the building from circulation. See Theodore Hughes's *Literature and Film in Cold War South Korea: Freedom's Frontier* (New York: Columbia University Press, 2012), 2, which discusses how South Korea has formed its postcolonial culture and identity on the basis of three major forms of disavowal, one of which is specifically concerned with the postcolonial treatment of colonialism: an "institutionalized forgetting" of the collaboration of Korean elites in the propagation of the imperialist project during the late colonial wartime mobilization period.

13. The critical concept of landscape helps us approach the ideological construction of the view or way of seeing the building. W. J. T. Mitchell approaches the representation of landscape as a signifying practice that functions as cultural power through a particular ideological effect. Such imaging of a landscape "naturalizes a cultural and social construction, representing an artificial world as if it were simply given and inevitable, and it also makes that representation operational by interpellating its beholder in some more or less determinate relation to its givenness as sight and site." A critical inquiry into landscape traces how the image becomes naturalized through the erasure of its own "readability" and

how the spectatorship constructed in this process shapes viewers' social identities. Mitchell, *Landscape and Power*, 2.

14. In this light, Choi Donghoon's 2009 fantasy film *Woochi* (*Chŏn Uch'i*) is a rigorously reflexive text that treats the subject of the colonial past as the image itself. The illusory and artificial facade of the movie set in the film stands in for the "historical real" in postcolonial cinema. See the "Coda" to this book for discussion of the film.

15. Many contemporary Korean filmmakers are keenly aware of the disavowal of colonial subject matter in cultural representation. In his 2006 interview with Ian Buruma, South Korean filmmaker Park Chan-wook points out that South Korean filmmakers would not face any serious censorship in the era of liberal democracy, with the exception of one taboo subject: the favorable depiction of Japanese colonial rule. He quips, "You could never say that the Japanese occupation of Korea had been beneficial. That would create more hostility than a movie praising North Korea. It would be like telling Jews that the Holocaust didn't exist." The interviewer, Buruma, ponders the feasibility of Park's analogy as he points out the material benefits that the colonial rule brought to Korea. He subsequently points out how the "cherished myths of nationalist history" remain unquestioned in liberal South Korean filmmaking. See Park Chan-wook, "Mr. Vengeance," interview by Ian Baruma, *New York Times Magazine*, April 9, 2006, 34.

16. I make an exception to discuss the horror film *Epitaph*, which was made in 2007. The film is included for its distinct notion of historical return and subconscious nostalgia for the Japanese Empire in South Korean cinema. While sharing the theme of resurgence of the repressed with the 1960s horror and revenge films, *Epitaph* takes the question of history and memory to a new level. For analysis of the film's unique significance, see chapter 5 on revenge horror films.

17. This pedagogic type of filmmaking is most evident in the filmic depiction of the patriotic heroes. The films of the postliberation era and the biopic films of the 1950s are examples of this cinematic tradition. I explore the filmic rendition of anticolonial nationalism in the next chapter.

18. According to the Korean Film Archive database, 208 narrative feature-length films are grouped under the keyword *ilche* (Japanese imperial/colonial era). In 1945–50 there were eleven such films; in 1951–60, eighteen; in 1961–70, fifty-eight; in 1971–80, fifty-five; in 1981–90, twenty-three; in 1991–2000, sixteen; in 2001–10, eighteen; and in 2011–16, nine.

19. It is thus hardly surprising that in subsequent decades these films have typically garnered adjectives such as *anticolonial* or *anti-Japanese*—designations that refer to a film's overall adherence to a resistentialist myth of nation, according to which most Korean people suffered from the violence of colonial rule but also resisted and struggled against it. I have drawn the notion of the resistentialist myth from Koen de Ceuster's work on South Korea's historiography. See his "The Nation Exorcised: The Historiography of Collaboration in South Korea," *Korean Studies* 25, no. 2 (2001): 207–42.

20. This is especially the case since nationalist discourse and historiography have decidedly shaped the ideal of Korean cinema. The case of the colonial film *Arirang* is a prime example. Even though this lost film does not feature a manifest anticolonial theme, historians and critics have valorized it as the epitome of the nationalist filmmaking practice. For a fuller exploration of the nationalist appraisal of Korean film history, see Lee Sunjin, "Yŏnghwasa sŏsul-gwa kusulsa pangbŏmnon" [Film historiography and the methodology

of oral history], in *Hanguk munhwa, munhak-kwa kusulsa* [Korean culture, literature and oral history], ed. Tongguk daehakkyo muhwa haksulwon han'gukmunhak yŏn'guso (Seoul: Tongguk taehakkyo chulpanbu, 2014), 79–118.

21. This area of critical neglect comes into sharp relief when we compare the canon of South Korean cinema to that of North Korean cinema. The canon of North Korean cinema overwhelmingly favors colonial-themed films.

22. Even colonial-themed films made by renowned Korean film directors have not fared well with critics. For instance, directors like Kim Kiyoung, Shin Sangok, Yu Hyŏnmok, and Yi Manhŭi all made films set in the colonial period. Yet these works have received little attention from film critics. The case of Kim Kiyoung's 1978 *Soil (Hŭk)* would be good example. Despite its fascinating depiction of the connections between cultural nationalism and a conjugal relationship, *Soil* has rarely been discussed a part of the auteur's oeuvre.

23. I am borrowing Christina Klein's insights into the importance of middlebrow culture here, as they offer a productive avenue for thinking about the workings of ideology and sentiment in the global order of the Cold War. According to Klein, ordinary Americans were able to relate affectively and intellectually to the Cold War's polarizing politics because of the works of middlebrow cultural producers and intellectuals. Despite the dismissal of sophisticated intellectuals, the new middlebrow cultural formation fostered the perception of the growing US power in Asia as the development of a new relationship and affinity with Asian peoples. See her *Cold War Orientalism: Asia in the Middlebrow Imagination, 1945–1961* (Berkeley: University of California Press, 2003), 7–8.

24. Postcolonial societies experienced the tensions and the tumultuous processes of nation building during this seismic shift toward the new global order. Kwon claims that neglecting the impacts of this transition led to "dehistoricization" of the very object of inquiry that postcolonial criticism aspires to examine and understand. Heonik Kwon, *The Other Cold War*, Columbia Studies in International and Global History (New York: Columbia University Press, 2010), 127–29.

25. Tonglin Lu reminds us of the structural misalignment between the reference of Japan and the formation of a new national identity in former colony states. He writes that "the colonial history of Japan, the only Asian empire builder of the modern period, serves as an important reference point for its former colonies as they reconfigure national identities" but that this reference point is unstable, "constructed through often-contradictory projections of the collective imagination" and "ultimately . . . characterized by inconsistency. Indeed, perceptions of the colonial past have little to do with historical realities, and more with current political needs." Drawing on Slavoj Žižek's notion of "parallax," Lu describes how "Taiwan's colonial past, viewed from various political angles and historical moments, has been portrayed 'parallactically,' as it has been incorporated into different political realities." Tonglin Lu, "A Cinematic Parallax View: Taiwanese Identity and the Japanese Colonial Past," *positions* 19, no. 3 (Winter 2011): 764.

26. The March 1st Movement of 1919 galvanized Koreans to protest against the brutal treatment of Koreans by the Japanese authorities. The colonial government subsequently modified its policy so that Koreans could exercise relative autonomy in the area of cultural activities and productions. The new film boom reflects the changing milieu of urban culture, as it paralleled and complemented the general growth of popular culture in the colonial Korea. For the cultural renaissance of the 1920s, see Michael Edson Robinson,

Korea's Twentieth-Century Odyssey: A Short History (Honolulu: University of Hawaii Press, 2007), 56–75.

27. The first homegrown talkie film, *Ch'unhyangjŏn*, premiered in 1935. The deferred development of sound film meant the prolonged production and circulation of the silent film, which had already garnered popular attention through the accompanying live performance of the *pyŏnsa*, who provided voices and narration for the featured film.

28. Brian Yecies and Ae-Gyoung Shim aptly state: "In this way, cinema in Korea was 'occupied' by economic, political, industrial, and cultural constraints brought to the peninsula by outsiders and then negotiated internally." See Brian Yecies and Ae-Gyoung Shim, *Korea's Occupied Cinemas, 1893–1948*, Routledge Advances in Film Studies (New York: Routledge, 2011), 5.

29. Most of these "collaborationist" films were recently discovered in various film archives outside Korea and "repatriated" back to the Korean Film Archive. They filled a gap in the archive of Korean cinema but also fueled controversies because of their outright pro-Japanese message, which had been largely glossed over in prior film history books. The issue of collaboration obviously has assumed a central significance in the new critical discourse of colonial Korean cinema. Moreover, these films have inspired a new direction in Korean film history scholarship by spurring reflection on the troubled question of colonial modernity.

30. For example, the effort by Korean film producer Yi Ch'angyong to comply with the state guidelines for pro-Japanese films did not translate into a business opportunity in the larger film markets of the metropole and other occupied areas. See O Sŏngji et al., *Koryŏ yŏnghwa hyŏphoe-wa yŏnghwa sinch'eje, 1936–1941* [The Korea Film Association and the new filmic system, 1936–1941] (Seoul: Han'guk Yŏngsang Charyowon, 2007).

31. A substantial body of scholarly works has offered nuanced readings of the contradictory dimensions of Korean identity caught in the state machinery of "assimilation" propaganda: that is, how the Korean person's path to salvation is repeatedly rendered comprehensible in terms of voluntary conversion into an imperial subject. Notable examples include Kim Ryŏsil, *T'usihanŭn cheguk, tusahanŭn singminji* [The imperial gaze and the colony on display] (Seoul: Samin, 2006); Yi Yŏngjae, *Cheguk Ilbon-ŭi Chosŏn yŏnghwa* [Korean cinema at the end of the Japanese Empire] (Seoul: Hyŏngsil Munhwa, 2008); Kyung Hyun Kim, the chapter "Viral Colony" in his *Virtual Hallyu: Korean Cinema of the Global Era* (Durham, NC: Duke University Press, 2011), 55–80. For a rigorous reading of the symptom of melancholia in the Korean male body in An Sŏkyŏng's *Volunteer Soldier* (*Chiwonbyŏng*, 1940), see Yi Yŏngjae's chapter "Hyŏpnyŏk-ŭi Simchŏng" in her *Cheguk Ilbon-ŭi Chosŏn yŏnghwa*, 45–115.

32. Kyung Hyun Kim, "Viral Colony."

33. The aforementioned criticisms tend to dwell on the moments of "hesitation" or "ambivalence" of Korean characters in order to muster the film's allegorical meanings. They help us gain insight into the structural instability of the state ideology itself, just as the transitory and contingent nature of the Korean identity also comes into fuller understanding vis-à-vis the dominant yet distant political power.

34. It must be noted that the empire in this context is not portrayed in association with coercion, or in the form of a force intruding on an individual's psyche. Missing from the picture is the negative depiction of colonial power as a surveillance mechanism that

postcolonial cinema would later take as the basic premise of historical representation of the colonial past. The atmosphere of film settings, e.g., the dark and ominous and claustrophobic atmosphere of a police state portrayed in postcolonial anticolonialist films as compared to the luminous and expansive realm of empire in colonial collaborationist films, therefore offers a point of comparison between two historically and politically divided cinemas that served two opposite ideologies.

35. Takashi Fujitani writes succinctly: "The drive to incorporate the Korean people into Japan's imperialist war unleashed a massive machinery of institutions and agents that sought to make all the people *visible* to power, and then worked to turn them into usable Japanese subjects." Takashi Fujitani, *Race for Empire: Koreans as Japanese and Japanese as Americans during World War II* (Berkeley: University of California Press, 2011), 293; also cited in Kelly Y. Jeong, "Enlightening the Other: Colonial Korean Cinema and the Question of Audience," *Review of Korean Studies* 18, no. 1 (2015): 26.

36. The image of the Korean in distress, which stands for the colonial subject's genuine interiority, functions as a new visual and visible component or trope in the taxonomy of the empire's visual registers—an image similar in effect to the trope of Korea as a local site in the service of the colonial gaze. On Korea as the object of the exotic gaze of the Japanese colonizer, see E. Taylor Atkins, *Primitive Selves: Koreana in the Japanese Colonial Gaze, 1910–1945* (Berkeley: University of California Press, 2010).

37. Michael Baskett reminds us that Japanese-sponsored films featured Japan's own narcissistic imperial projections on the screen. For instance, the images of new Japanese-built bridges, factories, or trains in colonies like Taiwan, Korea, and Manchuria were integral to the "construction of an *attractive modernist vision of empire*, where indigenous populations were presented as living in co-prosperity, ethnic harmony, and material abundance." See Michael Baskett, *The Attractive Empire: Transnational Film Culture in Imperial Japan* (Honolulu: University of Hawai'i Press, 2008), 8. Emphasis mine.

38. Here I draw upon the idea of connection from Yi Yŏngjae, *Cheguk Ilbon-ŭi Chosŏn yŏnghwa*, 32, 255.

39. I am indebted to the insight of Jini Kim Watson, who discusses the primacy of spatial themes in postcolonial cultural productions: "I suggest that there is a kind of postcolonial historical development whose primary process is spatial and architectural transformation, a process most clearly registered in the figures and displacements taken up in various fictional texts." Jini Kim Watson, *The New Asian City: Three-Dimensional Fictions of Space and Urban Form* (Minneapolis: University of Minnesota Press, 2011), 8.

40. This spatial feature of postcolonial films accords with visual metaphors and tropes evoked in the nationalist scenario of history. Nationalist discourse on colonialism typically resorts to negative spatiotemporal metaphors such as "dark times" (*ilche amhŭggi*) to render and signify the oppressive aura of colonial rule in Korea. Such descriptions give the generalized impression of the era as a rupture or void in the nation's history. Yi Yŏngjae, *Cheguk Ilbon-ŭi Chosŏn yŏnghwa*, 212.

41. Michel de Certeau's concepts of strategy and tactic are helpful in framing the question of the construction of colonial space from the viewpoint of the ex-colonized. Both strategy and tactic are defined by their relations to power, with different "spatial" orientations and effects. What distinguishes them are the "types of operations and the role of spaces: strategies are able to produce, tabulate and impose the controlled spaces, when those

operations take place, whereas tactics can only use, manipulate and divert these spaces." Strategies signify the manipulation of power relations that institutions or organizations exercise through their will and might: that is, the occupation and ownership of places. In contrast, the concept of tactics helps us come to terms with the condition of possibility of the colonized, who are deprived of their own space of political representation or autonomy but possess the unique subversive potential of actions. One of the key features of a tactic is its problematic location. As de Certeau writes, "[A] tactic is a calculated action determined by the absence of a proper locus. No delimitation of an exteriority, then, provides it with the condition necessary for autonomy." See Michel de Certeau, *The Practice of Everyday Life*, trans. Steven Rendall (Berkeley: University of California Press, 2011), 30, 37.

42. Partha Chatterjee, *The Nation and Its Fragments: Colonial and Postcolonial Histories* (Princeton, NJ: Princeton University Press, 1993), 6.

43. It is not too difficult to imagine the cultural logic behind such a draconic measure of suppression. The Japanese policy to assimilate Koreans into Japanese during the height of militarism created intense resistance and enmity among Koreans, which then found its channel of expression in the form of cinematic censorship after the liberation. The erasure of Japanese linguistic and literary references subsequently led to the stereotyping of Japanese in postcolonial Korean cinema. The actors who played Japanese characters had to speak their dialogues in Korean but with slight linguistic traits that alluded to Japanese Otherness, including intonation or accent variations. Particular headgear, such as the flat cap, was often used as a convention to register the wearer's pro-colonial Japanese ethnicity.

44. Even when films feature modern transportation sites like train stations, they often lack the aura of novelty or uniqueness commonly associated with modern technologies. A comparison of two of Shin Sangok's films helps us understand these contrasting characteristics. Both *The Houseguest and My Mother* (*Sarangbang sonnim-gwa ŏmŏni*, 1961) and *The Remembered Shadow of the Yi Dynasty* (*Ijo changyŏng*, 1967) feature the parting of lovers on and near a train station platform. The former film, which is set vaguely in postcolonial Korea, registers the resignation and sorrow of the male protagonist through the domineering presence of the train. The latter film, set in the colonial period, gives the train no such emotive charge. The station setting is devoid of emotional ambiance here; it is as alienating as any place in urban Seoul under the surveillance of the colonial power.

45. Kristen Whissel, *Picturing American Modernity: Traffic, Technology and the Silent Cinema* (Durham, NC: Duke University Press, 2008), 9.

46. Colonial films like *Sweet Dream* (*Mimong*; Yang Chunam, 1936) demonstrate all the hallmarks of urban modernity—its fascination with the novelty, movement, and spectacle of urban experience. In contrast, postcolonial cinema displays hardly any signs of interest in the perceptual mode of modernity under the colonial regime.

47. Most of the actions of resistance fighters occur around these places at nighttime, but their presence there is essentially transitory, so that we have no sense of the space as fully occupied.

48. The neighborhood space also characteristically lacks the aura of proximity or interaction among city dwellers. In fact, back alleys in traditional residential districts like the Chongno district of Seoul rarely feature local residents, passersby, or onlookers. The austerity and deadness of these places sharply contrasts with the aura of nostalgia and sensory stimulation often found in literary works. For instance, the Japanese novelist Kajiyama

Toshiyuki offers a vivid and lively sensory description of the shabby tavern in the back alley of Chongno in one of his novellas, showing the Japanese fascination with the Korean exotic: "Such a small shabby tavern would be one of the best places in which to enjoy typical folk food and drink. The environment in any alley was entirely different from that of the main street with its trams. The humid air in the dark, winding, narrow alley stank of filthy gutters and stale urine." Kajiyama Toshiyuki, *The Clan Records: Five Stories of Korea,* trans. Yoshiko Dykstra (Honolulu: University of Hawaii Press, 1995), 117.

49. In South Korean postliberation cinema, the depiction of negative space in terms of dark, drab, empty, and anxiety-producing urban microspaces, such as back alleys, naturally suggests stylistic and thematic similarities to an American film genre, film noir (though I would submit that South Korean films' rendition of negative space is far more artificial in ambiance, since it includes no onlookers or neighbors in the vicinity of the action). The striking resemblance reminds us that film noir may be understandable as a part of the global visual matrix of Cold War culture, rather than just as an intranational US phenomenon.

1. UNDER THE BANNER OF NATIONALISM

1. For instance, the Korean Film Alliance (Chosŏn Yŏnghwa Tongmaeng) submitted to USAMGIK a request for approval of the release of the documentary film *Chosŏn Ŭiyŏldan* (Ŭiyŏldan of Korea), which featured Kim Wonbong, a charismatic leader of the militant anarchist organization Ŭiyŏldan. USAMGIK rejected the request. The Korean Film Alliance criticized USAMGIK's decision and mobilized public opinion to oppose USAMGIK's stringent regulation over film exhibition. "Yŏnghwa sangyŏng hŏgaje chŏlp'yerŭl" [Calling for the abolition of film censorship by USAMGIK], *Chosŏn Ilbo,* October 23, 1946, 2.

2. In particular, the transfer of "enemy property" (*chŏksan*) theaters and the direct distribution of American films became the most contentious issues in the postliberation film scene in Korea. See Cho Hyejŏng, "Migunjŏngi yŏnghwa chŏngch'aek-e kwanhan yŏn'gu" [A study on American occupation era film policy] (PhD diss., Chungang University, 1997), 28–71.

3. In 1944, the colonial government in Korea consolidated the existing film companies into a single body called Chosŏn Yŏnghwasa. After liberation, all the properties of Chosŏn Yŏnghwasa were transferred to the new authority of USAMGIK. The productions of Chosŏn Yŏnghwasa were severely restricted as well, limited to a small number of newsreels and culture films. Han Sangŏn, *Haebang konggan-ŭi yŏnghwa, yŏnghwain* [Films and filmmakers in the space of liberation] (Seoul: Iron-gwa silchŏn, 2013), 23–30.

4. According to Chŏng Kŭnsik and Kyeonghee Choi, USAMGIK made a substantial effort to censor not only the press but films, reflecting a keen awareness of their propaganda effects. The organization was also aware of the political activism of leftist filmmakers in postliberation Korea. It is noteworthy that USAMGIK's regulation on moving pictures was declared in April 1946, preceding the regulation on newspapers and other regular print media in May 1946. See Chŏng Kŭnsik and Kyeonghee Choi, "Haebang hu kŏmnyŏl ch'eje-ŭi yŏn'gurŭl wihan myŏkkaji chilmun-gwa kwaje: Singminji yusan-ŭi chongsik-kwa chaepŏnsai-esŏ (1945–1952)" [A few questions and issues on the study of the postliberation censorship system: Between the closure and the continuity of the colonial legacy (1945–1952)], *Taedong Munhwa Yŏn'gu* 74 (2011): 7–70.

5. According to An Sŏkyŏng, a renowned colonial-era filmmaker, liberation resulted in systemic difficulties for Korean filmmakers as their film stock, development chemicals, and other filmmaking resources from Japan were suddenly cut off. See his oral account in "Yŏnghwa-ŭi chajenan, chŏngch'i munhwa-wa tongsi haegyŏl" [Shortage of film facilities should be solved along with the political and cultural problems], *Kyŏnghyang Sinmun*, December 15, 1946, 2.

6. The splitting of Korea into two inimical states led to a divergence in the anticolonial discourse of their films. As Travis Workman argues, the type of nationalist discourse that South Korean director Ch'oe Ing'yu illustrated in his films of the liberation era like *Hurrah! For Freedom* is very different from that in early North Korean films such as *My Home Village*. See Travis Workman, "Narrating and Aestheticizing Liberation in *Hurrah! For Freedom* and *My Home Village*," *Review of Korean Studies* 18, no. 1 (June 2015): 77–102.

7. These postwar years also witnessed the rise of a popular culture and film industry that paralleled and contributed to the spread of the Cold War logic and order in South Korea. Steven Chung argues that the popular films and discourses of 1950s South Korea show complex trajectories of interaction and dialogue with the global popular culture. See chapter 2 of *Split Screen Korea: Shin Sang-ok and Postwar Cinema* (Minneapolis: University of Minnesota Press, 2014), 47–81.

8. For an illuminating account of Shin's career in the 1960s, see chapter 3 of Chung's *Split Screen Korea*, 88–106.

9. Among these works only two films, *Hurrah! For Freedom* and *The Night before Independence Day*, are still in existence.

10. Two production companies, Kyemong Yŏnghwa Hyŏphoe and Koryŏ Yŏnghwa Hyŏphoe, made most of the films that purveyed this anticolonial nationalism. Kyemong Yŏnghwa Hyŏphoe financed the production of biographical historical films such as *The Chronicle of An Chunggŭn; The Chronicle of March 1st Revolution; Yun Ponggil, the Martyr;* and *Yu Kwansun*. Koryŏ Yŏnghwa Hyŏphoe, on the other hand, produced the nonbiographical nationalist films directed by Ch'oe In'gyu. The prominent film historian Yi Yŏngil points out that the senior filmmakers with a nationalist orientation played a decisive role in creating the cinematic rendition of anticolonial history. See his *Han'guk yŏnghwa chŏnsa* [A general history of Korean cinema], rev. ed. (Seoul: Sodo, 2004), 218–19.

11. I acknowledge that the historic partition of Korea makes the use of the term *Korea* or *South Korea* murky and complicated here. To be sure, political conflict and polarization had been brewing since liberation, which resulted in partition in 1948 and civil war in 1950. Such time lines make it difficult to discern the state origins of those films made before 1948. *Hurrah!* for instance, would be a Korean film but not a South Korean film according to this logic. The film was made during the incipient nation-state era under American military occupation (1945–48).

12. Travis Workman's article is a remarkable exception to the interpretive insulation surrounding *Hurrah!* It is the most sustained and nuanced reading of the film in recent years. Comparing this work to the first North Korean film, *My Home Village*, Workman brings attention to the historical specificity of two films by calling attention to their differing aesthetic constructions of liberation. See his "Narrating and Aestheticizing Liberation." My reading here builds upon his insights, particularly on the intensive use of melodramatic and gendered tropes of romance.

13. For instance, the film's male protagonist, Hanjung, is killed at the end according to the film script and other secondary sources, but his death is never depicted or shown in the damaged final film reel, and the sequence in which Hanjung (Chŏn Ch'anggŭn) and Mihyang (Yu Kyesŏn) talk about their relationship is so fragmented that it is nearly impossible to decipher the substance of their conversation. The damage to the film prints led even the prominent film historian Yi Yŏngil to misconstrue the basic story of the film in his magisterial *Han'guk yŏnghwa chŏnsa* (A general history of Korean cinema), where his summary (217–18) pays attention only to the interaction of the male protagonist Hanjung (Chŏn Ch'anggŭn) with the *kisaeng* Mihyang, overlooking Hanjung's important romance with the other female protagonist, Hyeja (played by Hwang Ryŏhŭi), and her crucial contribution to the nationalist struggle.

14. Yi Hyoin, "Haebang chikhu-ŭi Han'guk yŏnghwagye-wa yŏnghwa undong" [Korean film culture and activism in the postliberation era], in *Han'guk Yŏnghwa-ŭi P'unggyŏng, 1945–1959* [The landscape of Korean cinema, 1945–1959] (Seoul: Muhak Sasangsa, 2003), 23.

15. Workman, "Narrating and Aestheticizing Liberation."

16. The film ends with Hanjung and Hyeja running away from the hospital. This account of Hanjung's death is drawn not from the film but from other secondary sources. According to various secondary sources, Hanjung is shot and killed at daybreak on the day of the liberation.

17. Contrary to the convention of romance in popular film in which the woman is often the object of desire, Hanjung appears as the male subject of the female gaze, signaling an implicit link between having political authority and being the focus of women's desiring gaze.

18. Hence, the film departs from the typical scenario in popular cinema where the fulfillment of heterosexual romance parallels the resolution of the main conflict. I have in mind here the conventional norm of Hollywood, but in other commercial cinemas as well a heterosexual romance functions as a parallel story. See David Bordwell and Kristin Thompson, *Film Art: An Introduction,* 10th ed. (New York: McGraw-Hill, 2013).

19. It should be noted that *kisaeng* are not portrayed negatively in subsequent films. Im Kwont'aek's films in particular show the transformation of *kisaeng* for the nationalist cause. See chapter 4 on *kisaeng* and gangster films.

20. Mihyang later provides money to the nationalist camp in an effort to exonerate herself. But her effort to bring the "tainted" money to the revolutionaries enables Nambu to trace her to the nationalist camp and find Hanjung there. Thus Mihyang unintentionally brings trouble to the revolutionaries. In the police raid, Hanjung is taken captive and Mihyang dies in the crossfire. The film thus punishes Mihyang for her prior involvement with a collaborator and illustrates the negative representation of money in early films about the colonial period. For an examination of the changing meanings of money in the colonial representation, see chapter 3.

21. For the historical linkage between nationalism, Christianity, and melodrama in Korea, see Jinsoo An, "Screening the Redemption: Christianity in Korean Melodrama," in *South Korean Golden Age Melodrama: Gender, Genre, and National Cinema,* ed. Kathleen McHugh and Nancy Abelmann (Detroit, MI: Wayne State University Press, 2005), 65–97.

22. Workman points out that this domestic space of Hyeja is apolitical. My view is that while it appears to be apolitical, it is also the site of mobilization of female labor and devotion for the nationalist cause. See Workman, "Narrating and Aestheticizing Liberation," 93.

23. This theme, as I will illustrate, tends to resonate more strongly in biographical films of the late 1950s.

24. I would like to point out that Korean leaders were well aware that Japan had lost the war and were even contacted by the Japanese government regarding the transfer of power. For instance, Song Chinu, a moderate nationalist with untainted credentials, was approached by the Government-General between April 9 and 13 to be in charge of an interim administrative committee to secure law and order. He declined the offer, and on the morning of April 15 it was made to Yŏ Unhyŏng, who accepted. See Carter J. Eckert et al., *Korea Old and New: A History* (Seoul: Ilchogak, 1990), 329–30.

25. The film's damaged prints make it difficult to assess the details of the quarrel. However, they suggest that Hanjung apologizes for criticizing his fellow revolutionaries.

26. It would be possible, then, to read Hanjung's decision to continue fighting, which results in his unnecessary self-sacrifice, as a reflection of the filmmaker Ch'oe's overcompensating act of apology for his collaborationist work during the colonial period. More importantly, Ch'oe formulates a credo that far exceeds its utilitarian purpose. By fashioning nationalist resistance as individual, adventurous, excessive, and overtly uncompromising, Ch'oe manufactures tropes of nationalism that are reactionary in nature, limited in scope, and unfeasible in practice.

27. The active role of two filmmakers in the early years of filmmaking in postcolonial Korea deserves special consideration. Both Yun Pongch'un and Chŏn Ch'anggŭn started film careers in the colonial period but dropped them in order to avoid mounting pressures for collaboration toward the end of the colonial years. Chŏn in particular had been known in the industry for having personal contact with the prominent resistance leader Kim Ku of the provisional government-in-exile in Shanghai. And Chŏn later became the proselytizer of Kim Ku's nationalist politics after Kim's assassination by a South Korean military officer in 1949. As close friends in private life, both Yun and Chŏn played crucial roles in promulgating the nationalist view of colonial history in cinema through the practice of biographical filmmaking. Furthermore, they, along with their close associate film historian Yi Yŏngil, created the conceptual framework for a nationalist historiography of Korean cinema through their personal and firsthand accounts of colonial-era filmmaking and its culture. Yi later formulated his historical argument on realism as the foundation of Korean cinema, which is itself based on Yun's ideas of colonial cinema. The body of biographical films occupies a central place in the earnest and didactic mode of filmmaking that nearly achieved the status of official national history.

28. The list of nationalist heroes does not include radical leftist activists of the colonial period; these figures were structurally disavowed as subjects of filmmaking in South Korea.

29. Yun Pongch'un, the director who also contributed to the nationalist historiography of South Korean cinema, directed the first three films on the resistance leader Yu Kwansun in 1948, 1959, and 1966. Yu's ascendancy to the status of leader of the March 1st Movement hence derives in part from Yun's passionate advocacy for the cinematic treatment of Yu's heroism. Of the three versions, Yun's 1959 film received the highest critical acclaim.

30. Of the three versions, the 1959 film by Chŏn Ch'anggŭn, who also stars in the eponymous role, has become the canonized version.

31. The list of late 1950s biographical historical dramas includes *Yu Kwansun* (Yun Pongch'un, 1959), which focuses on the March 1st Movement of 1919. These films clearly show how South Korean cinema rehearsed the history of the Korean Empire to support the nationalist view of the colonial period that immediately ensued.

32. Though most biographical films focus on the heroic struggle of national leaders, Kim Kangyun's *Nameless Stars* (*Irŭmŏmnŭn pyŏldŭl*, 1959) is an exception. The film depicts the 1929 Kwangju student protest with an emphasis on the collective struggle of young people.

33. Im Hwasu, the film's producer, was arguably the most powerful and controversial figure in the film and entertainment business in the 1950s through his close association with Rhee's repressive political machine. He effectively functioned as Rhee's henchman and ideological mouthpiece in the culture industry. Im's positions include the presidency of the National Theater Association and the presidency of the Film Producers' Association. He also intimidated actors in the Anti-Communist Artist Association into giving speeches for Rhee's elections campaigns. His violent behavior toward actors, including an attack that resulted in the hospitalization of the then-leading comic actor Kim Hŭigap, was widely publicized in newspapers and caused public outrage.

34. The actual amount was 40 million *hwan,* and the matter was later discussed at a cabinet meeting of the Rhee administration. *"Chŏngnyŏn Rhee Syngman chejak, kongbosilsŏ sach'ŏnmanhwan"* [For production of *Young Syngman Rhee,* Division of Public Information provided 40 million *hwan*], *Chosŏn Ilbo,* May 18, 1960, 4.

35. Before producing *Independence Association,* Im had already made the biopic *Mansong Yi Kibung* (1958), a short forty-minute film about the titular man who became Rhee's running mate in the 1960 presidential election. The April Revolution of 1960 that toppled the Rhee administration also brought the resignation and subsequent death of Yi Kibung. For production details on *Mansong Yi Kibung,* see Kong Yŏngmin, "Saengaesa, Yi Sŏngch'ŏl" [A life history of Yi Sŏngch'ŏl], in *"2009 nyŏn han'guk yŏnghwasa kusul ch'aerok yŏn'gu sirijŭ"*[Korean film history oral interview series of 2009], 2009, Korean Film Archive, Seoul, cited in Lee Sunjin, "Hanguk chŏnjaeng hu naengjŏn-ŭi nolliwa singminji kiŏk-ŭi chaegusŏng" [The logic of the Cold War and the formation of the memory of colonial past in postwar Korea], *Kiok-kwa Chŏnmang* 23 (Winter 2010): 80.

36. This collaboration does not mean, however, that everything in the film is historically correct. As Lee Sunjin aptly points out, Rhee's subjective memories show inconsistencies with the key features of the film. In fact, the film helped turn the president's subjective account into an accepted truth. See Lee, "Hanguk chŏnjaeng hu," 98.

37. The Office of Presidential Security also gave film production various historical artifacts, props in the office's armory, to enhance the aura of historical authenticity. See Lee Sunjin, "Pak Haengch'ŏl," in *Yŏnghwaŭi koyangŭl chajasŏ* [In search of the home of cinema] (Seoul: Korean Film Archive, 2003), 121.

38. The film features virtually every major and minor actor of South Korean cinema in the late 1950s.

39. *Donga Ilbo,* November 20, 1959, evening edition, 4.

40. In the late 1950s the average number of screenings of a domestic film was somewhere between three and six. Lee, "Hanguk chŏnjaeng hu," 81.

41. See Kong, "2009 nyŏn Han'guk yŏnghwasa kusul," 197, cited in Lee, "Hanguk chŏnjaeng hu," 81.

42. The rigged presidential election of March 15, 1960, created widespread civilian protest and unrest. In the following month, the April Revolution of 1960 brought down the Rhee regime.

43. The dire circumstances of the war led filmmakers to produce documentary or newsreel films in support of the state's war effort. The personnel, technologies, and distribution channels of filmmaking had to rely heavily on the government's funding and support. Furthermore, the military information division of the US military played a key role in ensuring the continuation if not the stability of the filmmaking industry during the war and its aftermath.

44. The film was also a part of the larger promotional spectacle events of the late 1950s that emphasized the greatness of the current leader. These propaganda events included an exhibition (Unam chŏnsihoe), a play (Pungun), and news reels (such as one for the eighty-second birthday celebration of President Rhee) that all came out in 1957. These productions typically showcased Rhee as an exceptional leader of diplomatic skills during the colonial period. Lee, "Hanguk chŏnjaeng hu," 83.

45. Furthermore, Independence Association and other biopics of the era allude to a contemporaneous view of Chosŏn Korea very different from the colonialist appraisal of the premodern state and its failure. On the surface, the films appear to share the Japanese historical perspective on Chosŏn Korea as a stagnant, corrupt, and incompetent polity. However, I argue that Independence Association reframes its failure as a stage in a broader trajectory of growth, both for political leaders and for citizens who develop a keen historical consciousness.

46. Vivian Sobchack, "Surge and Splendor: A Phenomenology of Hollywood Historical Epic," Representations, no. 29 (Winter 1990): 26.

47. For an understanding of Shin Sangok's popular film aesthetics as well as his devotion to filmmaking, see Chung, Split Screen Korea, 129.

48. A Blood Bamboo was released on October 15, 1959, and Syngman Rhee on December 15, 1959.

49. Prasenjit Duara, Rescuing History from the Nation: Questioning Narratives of Modern China (Chicago: University of Chicago Press, 1995).

50. The fact that home never becomes the site of marriage or procreation shows the subordination of the domestic realm to a larger political purpose. This pattern of showing virtuous characters who sacrifice the joys of home and family to a greater political aim persists in movies about the colonial period in South Korean cinema in general.

51. At one point, Rhee brings all his earnings from his Korean language tutoring to his mother. However, the money hardly fills the emotional void that his impending departure creates. The scene underscores the moral integrity and sacrifice that Rhee's devotion to the nation entails.

52. Lee Sunjin argues that this conceptualization of Russia, rather than Japan, as the archenemy of Korea is a sign that the film transposes Cold War bipolar politics into the precolonial period. See her "Siguk yŏnghwa ttonŭn kinyŏmbi yŏnghwa" [A current affairs film or epic film], booklet in Kuhanmal sidaegŭk [Historical films about the Korean Empire], DVD boxed set (Seoul: Han'guk Yŏngsang Charyowon, 2012),15.

53. After the queen's assassination, the conservative faction seeks revenge on Kim Hongjip for his close association with the Japanese. Facing death, however, Kim does not resist or defend his position. Rather, he embraces their retribution. The film depicts Kim as a man of solemn demeanor, who in his last words quietly expresses his loyalty toward the king. Hence, the film brings out the pro-Japanese reformer's patriotic intentions rather than simply condemning him for his political miscalculation and ambition. That Rhee had developed the close ties with the pro-Japanese reform faction remains curiously downplayed in the film's depiction of his activities during this crucial period.

54. The Independence Gate (Tongnimmun) was established in 1897, after the first Sino-Japanese War, to celebrate Korea's independence from its previous status as tributary to China.

55. This middle segment of the film portrays a court torn apart and rendered ineffectual by political infighting. It focuses on the Kapshin coup, a failed three-day coup in 1884 that nearly toppled the monarchy. The coup, led by a group who wanted Korea to emulate the progressive reforms of Meiji Japan, included Kim Okkyun (1851–94) and Pak Yŏnghyo (1861–1939). It was quickly suppressed by a Chinese garrison in Korea, a development that led to the Chinese domination of Korea from 1885 to 1894. The film depicts the struggle over the reinstatement of Pak Yŏnghyo (1861–1939), the coup's alleged mastermind, who had fled to Japan. Rhee makes a strong appeal for pardoning Pak and his affiliate Sŏ Chaepil. But others vehemently oppose Rhee's request and accuse him of fomenting the culture of subversion. When the debate reaches an impasse, the king intervenes to break the deadlock. In real life the king at this point purged the group associated with Pak and Sŏ, but in the film the nature of the resolution is never specified and the issue is simply dropped from the narrative. As a result of this ellipse, the thorny question of Rhee's political loyalty to the monarchy remains unaddressed. The sequence illustrates how the film is structured around a series of blockages, distortions, and ellipses, all of which effectively obscure Rhee's affiliations in the volatile political contentions of his time. In particular, what is disavowed in the frame is the staunch pro-Japanese orientation of Pak's coup. Rhee's connection to the group of pro-Japanese reformers who backed the coup is downplayed in the film's depiction of court politics. This connection would have complicated, if not undermined, Rhee's later reputation for being a staunch anti-Japanese nationalist, which was central to his statesman image in postcolonial South Korea.

56. The newspaper even misreports his death in prison, turning him into a distant memory in the public mind. In short, Rhee is living on "borrowed time" at this point.

57. Liberation-era films are successful in focusing on the plights and struggles of individual characters, but they are not effective in constructing the complex image of the nationalist agent or leader who finds his worth among the people. That is, these films lack the communicative matrix of political orientation and authority that structure and naturalize the hegemonic status of anticolonial nationalism and the role of distinguished individual within it. Instead, they tend to dramatize and emphasize the anticolonial struggle of a more isolated and alienated male protagonist, set against a backdrop of a society in which many do not embrace or share his political creed. He acts to prove his faith in the nationalist cause. Hence, he is not automatically endowed with the aura of moral authority or power that later biographical films give their male protagonist. This aura is clearly related to the increasing use of such exceptional symbolic capital in Korean politics.

58. I owe this insight to Travis Workman, who argues that liberation, depicted through the "temporality of representing the recent past while simultaneously projecting a future for the postcolonial nation-state," is the central thematic feature of two postliberation films: *Hurrah! For Freedom* (1946) and *My Home Village* (1949). Differences in the depictions of liberation in the two films, he astutely points out, are linked to "the different views of colonial history that emerged under the U.S. and Soviet occupations." Workman, "Narrating and Aestheticizing Liberation," 2, 78. I value his insight into the primacy of liberation in these films, and slightly shift Workman's focus on the configuration of the political crisis in general to bring attention to the question of leadership in colonial or precolonial times of political crisis.

2. FILM AND THE *WAESAEK* CONTROVERSIES

1. Kwon Bodurae, "4.19nŭn wae kijŏgi toeji mothaenna" [Why did the April Revolution fail to become a miracle?], in *1960onyŏnŭl mutta* [To question 1960], by Kwon Bodurae and Chŏn Chŏnghwan (Seoul: Sangsang, 2012), 39.

2. Chŏn Chŏnghwan, "1960'ŭn wae Ilbon muhwarul choahaesŭlkka" [Why did the 1960s generation like Japanese culture?], in Kwon and Chŏn, *1960onyŏnŭl mutta,* 515.

3. A major popular magazine, *Arirang,* assigned translation of postwar Japanese literary works to young prominent Korean writers. Its release was advertised in the major newspaper *Tonga Ilbo,* and it garnered substantial attention, as its project represented the first major translation of Japanese literature in the postcolonial period. For details of this literary event, see Chŏn, "1960'ŭn wae ilbon muhwarul choahaesŭlkka," 517–25.

4. "Chaeppali ilbonyŏnghwa suip sinchŏng, ilbu ŏpcha t'aedo-e tanggukchadŭl tanghwang" [Advantageous request for Japanese film import permission catches the government agency off guard], *Tonga Ilbo,* May 5, 1960, 3.

5. "Yŏnghwa kŏmyŏrŭl wanhwa, ilhwa suipen ajik chujŏ" [Ministry relaxes film censorship but hesitates to allow Japanese film importation], *Han'guk Ilbo,* May 6, 1960, 3; "Ilyŏnghwa suip pŭlhŏ" [Japanese films not allowed], *Chosŏn Ilbo,* May 6, 1960, 3.

6. "Uri yŏnghwa taeil such'ul kyehoek, chehyŏpsŏ hŭimang chakp'ŭm chŏpsujung" [Producers' Association plans to export films to Japan, now gathers the list of films], *Han'guk Ilbo,* May 16, 1960, 4.

7. The notion of archipelago is drawn from Bruce Cumings's concept "archipelago of empire" in his book *Dominion from Sea to Sea: Pacific Ascendency and American Power* (New Haven, CT: Yale University Press, 2009), 393–96. The Asia-Pacific Film Festival was initially called the Southeast Asian Film Festival and later the Asian Film Festival. For more information on the early history of the film festival, see Lee Sangjoon, "The Emergence of the Asian Film Festival: Cold War Asia and Japan's Re-entrance into the Regional Film Festival in the 1950s," ed. Daisuke Miyao, *The Oxford Handbook of Japanese Cinema* (Oxford: Oxford University Press, 2014), 226–44.

8. Even though the government showed no signs of changing its policy, four of eleven items in the petition list were directly related to the (future) importation of Japanese films. "Pŏlssŏ ilhwa suipkwon nirigo honmihanŭn yŏnghwagye, chehyŏp yŏngbaega ch'ungdol" [Film industry shows signs of disarray over Japanese film importation as KFPA and distributors' association collide], *Han'guk Ilbo,* June 1, 1960, evening edition, 4.

9. The outright business calculation was only too apparent to film critics, importers, and distributors. Some articles expressed indignation that some sectors of the domestic film industry had failed to show contrition regarding their compliance with the propaganda campaign of the Rhee administration. See "Yŏmch'i ŏmnŭn sanghon" [Shameless commercialism], *Tonga Ilbo*, June 14, 1960, 4.

10. "Kwan-ŭi kŏmyŏlje p'yeji dung chehyŏpsŏ kŏnŭisŏ kolja" [Key ideas of the KFPA include the revision of government-led film censorship], *Kyŏnghyang Sinmun*, May 28, 1960, 4.

11. I was not able to track which four minutes were excised from the film.

12. The Hollywood films on the waiting list for review and release included *The Barbarian and the Geisha* (John Huston, 1958), *Sayonara* (Joshua Logan, 1957), and *House of Bamboo* (Samuel Fuller, 1955).

13. To be precise, the film is set in Okinawa Japan during the US occupation. A US captain Frisby is sent to Okinawa after World War II to promote democracy by establishing a school. The local people, however, want to have a teahouse instead.

14. Hollywood studios had to shoot films in Japan using Japanese staff and cast in order to circumvent the tax regulations on the film revenues in Japan. Hollywood stepped up coproduction in Europe during this period for the same reason. See Camille K. Yale, "Runaway Film Production: A Critical History of Hollywood's Outsourcing Discourse" (PhD diss., University of Urbana-Champaign, 2010).

15. Yu Hanchŏl, "Ilbongye yŏnghwa tŭngjangŭn sigi sangjo" [Too early to embrace Japanese films], *Chosŏn Ilbo*, August 17, 1960, evening edition, 4.

16. "Hŏgaŏpsi sangyŏngdoen ilhwa" [Screening Japanese films without permission], *Kyŏnghyang Sinmun*, September 25, 1960, 2.

17. "Kyoyuk kachi ittaedo ilhwa suip pparŭda" [Even with educational merit, release of Japanese films is not allowed], *Han'guk Ilbo*, September 27, 1960, 3.

18. For instance, Leni Riefenstahl's 1938 documentary *Olympia Part One: Festival of the Nations* garnered an enthusiastic response from Korean film audiences because it showcased the triumph of the Korean athlete Son Kijŏng in the marathon. The film was released twice in Korea: during the late colonial period (1940) and after liberation (1946). Its commercial success led to the release in subsequent years of culture films that featured international sports events. Hence, the sports-themed culture film was one of the most effective vehicles for conveying ideas and ideals of nationalism to film audiences. The release of *The Torch* was an attempt to benefit from the general commercial success of sports films. For details on the reception of *Olympia*, see Sim Hyegyŏng, "Han'guk sports minjok chuŭi-ŭi han kiwon" [A source of Korea's sports nationalism], in *Chiwŏnjin Han'guk yŏnghwasa: Munhwa yŏnghwaŭi an'gwa pak* [Erased Korean film history: Inside and outside the culture film], ed. Lee Sunjin et al. (Seoul: Han'guk Yŏngsang Charyowon, 2014), 187–227.

19. Serk-bae Suh, *Treacherous Translation: Culture, Nationalism, and Colonialism in Korea and Japan from the 1910s to 1960s* (Berkeley: University of California Press, 2013), 138.

20. "Ŏesaek yŏnghwa suip ch'uchŏne malssŏng" [Controversies over release permission for films of Japanese color], *Kyŏnghyang Sinmun*, November 6, 1962, 7.

21. "Ilbonsaek chit'ŭn mihwa" [American film with strong Japanese color], *Kyŏnghyang Sinmun*, December 28, 1963, 5.

22. See Ch'a T'aejin's opinion in "Chŏngdam: Hanil kuggyo yŏnghwagye-nŭn ŏttŏke toelkka?" [Interview: What are the prospects for film exchange in the time of normalization?], *Taehan Ilbo*, June 29, 1965, 5, and Yi Yŏngil's view in "Chisang t'oron: Chosok t'aegyŏl mudŭ-e tŭlttŭn yŏnye hanil kuggyo" [Debate: Status of the entertainment industry in the period of South Korea-Japan normalization], *Tonga Ilbo*, December 28, 1965, 5.

23. One anonymous critic went so far as to claim that the contemporary encroachment of Japanese film represented a cultural resurgence of Japan's late imperial ideology of the Greater Asia Co-Prosperity Sphere.

24. The most dramatic case would be the lopsided commercial success of Shin Sangok's *Sŏng ch'unhyang* over Hong Sŏnggi's *Chunhyangjŏn*. Both films were released almost simultaneously for the Chusŏk holiday, but Shin's film triumphed partly because of the appropriate color correction he applied to the film. Shin had to send the film prints to Japan for proper postproduction work.

25. "Tŭrop'i-ŭi yŏnggwang, aju yŏnghwaje" [The glory of the Asia-Pacific Film Festival], *Sŏul Sinmun*, May 20, 1962, 3.

26. The real practice of smuggling as well as the metaphor of smuggling appears frequently in the characterizations of the disreputable but uncontrollable cultural traffic between Japan and South Korea during the 1950s and early 1960s. "Meari" [Echo], *Han'guk Ilbo*, May 5, 1960, evening edition, 1.

27. "Kil t'ŭinŭn hanil yŏnghwa kyoru" [Opening the path for Korea-Japan film exchange], *Tonga Ilbo*, September 3, 1962, 5. Apparently, this shooting trip to Japan was a grueling task for cinematographer Chŏng Ilsŏng, as he and the director Kim had to use a midnight movie theater for lodging to cut expenses. See Yi Yŏnho, *Chŏngsol-ŭi nakin* [Signature of a legendary filmmaker] (Seoul: Han'guk Yŏngsang Charyowon, 2007), 32–33.

28. The Ministry of Information was also criticized for allowing the release of another "Japanese color" film, *The Bridge on the River Kwai*. An anonymous reporter criticized the board for overlooking the effect of antiwar ideology on Korean viewers, given the importance of military preparedness for waging a war against communism (*Pangong imchŏnt'aese*). "Panghwa-e sŭmyŏdŭn Ilbonsaek" [Japanese color in Korean cinema], *Kyŏnghyang Sinmun*, November 24, 1962, 8.

29. "Ilbon saekch'ae-wa yŏnghwagye: Kuksan chejakkyedo dilemma-e, *Hangbokhan Kodok*-ŭi keisŭ" [Japanese color and the Korean film industry: Dilemma within the domestic film scene, the case of *Happy Solitude*], *Tonga Ilbo*, December 8, 1963, 5.

30. The censorship documents housed at the Korean Film Archive show the injunction to eliminate images of "Japanese color." They are mostly urban scenes of Tokyo and images of Japanese dancers. "Kuksan yŏnghwa haenbokhan kodok sangyŏnghŏga" [Permission for release of the Korean film *Haengbokhan kodok*], in "*Haengbokhan kodok* kŏmyŏl sŏryu" [Censorship records of *Haengbokhan kodok*], 1963, in Han'guk Yŏngsang Charyowon kŏmyŏl sŏryu [Korean Film Archive censorship records] Korean Film Archive, Seoul.

31. Three more South Korean films set in contemporary Japan were slated for review and release: Kim Sŏngmin's *Black Glove* (*Kŏmŭn changgap*, 1963), Hong Sŏnggi and Pak Ch'an's *Tokyo Elegy* (*Tongkyŏng piga*, 1963), and Chang Ilho's *The Bridge over Hyŏnhaet'aan Strait* (*Hyŏnhaet'an-ŭi Kurŭmdari*, 1963).

32. "Ilbonsaekch'ae-ŭi yŏnghwa makaya hana" [Is it necessary to block Japanese films? The need for proper standards for film regulation], *Chosŏn Ilbo*, November 10, 1962, 5.

33. It is noteworthy that the problem of Japanese color was discussed in conjunction with other targets of film regulation, most notably the depiction of communism, and that restrictions on communism in film were one aspect of wide-ranging Cold War legislation against communist activity in Korea. The previous censorship board (the national committee on film ethics, from the Second Republic period [1960–61]) had already formalized subjects of prohibition: procommunist themes, materials harmful to public morality, and Japanese color, defined in terms of story line, physical background, and actors. (Language was not specified, although the general prohibition of Japanese color would have included prohibition of the Japanese language.) In 1962, in response to the growing complexity of the definition of Japanese color, the Ministry of Information promised flexible application, claiming that it would honor the regulations from the previous regime but carry out a "case-by-case" approach for each film under review. "Ŏesaek yŏnghwa suip ch'uchŏn-e malssŏng," 7.

34. Much of my account of the contention surrounding *Happy Solitude* is drawn from the "Ilbon saekch'ae-wa yŏnghwagye" newspaper article.

35. That said, the only permissible ground for Korean films' portrayal of Japanese people was a setting in Korea during the colonial era. This was why the ideal interethnic scenario came from Japanese literary works that visited the colonial period, such as Kajiyama Toshiyuki's *The Remembered Traces of Yi Dynasty* and *The Genealogy*, both of which were turned into films.

36. According to some estimates, forty domestic films of 1964 infringed on Japanese films. See "Hangukŭl nŏmbonŭn Ilyŏnghwa" [Japanese film aiming at Korean market], *Kyŏnghyang Sinmun*, July 10, 1965, 7. Others conjectured that almost 80 percent of all Korean films made at the time resorted to the poaching of Japanese narrative materials from one medium or another. See "Muŏsŭl makŭlkŏsin'ga" [Which element to block?], *Han'guk Ilbo*, April 30, 1964, 7.

37. "Muŏsŭl makŭlkŏsin'ga."

38. A newspaper reporter noted that all the screenplays of dubious or "nationless" origin in South Korean films were de facto Japanese works. See "Hyŏpsang 14-nyŏnmane noin hyŏnhaet'an-ŭi kagyo" [The bridge over Hyŏnhaet'an Strait that took fourteen years to build], culture section, *Sŏul Sinmun*, November 20, 1965, 1.

39. Both Yu Hanch'ŏl and Yu Hyŏnmok's views are drawn from the "Muŏsŭl makŭlkŏsin'ga" article.

40. Shin Sangok was not the director of the film. That title belongs to two directors: Im Wonsik and Na Ponghan. However, given the film's stature and scale, it would be safe to assume that Shin played a decisive role in its overall outcome. Shin also had a habit of assigning the title of directorship to his assistant when a finished film did not meet his expectations.

41. The film never received an approval for release. The year 1965 thus refers to the production year, not the release year.

42. "Hanilgan yŏbaeu kyoru" [Exchange of a Korean and a Japanese actress], *Tonga Ilbo*, April 27, 1965, 6.

43. Michi Kanako entered South Korea with a visitor's visa, worked on the film's shooting for forty days, and returned to Japan. "Hangukŭl nŏmbonŭn Ilyŏnghwa," 7.

44. For instance, in 1956 Shin Sangok started discussions with a Japanese film company and TV station about making *The Remembered Traces of Yi Dynasty*. This effort bore fruit

in 1967 with the film's release. Ibid., 7. *Romance of the Three Kingdoms* (*Samgukchi*) was also slated for coproduction. See Yi Yŏngil, "Chisang t'oron," 5.

45. The South Korean government kept stringent restrictions on civilian travel until 1989. Travel to foreign countries, including Japan, was allowed only for diplomatic, business, or education purposes.

46. Critics also noted the lack of dramatic verisimilitude in location films. The Korean characters act in exaggerated ways when they are set in a Japanese-location sequence, as if they are country bumpkins newly venturing into the dizzying urban space. See "Panghwa-e sŭmyŏdŭnŭn Ilbonjo" [The Japanese trend ingrained in Korean cinema], *Taehan Ilbo,* September 10, 1966, 5.

47. Another Zainichi actress, Yu Sumiae, appeared in Yu Hyŏnmok's 1963 film *Dreams of Youth Will Be Splendid* (*P'urŭn kkumŭn pinnari*).

48. In a rarely published discussion between Korean and Japanese film specialists in 1962, Korean film director Yu Tuhyŏn asks Japanese film critic Ogi Masahiro about the secret of Japanese film's success internationally. The latter answers by pointing out the attraction of exoticism. See "Yŏnghwain chwadamhoe: Il pyŏngron'ga-wa han kamdok" [Table talk: Japanese film critic and Korean film director], *Kyŏnghyang Sinmun,* May 18, 1962, evening edition, 4.

49. See "Chŏngdam: Hanil kuggyo, yŏnghwagye-nŭn ŏttŏggye toelga" [Debate: What would happen to the film industry after normalization?], *Taehan Ilbo,* June 29, 1965, 5, in which Korean film critics raise concerns about the wholesomeness of Japanese films and the threat of their encroachment on Korean life.

50. The release of the 1963 film *Happy Solitude* was still being blocked for violating film regulations (i.e., featuring a Japanese actor) when *Lonesome Goose* was in production in 1966.

51. "TBC-ŭi *Tonggyŏng Nagŭne,* ilbon hyŏnji chwaryŏng chungjiryŏng" [*Tokyo Vagabond* of TBC Station is ordered to stop filming], *Chungang Ilbo,* December 3, 1966, 5.

52. In the case of *Lonesome Goose,* the filmmaker never saw its completion and the Korean Film Archive database shows no trace of its production history whatsoever. It was completely erased from the official records of Korean film history. However, negative film prints and the screenplay of *Happy Solitude* are stored in the vault of the Korean Film Archive.

53. Chang Ilho's 1966 film *International Gold Robbery* (*Kukche kŭmgwe sagŏn*) also conveys an anticommunist message by showing espionage activities on behalf of North Korea in modern Japan.

54. Park Chung Hee took this position in his "Hanil hoedam t'agyŏl-e chŭŭmhan t'ŭkpyŏl tamhwamun" [Special address on agreement of normalization between South Korea and Japan], June 22, 1965, www.parkchunghee.or.kr/#!/detailed/analect/96.

3. THE MANCHURIAN ACTION FILM

1. Kim Soyoung, "Genre as Contact Zone: Hong Kong Action and Korean *Hwalkuk,*" in *Hong Kong Connections: Transnational Imagination in Action Cinema,* ed. Meaghan Morris, Siu Leung Li, and Stephen Chan Ching-kiu (Hong Kong: Hong Kong University Press, 2005), 97–110.

2. Andre Schmid, "Rediscovering Manchuria: Sin Ch'aeho and the Politics of Territorial History in Korea," *Journal of Asian Studies* 56 (1997): 26–46.

3. Ibid., 27.

4. Sin Ch'aeho, "Toksa sillon" [A new reading of history], *Taehan Maeil Sinbo*, 1908, reprinted in *Sin Ch'aeho yŏksa nonsŏljip* [Collection of Sin Ch'aeho's writings on history], ed. Chŏng Haeryŏm (Seoul: Hyŏndae Silhaksa, 1995), 57.

5. Schmid, "Rediscovering Manchuria," 34.

6. Andre Schmid, "Looking North toward Manchuria," in "Harbin and Manchuria: Place, Space and Identity," ed. Thomas Lahusen, special issue, *South Atlantic Quarterly* 99 (2000): 219–40.

7. Kim Tohyŏng, "Chŏng Kyo, Chang Chiyŏn, Yu Kŭn," in *Han'gukŭi yŏksaga-wa yŏksahak* [Korean historians and historiography], ed. Cho Tonggŏl, Han Yŏngu, and Pak Ch'ansŭng (Seoul: Ch'angjak-kwa Pipyŏngsa, 1994), 2:58.

8. Schmid, "Looking North," 229.

9. Ibid., 230.

10. Sin Ch'aeho and Chang Chiyŏn were not the only historians who shared the irredentist dream for Manchuria. Many nationalist historians who fled into exile in Manchuria during colonial times agreed on Manchuria's significance to Korea's national history as a whole. See Kim Kisŭng, "Pak Ŭnsik," in Cho, Han, and Pak, *Han'guk-ŭi yŏksaga-wa yŏksahak*, 2:100; Chŏn Uyong, "Kim Kyohŏn, Yi Sangryong," in Cho, Han, and Pak, *Han'guk-ŭi yŏksaga-wa yŏksahak*, 2:118–19.

11. Stefan Tanaka, *Japan's Orient: Rendering Pasts into History* (Berkeley: University of California Press, 1992).

12. For more on *Mansenshi*, see ibid., 246–49.

13. From the viewpoint of the Japanese Empire, Korean immigrants to Manchuria were functioning as colonial agents to carry out the "territorial osmosis" of imperialist expansion, Japan's unique empire building through encroachment into neighboring regions. See Hyun Ok Park, "Korean Manchuria: The Racial Politics of Territorial Osmosis," in "Harbin and Manchuria: Place, Space and Identity," ed. Thomas Lahusen, *South Atlantic Quarterly* 99 (Winter 2000): 193–215.

14. Schmid, "Looking North," 229.

15. Yi Hoeyŏng's life, for instance, exemplifies the hardships endured by anticolonial resisters in Manchuria. Born into one of the wealthiest and most powerful families in the late Chosŏn period, Yi liquidated his enormous family fortune to procure resources for the resistance movement when Chosŏn was annexed into Japan. He then moved to Manchuria to establish a military school for resistance guerrilla forces. He subsequently spent all his family fortune for the nationalist cause and faced extreme material hardship as a result. For an account of his tumultuous life, see Yi Tŏkil, *Anak'isŭtŭ Yi Hoeyŏng-gwa Chŏlmun Kŭdŭl* [Anarchist Yi Hoeyŏng and the young patriots] (Seoul: Ungjin Tatkŏm, 2001).

16. Robert Burgoyne, *Film Nation: Hollywood Looks at U.S. History* (Minneapolis: University of Minnesota Press, 1997), 8.

17. The preamble of South Korea's constitution makes clear this political heritage.

18. It should be noted that this interethnic romance is never actually shown in the film but is conveyed in the conversation between the Japanese higher official (future

father-in-law) and the Korean man (future son-in-law). The exclusion of the Japanese woman is not unusual in Manchurian action films, which showcase conflicts between men. In particular, the figuration of Japan and the Japanese as a military force in these films simply leaves little room for visibility of Japanese women.

19. This mode of adoption, in which marriage and adoption are conflated, is a clear violation of the immutable law of Korean family in two ways. First, it collides with the Korean rule of adoption whereby adopting a son with a different surname is prohibited. Moreover, the Korean family system treats an adopted son as a biological son. Consequently, the new adoption system would mean, in the eyes of Koreans, the permission of an incestuous relationship. Such practices met with fierce criticism and resistance from the Korean people. Hyunah Yang, "Envisioning Feminist Jurisprudence in Korean Family Law at the Crossroads of Tradition/Modernity" (PhD diss., New School of Social Research, 1998), 49–50.

20. Baek Moonim points out that *kisaeng* characters in popular colonial narratives often appear as the embodiment of traditional values, despite their dubious sexual reputations, and as the allegorical representation of the Korean nation. And because they represented violated corporal integrity, *kisaeng* women were often subject to abjection and abandonment by patriarchal and national authority. See her *Ch'unhyang-ŭi ttaldŭl: Han'guk yŏsŏng-ŭi panjjoktchari kyebohak* [Daughters of Ch'unhyang: The incomplete genealogy of Korean women] (Seoul: Ch'aeksesang, 2001), 96–98.

21. Kim Soyoung advances a similar argument regarding action films. She contends that the performativity of physical action exceeds the narrative logic and demonstrates some potentials of subversion to the dominant social ideology. See her "Genre as Contact Zone."

22. Han Sŏkchŏng, *Manchuguk kwon'guk-ŭi chaehaesŏk* [A new perspective on the formation of Manchukuo] (Pusan: Tonga University Press, 1999), 164–74.

23. Hughes, *Literature and Film*, 95.

24. Instead of using the generic term *Korean War film,* South Korean critics and filmmakers have historically used the catchall category of *anticommunist film (pan'gong yŏnghwa* in Korean) to signal a generically varied body of films that strictly comport with state politics. *Anticommunist film* signals cinematic terrain far broader and more representationally diverse than films narrowly featuring imagery of Korean War battles. It encompasses genres such as espionage, action, melodrama, film noir, musical, and children's animation. David Scott Diffrient aptly labels it an "umbrella genre" that not only corresponded to the ideological mandates of the authoritarian regimes but also entailed a greater degree of "genre intermixing." See David Scott Diffrient, "'Military Enlightenment' for the Masses: Genre and Cultural Intermixing in South Korea's Golden Age War Films," *Cinema Journal* 45, no. 1 (2005): 23.

25. Han Hyŏnmo's *March of Justice (Chŏngŭiŭi chin'gyŏk,* 1951) and Yun Pongch'un's *The Western Front (Sŏbu chŏnsŏn,* 1951) and *Footprints of the Barbarian (Orangkaeŭi paljach'wi,* 1951) are among the earliest cases of government-sponsored filmmaking. These films were designed to propagate the moral and political justification of the fight against North Korean aggression. *March of Justice* was, moreover, the first official documentary film on the Korean War to be produced by the Ministry of Defense. Lee Sunjin points out the film's significance on several registers. It was the first filmic attempt to chronicle the events of the ongoing Korean War, and it offered a cogent account of the war effort against communist aggression. The film also stresses the Korean War's international dimensions, which

filmic representations of the war in later decades have tended to downplay. See Lee Sunjin, "1950nyŏndae kongsanjuŭijaŭi chaehyŏn'gwa naengjŏnŭishik" [Representations of communists and Cold War consciousness in 1950s Korean films], in Kim Soyŏn et al., *Maehok-kwa hondon-ŭi sidae*, 138–39.

26. South Korea's capitalist mode of imagining anticolonial history becomes clear when it is juxtaposed against North Korea's cinematic rendition of the anticolonial struggle. Although the issue of money does appear in North Korean films, it never rises to the level of principal concern in the anticolonial campaign. Nor does it function as the irreplaceable kernel of the nationalist narrative. Rather, North Korean films are mainly preoccupied with the formation of national unity. The political enemy is located not only externally, that is, in the form of the Japanese enemy other, but also internally, in the form of factional strife and divisive infighting. The latter is often conceived as a more serious threat to the nationalist campaign. Much of North Korean cinema's narrative impetus is about overcoming divisive internal politics and forging a unified front for the struggle. Multivolume film series like *Star of Korea* (*Chosŏnŭi pyŏl*, Ŏm Kilsŏn, Cho Kyŏngsuk, 1980–87) and *Nation and Destiny* (*Minjoggwa unmyŏng*, numerous directors, 1991–) illustrate this thematic convention most clearly. In Shin Sangok's North Korean film *Salt* (*Sokŭm*, 1984), the female protagonist undergoes unending destitution and hardship. The abject poverty she suffers brings about the tragic disintegration of her family. Yet, despite the pressing economic issue, the film takes a dramatic turn at the end, underscoring her renewed class consciousness and determination to participate in the anticolonial struggle.

27. Slavoj Žižek, *The Plague of Fantasies*, 2nd ed. (London: Verso, 2008), 136–40.

28. Slavoj Žižek, *The Sublime Object of Ideology* (London: Verso, 1989), 65.

29. This aspect of Manchurian action films reminds us of the problematic neglect of local history and experiences that Heonik Kwon points out in his study of the Cold War discourse and imaginary. See his *Other Cold War*, 122.

30. In *The Good, the Bad, the Weird* (*Choŭnnom nappunnom isanghannom*, Kim Jeeun, 2008), Yun T'aegu, the "weird" character played by Song Kangho, gives a forceful articulation of this scavenging logic. Placed in fierce competition with two other men, that is, the good and the bad, in pursuit of the treasure map, Yun states that even thieves should respect others when it comes to stealing. He reasons that those who take action first, referring to himself, should claim ownership of the property.

4. IN THE COLONIAL ZONE OF CONTACT

1. Although I use the adjective *generic* to refer to an aggregate of films that share recurring tropes, imagery and narrative, and thematic conventions, my use of the term *genre* includes the more historically specific development of the film cycle. I elaborate on this dimension of film terminology in more detail later.

2. In this regard, the South Korean gangster film differs from its American counterpart, although the two do seem to share thematization of the individual struggle for success in times of political turmoil and social crisis. In the case of classic Hollywood gangster films, the archetypical films emerged during the Great Depression.

3. The colonial discourse of the *kisaeng* courtesan takes us into quite different historical implications. The *kisaeng* effectively became an icon of colonial Korea through modern

technologies of image reproduction. Under colonial rule, the image of *kisaeng* proliferated in many visual materials, particularly in tourism promotions, and inculcated particular ways of perceiving the figure of female entertainer as an object of fascination and desire for the beholder. Often featured against a backdrop of landmark architecture of the bygone era, such images of *kisaeng* naturalized and privileged the colonizers' modern subjecthood through the colonialist gaze. Yet the early gangster films seem to counteract the colonialist view of the *kisaeng*, often by pairing her with the agile and muscular Korean protagonist. For the *kisaeng* as icon of Korean culture and as object of colonizers' fascination, see Atkins, *Primitive Selves*.

4. Though these *kisaeng* films are set in the colonial period, the 1960s and 1970s saw a surge of *kisaeng*-themed films set in postcolonial, contemporary settings, such as *Mother Kisaeng* (*Ŏmma Kisaeng*; Pak Yun'gyo, 1968), *I Demand No Condition* (*Na-ege chogŏnŭn ŏptta*; Kang Taesŏn, 1971), *Although We Are Now Strangers* (*Chigŭmŭn namijiman*; Cho Munjin, 1971), and *Live Well, My Daughters* (*Chal saradao nae ttaldŭra*; Kim Sŏn'gyŏng, 1972).

5. The dramatic arc of the latter group is similar to that of a subset of social problem films in Hollywood called the "fallen woman" film cycle of the silent and early talkie film era. These films typically salaciously thematized the subject of female prostitution and its moral and social consequences. See Lea Jacobs, *The Wages of Sin: Censorship and the Fallen Woman Film, 1928–1942* (Berkeley: University of California Press, 1997).

6. To be precise, the heyday of *kisaeng* films predates that of gangster films. Manchurian action films and swordplay films (*muhyŏpmul*) are antecedent action films (*hwalguk*) of the mid-1960s and 1970s. In the case of Manchurian action films, the theme of nationalist struggle against the colonial forces is explicit and central.

7. In contrast, the gangster is not the destined mate for the *kisaeng* character in *kisaeng* films. The heterosexual couple consists of an upper-class man of the Korean elite and a *kisaeng*, a disparity that results in her eventual demise.

8. Rey Chow, "Film as Ethnography: Or, Translation between Cultures in the Postcolonial World," in *The Rey Chow Reader*, ed. Paul Bowman (New York: Columbia University Press, 2010), 150, 153.

9. Ibid., 150, 152.

10. Ibid., 153.

11. Ibid.

12. Most notably, I owe an intellectual debt to Heonik Kwon, whose comprehensive critical overview on the epistemological contours of the modern bipolar political order called the Cold War shaped my approach to filmic representation of colonialism as a part of the South Korea's cultural production of the Cold War. See Heonik Kwon, *Other Cold War*.

13. Zaki Laïdi, *A World without Meaning: A Crisis of Meaning in International Politics* (New York: Routledge, 1998), 17, cited in Heonik Kwon, *Other Cold War*, 5.

14. Christian G. Appy, "Introduction: Struggling for the World," in *Cold War Constructions: The Political Culture of United States Imperialism, 1945–1966*, ed. Christian G. Appy (Amherst: University of Massachusetts Press, 2000), 3, cited in Kwon, *Other Cold War*, 6.

15. Kwon, *Other Cold War*, 122; Seungsook Moon, *Militarized Modernity and Gendered Citizenship in South Korea* (Durham, NC: Duke University Press, 2005).

16. Indeed, this intersection in my view remains woefully underexamined in Korean film studies. The political rhetoric and discourse of the dominant-imaginary Cold War have

always permeated and affected the local memories of violent political upheavals, although those local memories have maintained a contrarian integrity and voice.

17. It is through the subordination and adjustment of local knowledge to the larger schema of global politics that the dominant Cold War political agenda holds great discursive efficiency and sway over the population. As Heonik Kwon repeatedly reminds us in *Other Cold War*, the modern reality of the Cold War comes into full view only through dialectical understanding of two seemingly incompatible visions: the global construction of it in the West and local experiences of it in the postcolonial world.

18. Out of six films he directed in 1967, four directly or indirectly deal with the theme of colonialism. These colonial-themed films are *I Yearn to Go, Youth Theater, Kang Myŏnghwa,* and *Miracle of Gratitude (Poŭn-ŭi kijŏk).*

19. Examples of *kisaeng* films set in the colonial era include *The Lady of Myŏngwŏlgwan* (*Myŏngwŏlgwan ass;* Pak Chongho, 1967), *Blue Light, Red Light* (*Chŏngdŭng hongdŭng;* Yi Hyŏngp'yo, 1968), *Jade Hairpin* (*Okpinyŏ;* Kang Taejin, 1968), *Goodbye Seoul* (*Sŏuriyŏ annyŏng;* Chang Ilho, 1969), and *A Camellia Blossoms and Falls* (*Tongbaekkot p'igo chigo;* Chŏng Chinu, 1970). *Kang Myŏnghwa* was also noteworthy for catapulting the little-known actress Yun Chŏnghŭi, who played the title role, to stardom. She subsequently ended up playing the female lead in over thirty films by the end of the decade.

20. Yi Yŏngil criticizes reactionary *sinpa* melodramas for their inattention to contemporary social change and cultural developments and compares them unfavorably to early 1960s family melodramas, in which present conflicts between social values and individual agency come into clear view. I would note, however, that this criticism does not properly consider the late 1960s resurgence of films portraying colonial culture. *Kisaeng* films should be viewed as reacting against the previous film depictions of the colonial era, which mostly did not assess colonial culture. See his *Han'guk yŏnghwa chŏnsa,* 353–54.

21. Kwon Bodurae, *Yŏnae-ŭi sidae: 1920-yŏndae ch'oban ŭi munhwa wa yuhaeng* [Age of Love: Culture and trends of the early 1920s] (Seoul: Hyŏnsil munhwa yŏn'gu, 2003).

22. According to Kwon Bodurae (in ibid.), Chang did not commit suicide for love immediately after Kang's death. Rather, he led a life of debauchery for nearly a year before he committed suicide. There are different accounts of his death in subsequent popular narratives. A 1927 novel by Yi Haegwan recounts it as a ghost story in which the resentful ghost of Kang brings about Chang's downfall. An anonymous 1935 version of the tale portrays his death as the result of his abysmal despair over the loss of love. The film version is closer in spirit to the later version, which emphasizes the couple's enduring bond of love.

23. See Paek Munim, "1950 nyŏndae huban 'munye'rosŏ sinario-ŭi ŭimi" [Meaning of the screenplay as literary art in the late 1950s], in Kim Soyŏn et al., *Maehokkwa hondon-ŭi sidae.*

24. An image of student youth being rowdy presupposes implicit social tolerance and sanction, which register the unique and stable terrain of urban culture in cinematic representation. That is, the highlighted enjoyment of social privilege presupposes the lack of a nationalist consciousness or concerns for reclaiming sovereignty and independence. Instead, the focus has shifted to a reality where colonial rule is now firmly established.

25. In films such as *Nameless Stars* (*Irŭmŏmnŭn pyŏldŭl*) or *Evergreen* (*Sangnoksu*), students embody ideal types of leadership: devoting oneself to the cause of the nation and embracing the dire consequences of doing so. In other words, they emerge as icons of an enlightenment project that captured the imagination of many intellectuals in the early years

of the colonial period. For a more detailed articulation of the enlightenment in Korean cinema, see Chung, *Split Screen Korea*.

26. It should be noted that in previous films about the colonial era the nighttime urban streets are sterile and empty, and there is no sense of neighborly connection among Koreans (or with the Japanese). Neighborly social interaction itself is largely missing from filmic representations of the colonial past.

27. There is, of course, an opposite case as well. *Evil Flower Pae Chŏngja* (*Yohwa Pae Chŏngja;* Yi Kyuung, 1966) features the notorious historic female collaborator Pae Chŏngja, who makes herself available only to powerful Japanese figures. Her sexuality is one of the most explicit markers of Otherness that incites the anger and indignation of Koreans.

28. Myŏngwŏlgwan is a renowned Korean-cuisine restaurant in Seoul that frequently appears in *kisaeng* narratives. It has become a metonym for all *kisaeng* houses in cinematic representation. Instead of using fictitious names, *kisaeng*-themed films frequently invoke this restaurant, turning it into a near-iconic brand of the business. According to records, the dance performances of *kisaeng* were the main attraction at Myŏngwŏlgwan. During the colonial period, *kisaeng* houses like Myŏngwŏlgwan were one of the main attractions for Japanese tourists in Korea.

29. In many postcard photos from the colonial era, *kisaeng* do not register this visual misalignment. They are discursively constructed to embody Korea's passive femininity. Often juxtaposed with nostalgia-inducing images of Korea's past such as palaces and other premodern landmark sites, the imaged *kisaeng* gaze back at the anonymous viewer in order to anchor, stabilize, and naturalize the colonial observer's fascination with the colonized body. The aura of melancholia associated with the *kisaeng* image has to do in part with this particular positioning of passivity, which the film *Kang Myŏnghwa* largely dispels in the *kisaeng* house sequence here. For a detailed examination of the *kisaeng* image in colonial photography, see Yi Kyŏngmin, *Kisaengŭn ottŏkke mandŭrŏjŏnnŭn'ga* [How *kisaeng* was constructed] (Seoul: Sajin Akaibŭ Yŏn'guso, 2004).

30. We find a similar instance of a female entertainer forced to pour a glass in Im Kwont'aek's *Sopyonje*, in which a young girl, Songhwa, who is ignorant of the act's sexual implications, complies with the elderly men who press her to do so. Songhwa's father Yubong intervenes, only to face humiliation by the unruly male clients. Yubong later violently punishes Songhwa for thoughtlessly submitting to the men's pressure.

31. The imagery of this leisurely nighttime stroll once again dispels the aura of danger and surveillance that other films in a colonial urban setting habitually depict. Instead, it echoes and adheres to visual tropes of romance in other postwar Korean melodrama films, most notably *Drifting Island* (*P'yorudo;* Kwon Yŏngsun, 1960), which uses the serene streets in the vicinity of the old palace as the principal space of romance.

32. Their most cherished plan for their daughter's future is to marry her off to a wealthy man as a concubine.

33. The couple ultimately return to the same room in the resort to commit double suicide.

34. This sense of new possibility is accentuated by the reversed domestic gender roles of the honeymoon couple: Chang prepares dinner to please his wife Kang.

35. How did this positive depiction of Japanese life pass the watchful inspection of film censors? As it turned out, the censorship board ordered the removal of the sequence and the production company complied. The existing film print at the Korean Film Archive shows

the sequence intact because the film prints archived there are often early versions that have not yet undergone their prerelease review and censorship by state authorities. That said, the existing film prints at the Korean Film Archive are not the actual release in many cases. Cases of disparity between the release prints and archival prints are too numerous to list. Notable examples include such prominent works as Shin Sangok's *Romance Papa* (*Romaensŭ ppappa*, 1960), Kim Kiyoung's *The Housemaid* (*Hanyŏ*, 1960), and Yu Hyŏnmok's *Spring Dream* (*Ch'unmong*, 1965). Problematic dialogues and scenes have been removed from the original prints. *Spring Dream* is one of the most extreme cases, for the film was excessively censored and the director faced criminal charges for violating obscenity rules on the screen. The archive's print, however, shows no signs of excisions by authorities.

36. The most renowned film example would be Shin Sangok's 1967 film *The Remembered Traces of the Yi Dynasty* (*Ijojanyŏng*).

37. For elaboration on this conceptualization of money, see chapter 3 on the Manchurian action film.

38. The failure of the colonial police is later compounded by their complicity with the local Japanese gang as a supplement to the state apparatus to conquer and dominate the hidden enclave of Koreans.

39. This performative feature reminds us of the role that the prologue character plays at the beginning of many films. A prologue character appears as someone outside the diegetic world of drama, often telling the audience what to expect from the ensuing dramatic presentation. The central dynamic here is how the prologue character leads the audience to suspend disbelief in the dramatic events that follow.

40. I draw my reading here from Slavoj Žižek's insight into the conditional nature of belief and the function of the prologue character. See *The Pervert's Guide to Cinema* (dir. Sophie Fiennes, 2008).

41. Na Kwanjung is the best-dressed gangster in the film. His poise and charisma are signaled by the immaculate Western suit he wears. As in many gangster films, the suit connotes mature masculinity and urban material aspiration.

42. It is revealing that the meeting takes place at a Western-style tavern. The place registers social activities and cultural interactions distinct from those of the *kisaeng* house. The latter functions as the indigenous site of local ritual and custom, as it has the aura of a private home in the film.

43. She is also an orphan, like Tuhan is. Later, she represents the moral principle of uncompromising resistance to Japanese aggression and violence.

44. After being humiliatingly defeated by Shinmajŏk's attack, Tuhan takes refuge at a remote Buddhist temple, where the film chronicles his speedy recovery and his subsequent physical training for combat. Tropes of martial arts films are unmistakable in this sequence. Tuhan appears as a martial artist who retreats from public life for training after witnessing the successful attack against of his training school. The film builds anticipation for Tuhan's revenge, not only through his strenuous exercise, but also through the moral encouragement of his *kisaeng* girlfriend Sŏlhwa and his student subordinate Sŏngmin. Sŏlhwa practically functions as a wife, tending to him as he recovers and trains to perfect his art. She is also the voice of absolute moral principle, as she demands that Tuhan take righteous revenge. Hence, even in the absence of Na, Tuhan's education continues, and the student subordinate Sŏngmin bears witness to this moral teaching.

45. The wedding indicates how this gangster film is preoccupied with the staging of social rituals. Despite the series of crises in which he is embroiled, Tuhan is able to participate in ritual events, restoring to the Koreans an ambiance of everyday social life, internal order, and a sense of continuity that is typically impossible in the conventional imagination of films set in the colonial situation. It should be noted that the wedding itself is totally anachronistic, for it does not offer even a minimal sense of historical authenticity. It is the performative dimension of the social act that is important here. Rather than bringing attention to realistic details of the wedding as a social event in the colonial era, the film emphasizes the ideological effects of ritual. The wedding is also the occasion of social cohesion in that the beggars also join in the celebration.

46. The Japanese boss is quite clear about his intention: his sexual violence against Sŏlhwa is designed to anger Tuhan. This is a barbarous act that changes the very nature of the resistance struggle. Because the damage that the Japanese inflicts is grossly excessive, it cannot be reciprocated in exact terms. Nor can any meaningful value be drawn from the retribution. The subsequent action by Tuhan's forces is not about avenging the dead, but about appropriating the event of Sŏlhwa's rape and murder for the agenda of defeating the rival Japanese gang. This dilemma characterizes many of the rape-themed revenge films of the 1970s that are set in the colonial era.

47. In fact, Sŏlhwa's death results in part from her giving advice to her husband on propriety regarding a death. When Tuhan is engulfed in the anger over the death of his subordinate and brother-in-law, Sŏngmin, she asks him to postpone taking action and instead to visit Chiyŏng, a young widow who is grieving over the loss of her beloved husband. Tuhan follows her advice, but his departure leaves Sŏlhwa completely vulnerable to the Japanese assault.

48. However, Shinmajŏk dies in the battle at the end, an outcome that seems to underscore the nationalist ideology that the figure of dual affiliations should be eliminated.

5. HORROR AND REVENGE

1. The film's release year (1966) immediately followed the normalization treaty between Japan and Korea in 1965, which had a profound impact on the subsequent filmic representation of Japan as the former colonizer. The fact that *Yeraishang* sets its drama against the backdrop of the April Revolution of 1960s further complicates the renewed urgency for decolonization that seems to pervade the films of the postnormalization period.

2. *Epitaph* is the only film outside the general range of the period that this manuscript covers, which is from 1945 to the 1970s. I justify its inclusion in part because as a horror film it holds a unique place in the constellation of colonial representation in South Korean cinema. In addition, the film's portrayal of a fascination with and nostalgia for an alluring colonial order offers a stark contrast to the subversive theme of memory and violence in *Yeraishang*.

3. The film is the story of a female protagonist, Wŏlhyang, whose dual devotion to her brother (a nationalist resistance fighter) and her husband (a successful businessman) leads her to choose the life of a *kisaeng* courtesan. This decision later stigmatizes her, and a series of destabilizing events, including her husband's betrayal, her exposure to a murder scheme, and poor health lead to her unjust death. Wŏlhyang then resurfaces as a vengeful ghost, going after individuals responsible for her suffering and death. Refashioning the motif of the

traditional ghost narrative, the film presents the female ghost as a vengeful but essentially moral figure whose pent-up resentment of injustice demands the repentance of others. The film's ending offers the fulfillment of the dramatic premise, as the husband now regrets his wrongdoing and pledges in front of her grave that he will honor her sacrifice and look after their child's upbringing.

4. For instance, Paek Munim argues that the female ghost has been an important motif in popular cinema to thematize the complex problem of colonial experience. Kyung Hyun Kim points out that the female protagonist Wŏlhyang possesses a surprising agency and power as a vengeful figure despite her initial position as *nui tongsaeng* (sister) to others. See Baek Moonim, *Wŏlha-ŭi yŏgoksŏng: Yŏgwiro ingŭn Han'guk* [Scream under the moon: Reading Korea through the figure of the female ghost] (Seoul: Ch'aeksesang, 2008); Kyung Hyun Kim, *Virtual Hallyu*, 73, 74.

5. The film makes clear its linkage to the horror genre early on by showcasing semantic properties of the genre even prior to the appearance of the monster narrator. By *semantic properties,* I am referring to the vista of the cemetery, the high-pitched theremin sound, the floating will-o'-the-wisp, and the high scream of a woman that make up the brief opening credit sequence.

6. *Public Cemetery* belongs to a low-budget horror film cycle of the late 1960s that was based on a provincial network of film production, distribution, and exhibition, in contrast to high-budget film productions, which typically were financed by investment capital drawn from greater Seoul-area theater chains. The limited budget in part explains the film's resort to the receding but resilient *sinpa* form.

7. From the 1950s, *sinpa* drama and *pyŏnsa* narration, in particular, were continuously criticized and devalued. The *sinpa* mode has been criticized for its overt sentimentalism and its embrace of a fatalistic worldview. Critics often regarded (social) realism as a politically sound corrective to the corrupting influence of the *sinpa* mode.

8. Bliss Cua Lim, *Translating Time: Cinema, the Fantastic, and Temporal Critique* (Durham, NC: Duke University Press, 2009).

9. Bruce Cumings, *Korea's Place in the Sun: A Modern History* (New York: W. W. Norton, 1997), 345.

10. The conventional historical account of the April Revolution tends to focus almost entirely on the merit of the narrowly defined political achievement, that is, the democratic victory that ended a corrupt and authoritarian regime. Because the reactionary coup in 1961 eclipsed the revolution within a year, the revolution was narrowly characterized as a student-led rebellion of youthful energy and untainted innocence but also as the wellspring of subsequent social disarray, confusion. and corruption.

11. To understand the illustrious career of Chung Chang Wha as a master of the action genre in Korea and Hong Kong, see Aaron Han Joon Magnan-Park, "Restoring the Transnational from the Abyss of Ethnonational Film Historiography: The Case of Chung Chang Wha," *Journal of Korean Studies* 16, no. 2 (Fall 2011): 249–84.

12. The film *Yeraishang* is based on a daily radio drama of the same title by Kim Sŏkya. The series aired during evening prime time on TBC Radio in 1965. The title *Yeraishang* is a Korean rendition of the Chinese pronunciation of the word for night-blooming jasmine (*yè lái xiāng* 夜來香), an evergreen woody shrub known for its powerful nocturnal fragrance. In the film, it is a nickname of the female protagonist, a nightclub waitress.

13. In this regard, *Yeraishang* shares with contemporaneous Manchurian action films the moral and political justification of the use of violence to deal with the historical dilemma of colonialism. See An Jinsoo, "Manju action yŏnghwa-ŭi mohohan minjok chuŭi" [Ambiguous nationalism in Manchurian action films], *Manju Hakhoe* 8 (2008): 199–229.

14. This does not mean, however, that all social malice and problems are eliminated by the revolution. The film diverges from the historicist frame of reference by setting the entire arc of diegetic events in the prolonged ambiance of revolution.

15. The pattern of their courtship illustrates how the film resorts to the ideology of national unity typically found in films of militant anticolonial struggle, most notably Manchurian action films. Films such as *Farewell to Tumen River* and *Continent on Fire* underscore the utility of woman's labor, specifically the type of labor visible in the pleasure quarters of society, in forging a nationalist coalition to fight against colonial oppression. According to this scenario, the female character working outside the domain of traditional domesticity is not denigrated for her disreputable profession. If anything, these films regard her ability to lure enemy men as a valuable intelligence asset to the larger nationalist cause. Concurrently, there is no equivocation on the virtuousness of her character, as she remains completely faithful to the Korean man she loves. It is her unwavering support and loyalty that distinguishes the Korean men who are in competition with other ethnic men. *Yeraishang* hence restages the gendered configuration of the anticolonial struggle in its valorization of the romantic relationship. See chapter 3 above on Manchurian action films.

16. Once again, *Arirang* illustrates the workings of this gendered pattern of the nationalist imaginary par excellence. The antagonist Kiho's sexual assault on Yŏnghui, which subsequently triggers the violent retaliatory response of the protagonist, Yŏngjin, is almost always understood as an allegory of the nation according to which the nation's subjugation to colonial rule takes a distinctively gendered, that is, feminized, form. Im Kwont'aek's film *Sopyonje* (1993) replicates this gendered pattern of the nationalist imaginary through a story of the traditional art of *pansori* singing in decline.

17. See chapter 3 above on Manchurian action films for an analysis of the significance of money.

18. For an illuminating discussion of colonial collaboration and its social and historiographical dimensions, see De Ceuster, "Nation Exorcised."

19. After the fall of the Rhee administration, Park immediately senses the drastic change. He orders his right-hand man to send money, which was originally designated to bribe corrupt politicians, to a relief fund. He also makes sure that his "humanitarian" endeavor receives full press coverage. His actions illustrate the successful modus operandi of an ex-collaborator businessman: opportunism, bribery, and public relations.

20. Korean horror films are typically released during summer to appeal to the young teenage audience. *Epitaph* was one of five horror films to appear in the summer of 2007. Perhaps because of fierce competition, the film did not do well at the box office but received highly favorable critical reviews. Despite the film's poor commercial performance, an audience campaign led to the film's re-release, a phenomenon that testifies to the film's exceptional quality and the existence of a core audience group. It is now considered one of the finest films of 2007.

21. For close analysis of aesthetic strategies in *A Tale of Two Sisters*, see Jinhee Choi, *The South Korean Film Renaissance: Local Hitmakers, Global Provocateurs* (Middletown, CT: Wesleyan University Press, 2010), 160–63.

22. For a treatment of all three episodes, see Kyung Hyun Kim, *Virtual Hallyu*, 75–79.

23. She is a benevolent manager-owner whose Japanese ethnicity never becomes an issue among Koreans working in the hospital. Despite her ethnic difference, Korean doctors and nurses alike show respect toward her, and she reciprocates with expected civility toward her employees.

24. In contrast, the Japanese female monk who officiates the ritual is clearly shown to viewers but with a strange sense of unfamiliarity and uncanniness.

25. In the second episode, the modern method of psychoanalysis fails to figure out the root cause of a child's trauma, whereas the last episode similarly emphasizes the downfall of a couple who do not know the origins of their suffering.

26. Although striking in its bold expression of interethnic romance, this sort of unabashed consummation is not the first instance in the history of South Korean cinema. Maverick filmmaker Kim Kiyoung, who is known for his "diabolic" imagination in the domestic horror thriller genre, first foregrounded this theme in his 1961 film *Over Hyŏnhaetanŭn* (*Hyŏnhaetanŭn algo itta;* aka *The Sea Knows*). In Kim's film, the Korean male protagonist chooses marriage with a Japanese woman over the nationalist call to join the resistance army to fight the Japanese Empire.

27. Here I am relying on the psychoanalytic notion of fantasy as the possible answer to the impossible question and demand of the unfathomable Other.

28. For instance, he is excluded from the funeral ceremony that the Japanese monk was officiating, even though he is working at the morgue.

29. I am borrowing the notion of perversion that Slavoj Žižek elaborated with regard to the big Other, i.e., the symbolic order that offers and regulates the meanings of one's existence. According to Žižek, the pervert is the person who identifies himself with the symbolic Law and further imagines himself as its instrument, all because he attempts to evade the nonexistence of the big Other. "Perversion is a double strategy to counteract this nonexistence: an (ultimately deeply conservative, nostalgic) attempt to install the law artificially, in the desperate hope that we will then take this self-posited limitation 'seriously,' and in a complementary way, a no less desperate attempt to codify the very transgression of the Law." See Slavoj Žižek, *The Puppet and the Dwarf: The Perverse Core of Christianity* (Cambridge, MA: MIT Press, 2003), 53.

30. Aoi's tears can be read as genuine sympathy from the true victim toward the subject (Chŏngnam), who fails to confront or understand the cause of the historic injustice.

31. There seems to be an implicit understanding that recent films that dramatize the colonial experience are revisionist in orientation, as they foreground the lure of the urban attractions associated with colonial modernity. The case of *Epitaph,* however, informs us otherwise: it stages an intransigent, perverse desire for the eternity and permanence of the Japanese Empire at the heart of the ghost narrative.

CODA

1. The film faithfully follows the "aesthetics of verticality"—a distinctive feature of CGI-dominated Hollywood blockbuster films in which the individual's agency to overcome the physical laws of nature through vertical movement, i.e., flying through the air and levitating, finds its most distinctive manifestation. The film's action climax hence testifies to the global circulation of Hollywood blockbuster aesthetics through its imaginative appropriation by

non-Hollywood filmmaking machinery. Kristen Whissel, "Tales of Upward Mobility: The New Verticality and Digital Special Effects," *Film Quarterly* 59, no. 4 (Summer 2006): 23–34.

2. Michael Robinson, "Contemporary Cultural Production in South Korea: Vanishing Meta-narratives of Nation," in *New Korean Cinema*, ed. Shin Chi-Yun and Julian Stringer (New York: New York University Press, 2005), 15–31.

3. Here I am referring to the publication of such books as Kim Chinsong's *Permit Dance Halls in Seoul* (*Sŏul e ttansŭhorŭl hŏhara*), which galvanized public interest in the popular and urban culture of the colonial period. This "cultural turn" toward the colonial period also triggered a continuing debate on the nature of colonial modernity, significantly challenging the nationalist historiography. Kim Chin-song, *Sŏul e ttansŭhorŭl hŏhara: Hyŏndaesŏng ŭi hyŏngsŏng* [Permit dance halls in Seoul: The formation of modernity] (Seoul: Hyŏnsil Munhwa Yŏn'gu Yŏn'gusil, 1999).

4. I made an exception to include the 2007 film *Epitaph* in the main body of this book because of its unique status within horror film. As I explained in the main section of chapter 5, horror and revenge drama is preoccupied with the distinctive thematic convention of "the return," which straddles the epistemological divide between the colonial past and the postcolonial present. Although *Epitaph* shares some of the key characteristics of the post-2000 films on the colonial past, its thematic resonance with pre-2000 films needs to be underscored. That is, the genre film's stringent adherence to the question of unaddressed past injustice through the theme of a "return of the repressed"—as well as to perverse desire and nostalgia for the Japanese other—sets *Epitaph* apart from its contemporary works.

BIBLIOGRAPHY

An, Jinsoo. "Manju action yŏnghwa-ŭi mohohan minjok chuŭi" [Ambiguous nationalism in Manchurian action films]. *Manju Hakhoe* 8 (2008): 199–229.

———. "Screening the Redemption: Christianity in Korean Melodrama." In *South Korean Golden Age Melodrama: Gender, Genre, and National Cinema,* edited by Kathleen McHugh and Nancy Abelmann, 65–97. Detroit, MI: Wayne State University Press, 2005.

An, Sŏkyŏng. "Yŏnghwa-ŭi chajenan, chŏngch'i munhwa-wa tongsi haegyŏl" [Shortage of film facilities should be solved along with the political and cultural problems]. *Kyŏnghyang Sinmun,* December 15, 1946, 2.

Anderson, Benedict. *Imagined Communities: Reflections on the Origin and Spread of Nationalism.* New York: Verso, 2006.

Appy, Christian G., ed. "Introduction: Struggling for the World." In *Cold War Constructions: The Political Culture of United States Imperialism, 1945–1966.* Amherst: University of Massachusetts Press, 2000.

Atkins, E. Taylor. *Primitive Selves: Koreana in the Japanese Colonial Gaze, 1910–1945.* Colonialisms. Berkeley: University of California Press, 2010.

Baek, Munim. "1950 nyŏndae huban 'munye'rosŏ sinario-ŭi ŭimi" [The meaning of the screenplay as literary art in the late 1950s]. In Kim Soyŏn et al., *Maehok-kwa hondon-ŭi sidae,* 205.

———. *Ch'unhyang-ŭi ttaldŭl: Han'guk yŏsŏng-ŭi panjjoktchari Kyebohak* [Daughters of Ch'unhyang: The incomplete genealogy of Korean women]. Seoul: Ch'aeksesang, 2001.

———. *Wŏlha-ŭi yŏgoksŏng: Yŏgwiro ingŭn Han'guk* [Scream under the moon: Reading Korea through the figure of the female ghost]. Seoul: Ch'aeksesang, 2008.

Baskett, Michael. *The Attractive Empire: Transnational Film Culture in Imperial Japan.* Honolulu: University of Hawai'i Press, 2008.

Bordwell, David, and Kristin Thompson. *Film Art: An Introduction.* 10th ed. New York: McGraw-Hill, 2013.

Burgoyne, Robert. *Film Nation: Hollywood Looks at U.S. History.* Minneapolis: University of Minnesota Press, 1997.

Certeau, Michel de. *The Practice of Everyday Life.* Translated by Steven Rendall. Berkeley: University of California Press, 2011.

Ceuster, Koen de. "The Nation Exorcised: The Historiography of Collaboration in South Korea." *Korean Studies* 25, no. 2 (2001): 207–42.

———. "Wholesome Education and Sound Leisure: The YMCA Sports Programme in Colonial Korea." *European Journal of East Asian Studies* 2, no. 1 (2003): 53–88.

Ch'a, T'aejin. "Chŏngdam: Hanil kuggyo yŏnghwagye-nŭn ŏttŏke toelkka?" [Interview: What are the prospects for film exchange in the era of normalization?]. *Taehan Ilbo,* June 29, 1965, 5.

"Chaeppali ilbonyŏnghwa suip sinchŏng, ilbu ŏpcha t'aedo-e tanggukchadŭl tanghwang" [Advantageous request for Japanese film import permission catches the government agency off guard]. *Tonga Ilbo,* May 5, 1960, 3.

Chatterjee, Partha. *The Nation and Its Fragments: Colonial and Postcolonial Histories.* Princeton, NJ: Princeton University Press, 1993.

Cho, Hyejŏng. "Migunjŏngi yŏnghwa chŏngch'aek-e kwanhan yŏn'gu" [A study on American occupation era film policy]. PhD diss., Chungang University, 1997.

Cho, Tonggŏl, Han Yŏngu, and Pak Ch'ansŭng, eds. *Han'guk-ŭi yŏksaga-wa yŏksahak* [Korean historians and historiography]. Vol. 2. Seoul: Ch'angjak-kwa Pip'yŏngsa, 1994.

Choi, Jinhee. *The South Korean Film Renaissance: Local Hitmakers, Global Provocateurs.* Wesleyan Film. Middletown, CT: Wesleyan University Press, 2010.

Chŏn, Chŏnghwan. "1960'ŭn wae Ilbon muhwarul choahaesŭlkka" [Why did the 1960s generation like Japanese culture?]. In *1960onyŏnŭl mutta* [To question 1960], by Kwon Podŭre and Chŏn Chŏnghwan, 515. Seoul: Sangsang, 2012.

Chŏn, Uyong. "Kim Kyohŏn, Yi Sangryong." In Cho, Han, and Pak, *Han'guk-ŭi yŏksaga-wa yŏksahak,* 2:118–19.

Chŏng, Kŭnsik, and Kyeonghee Choi. "Haebang hu kŏmnyŏl ch'eje-ŭi yŏn'gurŭl wihan myŏkkaji chilmun-gwa kwaje: Singminji yusan-ŭi chongsik-kwa chaep'ŏnsai-esŏ (1945–1952)" [A few questions and issues on the study of the postliberation censorship system: Between the closure and the continuity of the colonial legacy (1945–1952)]. *Taedong Munhwa Yŏn'gu* 74 (2011): 7–70.

"Chŏngdam: Hanil kuggyo, yŏnghwagye-nŭn ŏttŏggye toelga" [Debate: What would happen to the film industry after normalization?]. *Taehan Ilbo,* June 29, 1965, 5.

Chow, Rey. "Film as Ethnography; or, Translation between Cultures in the Postcolonial World." In *The Rey Chow Reader,* edited by Paul Bowman, 148–70. New York: Columbia University Press, 2010.

Chung, Steven. *Split Screen Korea: Shin Sang-ok and Postwar Cinema.* Minneapolis: University of Minnesota Press, 2014.

Cumings, Bruce. *Dominion from Sea to Sea: Pacific Ascendency and American Power.* New Haven, CT: Yale University Press, 2009.

———. *Korea's Place in the Sun: A Modern History.* New York: W. W. Norton, 1997.

Diffrient, David Scott. "Han'guk Heroism: Cinematic Spectacle and the Postwar Cultural Politics of *Red Muffler.*" In *South Korean Golden Age Melodrama: Gender, Genre and*

National Cinema, edited by Kathleen McHugh and Nancy Abelmann, 151–83. Detroit, MI: Wayne State University Press, 2005.

——. "'Military Enlightenment' for the Masses: Genre and Cultural Intermixing in South Korea's Golden Age War Films." *Cinema Journal* 45, no. 1 (Autumn 2005): 22–49.

Duara, Prasenjit. *Rescuing History from the Nation: Questioning Narratives of Modern China*. Chicago: University of Chicago Press, 1995.

Eckert, Carter J., Ki-baek Yi, Young Ick Lew, Michael Robinson, and Edward W. Wagner, eds. *Korea Old and New: A History*. Seoul: Ilchogak, 1990.

Fujitani, Takashi. *Race for Empire: Koreans as Japanese and Japanese as Americans during World War II*. Berkeley: University of California Press, 2011.

Han, Sŏkchŏng. *Haebang konggan-ŭi yŏnghwa, yŏnghwain* [Films and filmmakers in the space of liberation]. Seoul: Iron-gwa silchŏn, 2013.

——. *Manchuguk kwon'guk-ŭi chaehaesŏk* [A new perspective on the formation of Manchukuo]. Pusan: Tonga University Press, 1999.

"Hangukŭl nŏmbonŭn Ilyŏnghwa" [Japanese film aiming at Korean market]. *Kyŏnghyang Sinmun*, July 10, 1965, 7.

"Hanilgan yŏbaeu kyoru" [Exchange of a Korean and a Japanese actress]. *Tonga Ilbo*, April 27, 1965, 6.

"Hŏgaŏpsi sangyŏngdoen ilhwa" [Screening Japanese films without permission]. *Kyŏnghyang Sinmun*, September 25, 1960, 2.

Hong, Kal. *Aesthetic Constructions of Korean Nationalism: Spectacle, Politics, and History.* Asia's Transformations. New York: Routledge, 2011.

Hughes, Theodore H. *Literature and Film in Cold War South Korea: Freedom's Frontier*. New York: Columbia University Press, 2012.

"Hyŏpsang 14-nyŏnmane noin hyŏnhaet'an-ŭi kagyo" [The bridge over Hyŏnhaet'an Strait that took fourteen years to build]. Culture section. *Sŏul Sinmun*, November 20, 1965, 1.

"Ilbonsaekch'ae-ŭi yŏnghwa makaya hana" [Is it necessary to block Japanese films? The need for proper standards for film regulation]. *Chosŏn Ilbo*, November 10, 1962, 5.

"Ilbon saekch'ae-wa yŏnghwagye: Kuksan chejakkyedo dilemma-e, *Hangbokhan Kodok*-ŭi keisŭ" [Japanese color and the Korean film industry: Dilemma within the domestic film scene, the case of *Happy Solitude*]. *Tonga Ilbo*, December 8, 1963, 5.

"Ilbonsaek chit'ŭn mihwa" [American film with strong Japanese color]. *Kyŏnghyang Sinmun*, December 28, 1963, 5.

"Ilyŏnghwa suip pŭlhŏ" [Japanese films not allowed]. *Chosŏn Ilbo*, May 6, 1960, 3.

Jacobs, Lea. *The Wages of Sin: Censorship and the Fallen Woman Film, 1928–1942*. Berkeley: University of California Press, 1997.

James, David E., and Kyung Hyun Kim, eds. *Im Kwon-Taek: The Making of a Korean National Cinema*. Detroit, MI: Wayne State University Press, 2002.

Jeong, Kelly Y. "Enlightening the Other: Colonial Korean Cinema and the Question of Audience." *Review of Korean Studies* 18, no. 1 (2015): 26.

Jin, Jong-Heon. "Demolishing Colony: The Demolition of the Old Government-General Building of Chosŏn." In *Sitings: Critical Approaches to Korean Geography*, edited by Timothy R. Tangherlini and Sallie Yea. Hawai'i Studies on Korea. Honolulu: University of Hawai'i Press, Center for Korean Studies, 2008.

Kajiyama, Toshiyuki. *The Clan Records: Five Stories of Korea.* Translated by Yoshiko Kurata Dykstra. Honolulu: University of Hawai'i Press, 1995.

"Kil t'ŭinŭn hanil yŏnghwa kyoru" [Opening the path for Korea-Japan film exchange]. *Tonga Ilbo,* September 3, 1962, 5.

Kim, Chin-song. *Sŏul e ttansŭhorŭl hŏhara: Hyŏndaesŏng ŭi hyŏngsŏng* [Permit dance halls in Seoul: The formation of modernity]. Seoul: Hyŏnsil Munhwa Yŏn'gu Yŏn'gusil, 1999.

Kim, Kisŭng. "Pak Ŭnsik." In Cho, Han, and Pak, *Han'guk-ŭi yŏksaga-wa yŏksahak,* 2:100.

Kim, Kyung Hyun. *The Remasculinization of Korean Cinema.* Asia-Pacific. Durham, NC: Duke University Press, 2004.

——. "The Transnational Constitution of Im Kwon-Taek's Minjok Cinema in Chokpo, Sŏp'yŏnje, and Ch'wihwasŏn." *Journal of Korean Studies* 16, no. 2 (2011): 231–48.

——. *Virtual Hallyu: Korean Cinema of the Global Era.* Durham, NC: Duke University Press, 2011.

Kim, Ryŏsil. *T'usihanŭn cheguk, tusahanŭn singminji* [The imperial gaze and the colony on display]. Seoul: Samin, 2006.

Kim, Soyŏn, et al., eds. *Maehok-kwa hondon-ŭi sidae* [Age of fascination and chaos]. Seoul: Sodo, 2003.

Kim, Soyoung. "Genre as Contact Zone: Hong Kong Action and Korean *Hwalkuk.*" In *Hong Kong Connections: Transnational Imagination in Action Cinema,* edited by Meaghan Morris, Siu Leung Li, and Stephen Chan Ching-kiu, 97–110. Hong Kong: Hong Kong University Press, 2005.

Kim, Tohyŏng. "Chŏng Kyo, Chang Chiyŏn, Yu Kŭn." In Cho, Han, and Pak, *Han'gukŭi yŏksaga-wa yŏksahak,* 2:58.

Klein, Christina. *Cold War Orientalism: Asia in the Middlebrow Imagination, 1945–1961.* Berkeley: University of California Press, 2003.

"Kwan-ŭi kŏmyŏlje p'yeji dung chehyŏpsŏ kŏnŭisŏ kolja" [Key ideas of KFPA include the revision of government-led film censorship]. *Kyŏnghyang Sinmun,* May 28, 1960, 4.

Kwon, Heonik. *The Other Cold War.* Columbia Studies in International and Global History. New York: Columbia University Press, 2010.

Kwon, Bodurae. "4.19nŭn wae kijŏgi toeji mothaenna" [Why did the April Revolution fail to become a miracle?]. In *1960nyŏndaerŭl mutta* [To question the 1960s], by Kwon Bodurae and Chŏn Chŏnghwan, 39. Seoul: Sangsang, 2012.

——. *Yŏnae-ŭi sidae: 1920-yŏndae ch'oban ŭi munhwa wa yuhaeng* [Age of Love: Culture and trends of the early 1920s]. Seoul: Hyŏnsil munhwa yŏn'gu, 2003.

"Kyoyuk kachi ittaedo ilhwa suip pparŭda" [Even with educational merit, release of Japanese films is not allowed]. *Han'guk Ilbo,* September 27, 1960, 3.

Laïdi, Zaki. *A World without Meaning: A Crisis of Meaning in International Politics.* New York: Routledge, 1998.

Lee, Sunjin. "Hanguk chŏnjaeng hu naengjŏn-ŭi nolliwa singminji kiŏk-ŭi chaegusŏng" [The logic of the Cold War and the formation of the memory of colonial past in postwar Korea]. *Kiok-kwa Chŏnmang* 23 (Winter 2010): 80–89.

——. "1950nyŏndae kongsanjuŭijaŭi chaehyŏn'gwa naengjŏnŭisik" [Representations of communists and the Cold War consciousness in 1950s Korean films]. In Kim Soyŏn et al., *Maehok-kwa hondon-ŭi sidae,* 138–39.

———. "Siguk yŏnghwa ttonŭn kinyŏmbi yŏnghwa" [A current affairs film or epic film]. Booklet in *Kuhanmal sidaegŭk* [Historical films about the Korean Empire]. DVD boxed set, 12–13. Seoul: Han'guk Yŏngsang Charyowon, 2012.

———. "Yŏnghwasa sŏsul-gwa kusulsa pangbŏmnon" [Film historiography and the methodology of oral history]. In *Hanguk munhwa, munhak-kwa kusulsa* [Korean culture, literature and oral history], edited by Tongguk daehakkyo muhwa haksulwon han'gukmunhak yŏn'guso, 79–118. Seoul: Tongguk taehakkyo chulpanbu, 2014.

Lim, Bliss Cua. *Translating Time: Cinema, the Fantastic, and Temporal Critique*. Durham, NC: Duke University Press, 2009.

Lu, Tonglin. "A Cinematic Parallax View: Taiwanese Identity and the Japanese Colonial Past." *Positions* 19, no. 3 (Winter 2011): 763–65.

Magnan-Park, Aaron Han Joon. "Restoring the Transnational from the Abyss of Ethnonational Film Historiography: The Case of Chung Chang Wha." *Journal of Korean Studies* 16, no. 2 (Fall 2011): 249–84.

"Meari" [Echo]. *Han'guk Ilbo*, May 5, 1960, evening edition, 1.

Mitchell, W. J. T. *Landscape and Power*. 2nd ed. Chicago: University of Chicago Press, 2002.

Moon, Seungsook. *Militarized Modernity and Gendered Citizenship in South Korea*. Durham, NC: Duke University Press, 2005.

"Muŏsŭl makŭlkŏsin'ga" [Which element to block?]. *Han'guk Ilbo*, April 30, 1964, 7.

O, Sŏngji, Hieyoon Kim, Lee Sunjin, and Lee Hwajin. *Koryŏ yŏnghwa hyŏphoe-wa yŏnghwa sinch'eje, 1936–1941* [Korea Film Association and the new film system, 1936–1941]. Seoul: Han'guk Yŏngsang Charyowon, 2007.

"Ŏesaek yŏnghwa suip ch'uchŏn-e malssŏng" [Controversies over release permission for films of Japanese color]. *Kyŏnghyang Sinmun*, November 6, 1962, 7.

"Panghwa-e sŭmyŏdŭn Ilbonsaek" [Japanese color in Korean cinema]. *Kyŏnghyang Sinmun*, November 24, 1962, 8.

"Panghwa-e sŭmyŏdŭnŭn Ilbonjo" [The Japanese trend ingrained in Korean cinema]. *Taehan Ilbo*, September 10, 1966, 5.

Park, Chan-wook. "Mr. Vengeance." Interview by Ian Buruma. *New York Times Magazine*, April 9, 2006.

Park, Chung Hee. "Hanil hoedam t'agyŏl-e chŭŭmhan t'ŭkpyŏl tamhwamun" [Special address on agreement of normalization between South Korea and Japan]. June 22, 1965. www.parkchunghee.or.kr/#!/detailed/analect/96.

Park, Hyun Ok. "Korean Manchuria: The Racial Politics of Territorial Osmosis." In "Harbin and Manchuria: Place, Space and Identity," edited by Thomas Lahusen, special issue, *South Atlantic Quarterly* 99 (Winter 2000): 193–215.

"Pŏlssŏ ilhwa suipkwon nirigo honmihanŭn yŏnghwagye, chehyŏp yŏngbaega ch'ungdol" [Film industry shows signs of disarray over Japanese film importation as KFPA and distributors' association collide]. *Han'guk Ilbo*, June 1, 1960, evening edition, 4.

Robinson, Michael Edson. "Contemporary Cultural Production in South Korea: Vanishing Meta-narratives of Nation." In *New Korean Cinema*, edited by Chi-Yun Shin and Julian Stringer, 15–31. New York: New York University Press, 2005.

———. *Korea's Twentieth-Century Odyssey: A Short History*. Honolulu: University of Hawai'i Press, 2007.

Schmid, Andre. "Looking North toward Manchuria." In "Harbin and Manchuria: Place, Space and Identity," edited by Thomas Lahusen, special issue, *South Atlantic Quarterly* 99 (2000): 219–40.

———. "Rediscovering Manchuria: Sin Ch'aeho and the Politics of Territorial History in Korea." *Journal of Asian Studies* 56 (1997): 26–46.

Shim, Hun. *Sanroksu* [Evergreen]. Seoul: Samjungdang, 1990. First published in *Tonga Ilbo,* September 10, 1935–February 15, 1936.

Sim, Hyegyŏng. "Han'guk sports minjok chuŭi-ŭi han kiwon" [A source of Korea's sports nationalism]. In *Chiwŏnjin Han'guk yŏnghwasa: Munhwa yŏnghwaŭi an'gwa pak* [Erased Korean film history: Inside and outside the culture film], edited by Lee Sunjin et al., 187–227. Seoul: Han'guk Yŏngsang Charyowon, 2014.

Sin, Ch'aeho. "Toksa sillon" [A new reading of history], *Taehan Maeil Sinbo* [Korea Daily News] (1908). Reprinted in *Sin Ch'aeho yŏksa nonsŏljip* [Collection of Sin Ch'aeho's writings on history], edited by Chŏng Haeryŏm, 57. Seoul: Hyŏndae Silhaksa, 1995.

Sobchack, Vivian. "Surge and Splendor: A Phenomenology of Hollywood Historical Epic." *Representations* 29 (Winter 1990): 26.

Tanaka, Stefan. *Japan's Orient: Rendering Pasts into History.* Berkeley: University of California Press, 1992.

"TBC-ŭi *Tonggyŏng Nagŭne,* ilbon hyŏnji chwaryŏng chungjiryŏng" [Tokyo vagabond of TBC Station is ordered to stop filming]. *Chungang Ilbo,* December 3, 1966, 5.

Toshiyuki, Kajiyama. *The Clan Records: Five Stories of Korea.* Translated by Yoshiko Dykstra. Honolulu: University of Hawai'i Press, 1995.

"Tŭrop'i-ŭi yŏnggwang, aju yŏnghwaje" [The glory of the Asia-Pacific Film Festival]. *Sŏul Sinmun,* May 20, 1962, 3.

"Uri yŏnghwa taeil such'ul kyehoek, chehyŏpsŏ hŭimang chakp'ŭm chŏpsujung" [Producers' Association plans to export films to Japan, now gathers the list of films]. *Han'guk Ilbo,* May 16, 1960, 4.

Watson, Jini Kim. *The New Asian City: Three-Dimensional Fictions of Space and Urban Form.* Minneapolis: University of Minnesota Press, 2011.

Whissel, Kristen. *Picturing American Modernity; Traffic, Technology and the Silent Cinema.* Durham, NC: Duke University Press, 2008.

———. "Tales of Upward Mobility: The New Verticality and Digital Special Effects." *Film Quarterly* 59, no. 4 (Summer 2006): 23–34.

Workman, Travis. "Narrating and Aestheticizing Liberation in *Hurrah! For Freedom* and *My Home Village.*" *Review of Korean Studies* 18, no. 1 (June 2015): 77–102.

Yale, Camille K. "Runaway Film Production: A Critical History of Hollywood's Outsourcing Discourse." PhD diss., University of Urbana-Champaign, 2010.

Yang, Hyunah. "Envisioning Feminist Jurisprudence in Korean Family Law at the Crossroads of Tradition/Modernity." PhD diss., New School for Social Research, New York, 1998.

Yecies, Brian, and Ae-Gyoung Shim. *Korea's Occupied Cinemas, 1893–1948.* Routledge Advances in Film Studies. New York: Routledge, 2011.

Yi, Hyoin. "Haebang chikhu-ŭi han'guk yŏnghwagye-wa yŏnghwa undong" [Korean film culture and activism in the postliberation era]. In *Han'guk yŏnghwa-ŭi p'unggyŏng, 1945–1959* [The landscape of Korean cinema, 1945–1959], 23. Seoul: Muhak Sasangsa, 2003.

Yi, Kyŏngmin. *Kisaengŭn ottŏkke mandŭrŏjŏnnŭn'ga* [How *kisaeng* was constructed]. Seoul: Sajin Akaibŭ Yŏn'guso, 2004.

Yi, Tŏkil. *Anak'isŭtŭ Yi Hoeyŏng-gwa Chŏlmun Kŭdŭl* [Anarchist Yi Hoeyŏng and the young patriots]. Seoul: Ungjin Tatk'ŏm, 2001.

Yi, Yŏngil. "Chisang t'oron: Chosok t'agyŏl mudŭe tŭlttŭn yŏnye hanil kukkyo" [Debate: Status of the entertainment industry in the period of South Korea-Japan normalization]. *Tonga Ilbo*, December 28, 1965, 5.

——. *Han'guk yŏnghwa chŏnsa* [A general history of Korean cinema]. Rev. ed. Seoul: Sodo, 2004.

Yi, Yŏngjae. *Cheguk Ilbon ŭi Chosŏn yŏnghwa* [Korean cinema at the end of the Japanese Empire]. Seoul: Hyŏnsil Munhwa, 2008.

Yi, Yŏnho. *Chŏngsol-ŭi nakin* [Signature of a legendary filmmaker]. Seoul: Han'guk Yŏngsang Charyowon, 2007.

"Yŏmch'i ŏmnŭn sanghon" [Shameless commercialism]. *Tonga Ilbo*, June 14, 1960, 4.

"Yŏnghwain chwadamhoe: Il pyŏngron'ga-wa han kamdok" [Table talk: Japanese film critic and Korean film director]. *Kyŏnghyang Sinmun*, May 18, 1962, evening edition, 4.

"Yŏnghwa kŏmyŏrŭl wanhwa, ilhwa suipen ajik chujŏ" [Ministry relaxes film censorship but hesitates to allow Japanese film importation]. *Han'guk Ilbo*, May 6, 1960, 3.

"Yŏnghwa sangyŏng hŏgaje chŏlp'yerŭl" [Calling for the abolition of film censorship by USAMGIK]. *Chosŏn Ilbo*, October 23, 1946, 2.

Yu, Hanchŏl. "Ilbongye yŏnghwa tŭngjangŭn sigi sangjo" [Too early to embrace Japanese films]. *Chosŏn Ilbo*, August 17, 1960, evening edition, 4.

Žižek, Slavoj. *The Plague of Fantasies.* 2nd ed. The Essential Žižek Series. London: Verso, 2008.

——. *The Puppet and the Dwarf: The Perverse Core of Christianity.* Cambridge, MA: MIT Press, 2003.

——. *The Sublime Object of Ideology.* London: Verso, 1989.

colonial violence repression: overview, 3, 107; April revolution and colonial resentment, 110–11; *Epitaph*, 118–24; return of in horror and revenge, 107–24; temporality and representation in horror genre as, 107–10; *Yeraishang* and the melodramatic reckoning of violence, 111–18, 124
colonial visual culture, emergence of suppressed legacies of, 12
Confucianism, 28, 33
The Continent on Fire (*Pulputnŭn taeryuk*, 1965) (Yi Yongho), 57–64; female labor values, 162n15; Han Tongmin (character), 58–63, 64 *fig.*5; Kang Chisŏk (character), 64 *fig.*5; Misa'e (character), 58–61, 63; reconception of money in, 69; Soryŏ (character), 60
contrarian gestures, 22, 138n31
conversion themes, 6, 128
coproduction, 46, 48
counterinsurgency campaigns, 55
crime investigation, in post-2000s film, 128
cultural activities autonomy, 137n26
cultural discourse: Cold War bipolarity and, 4; cultural attitude shifts, 15; cultural autonomy, 137n26; cultural constraints, 138n28; cultural dialogue, 35; cultural heritage debate, 78; cultural identity debate, 11; cultural memories, 82; cultural production control, 6; decolonization, 36, 39–40; film exchange with Japan and, 35; problematizing culture, 78–81
cultural exchange: anticolonial nationalism and, 38–39; parameter confusion, 49–50; themes of, 50; Yu Hanchŏl on, 39–40
cultural productions: autonomy of, 137n26; culture film category, 40; normalization treaty and, 11; regulation of, 5; USAMGIK control of, 14, 141nn1,3,4, 146n43

"dark times" (*ilche amhŭggi*) metaphors, 10, 139n40
Daughter of the Governor General (*Ch'ongdok-ŭi ttal*, 1965) (Cho Kŭngha), 46–48, 47 *fig.*4
decolonization, 11, 12, 15, 35–36, 39–40, 160n1
diaspora Koreans (Zainichi), 48, 50, 52, 152n47
disavowal concept, 3, 11, 36, 38, 39, 46, 87, 126, 135n12, 136n15
discrimination, 82, 130
discursive practices, 4, 11
distribution networks, 25, 146n43
Division of Culture, 40
Division of Public Information, 25

domestic spaces: in *The Continent on Fire* (*Pulputnŭn taeryuk*, 1965), 58; in *Hurrah!* 18; in *The Independence Association and Young Syngman Rhee* (*Tongnip Hyŏphoewa Chŏngnyŏn Rhee Syngman*, 1959) (Shin Sangok), 28–29; and nationalist cause, 143n22; political purpose and, 146n50
Dreams of Youth Will Be Splendid (*P'urŭn kkumŭn pinnari*, 1963) (Yu Hyŏnmok), 152n47
Drifting Island (*P'yorudo*, 1960) (Kwon Yŏngsun), 158n31

economics: economic constraints, 138n28; economic incentives, 41; economic partnership, 10; economic privation, 15; economic reciprocity, 42; in gangster films, 106; Japan as model for development in, 51; Japanese economic assistance, 73; of Manchurian action films, 69–70; of warfare, 53
elitism, 40, 41, 49, 50, 135n12
"enemy property" (*chŏksan*) theaters, 141n2
enlightenment discourse of progress, 12, 28, 157n25
Epitaph (*Kidam*, 2007) (Chŏng Shik & Chŏng Pŏmshik), 118–24; overview, 13, 107, 136n16; Chŏngnam in, 120 *fig.*10; commercial performance of, 162n20; Japanese empire in, 163n31; medical science theme, 128; uniqueness of, 160n2, 164n4; Wŏlhyang (character), 160n3
equalization, 51, 92
espionage, 50, 60, 102
ethnic differences, 7, 130, 139n37
ethnography, origins of, 78
Evergreen (*Sangnoksu*), 157n25
Evil Flower Pae Chŏngja (*Yohwa Pae Chŏngja*, 1966) (Yi Kyuung), 158n27
exclusion/inclusion logic, 77, 82
exoticism, 59, 141n48, 152n48
extranational space, 131

fallen woman motif, 107, 111, 156n5
family issues: family law practices, 58, 62, 154n19; family melodrama genre, 81; family name systems, 57–58, 62; family registration, 58, 62, 154n19
fantasy genre, *The Taoist Wizard* (*Choi Donghoon*), 125, 126 *fig.*11
Farewell to Tumen River (*Tumanganga charigŏra*, 1962) (Im Kwŏnt'aek), 52, 59, 69, 133n1, 162n15
fatalism, 91, 125, 134n4, 161n7

Some formalist mention, but only superficeley

CPSIA information can be obtained
at www.ICGtesting.com
Printed in the USA
LVHW04s0842250518
578443LV00002B/2/P

9 780520 295308